(Frontispiece.)

ODIN.

MYTHS OF NORTHERN LANDS

NARRATED WITH SPECIAL REFERENCE TO
LITERATURE AND ART

BY

H. A. GUERBER

AUTHOR OF "MYTHS OF GREECE AND ROME"

"Wake again, Teutonic Father ages,
Speak again, beloved primæval creeds;
Flash ancestral spirit from your pages,
Wake the greedy age to noble deeds."
CHARLES KINGSLEY

NEW YORK ·:· CINCINNATI ·:· CHICAGO
AMERICAN BOOK COMPANY

293
g 93 m

643

DEDICATED

TO

MY PARENTS.

PREFACE.

THE aim of this handbook of Northern mythology is to familiarize the English student of letters with the religion of his heathen ancestors, and to set forth, as clearly as possible, the various myths which have exercised an influence over our customs, arts, and literature.

As Norwegians, Danes, Swedes, Icelanders, Germans, English, and French all came originally from the same stock and worshiped the same gods, so these tales formed the basis not only of their religious belief, but also of their first attempts at poetry. They are the classics of the North, and deserve as much attention at our hands as the more graceful and idyllic mythology of the South.

The most distinctive traits of the Northern mythology are a peculiar grim humor which is found in the religion of no other race, and a dark thread of tragedy which runs throughout the whole woof. These two characteristics, touching both extremes of the scale, have colored Northern thought, and have left their indelible imprint upon all our writings even to this day.

The mythology of Greece and Rome, growing as spontaneous and luxuriant as the tropical vegetation, came to its full fruition and began to decay before the introduction of Christianity. But Northern mythology, of slower growth, was arrested in mid-career before it had attained its complete development.

5

A glossary, and complete index have been added to adapt this book for general use in libraries and public schools. Author and publishers sincerely trust that this little work will be as kindly received and as well appreciated as has been the case with its predecessor, "Myths of Greece and Rome," the first volume of this series.

CONTENTS.

CHAP.		PAGE
I.	The Beginning of All Things	9
II.	Odin	23
III.	Frigga	46
IV.	Thor	61
V.	Tyr	84
VI.	Bragi	93
VII.	Idun	100
VIII.	Niörd	107
IX.	Frey	112
X.	Freya	124
XI.	Uller	131
XII.	Forseti	134
XIII.	Heimdall	137
XIV.	Hermod	144
XV.	Vidar	147
XVI.	Vali	150
XVII.	The Norns	154
XVIII.	The Valkyrs	160
XIX.	Hel	166
XX.	Ægir	171
XXI.	Balder	182
XXII.	Loki	198
XXIII.	The Giants	210
XXIV.	The Dwarfs	217
XXV.	The Elves	221
XXVI.	The Sigurd Saga	225
XXVII.	The Twilight of the Gods	263
XXVIII.	Greek and Northern Mythologies—A Comparison	274
	Index to Poetical Quotations	293
	Index and Glossary	295

LIST OF ILLUSTRATIONS.

ODIN		*Frontispiece*
NORTH CAPE AND THE MIDNIGHT SUN	*To face page*	9
VALHALLA — Hoffmann	"	25
THE PIED PIPER OF HAMELIN — H. Kaulbach	"	32
FRIGGA	"	48
EÁSTRE, OR OSTARA	"	57
THOR	"	69
FREY	"	112
FREYA	"	124
THE WITCHES DANCE (VALPURGISNACHT) — Von Kreling.	"	129
VALKYRS RIDING TO BATTLE — P. N. Arbo	"	160
LORELEI AND THE FISHERMAN — Paul Thumann	"	180
BALDER	"	188
LOKI AND SIGYN — Carl Gebhardt	"	200
NORWEGIAN WATERFALL	"	208
TORGHATTEN, NORWAY	"	213
DANCE OF THE WILL-O'-THE-WISPS — W. Kray	"	221
OLD HOUSES WITH CARVED DOORPOSTS, NORWAY	"	224
THE BRANSTOCK — Hoffmann	"	229
SIGURD AND THE DRAGON — K. Dielitz	"	245
BRUNHILD'S AWAKENING — Th. Pixis	"	249
GUDRUN GIVING THE MAGIC DRINK TO SIGURD — Th. Pixis	"	252
BRUNHILD — Th. Pixis	"	256
HÖGNI THROWING THE TREASURE INTO THE RHINE — Julius Schnorr	"	260

NORTH CAPE AND THE MIDNIGHT SUN

(Opp. p. 5.)

MYTHS OF NORTHERN LANDS.

CHAPTER I.

THE BEGINNING OF ALL THINGS.

ALTHOUGH the Aryan inhabitants of northern Europe are supposed by some authorities to have come originally from the plateau of Iran, in the heart of Asia, the climate and scenery of the countries where they finally settled had great influence in shaping their early religious beliefs, as well as in ordering their mode of living.

The grand and rugged landscapes of Northern Europe, the midnight sun, the flashing rays of the aurora borealis, the ocean continually lashing itself into fury against the great cliffs and icebergs of the arctic circle, could not but impress the people as vividly as the almost miraculous vegetation, the perpetual light, and the blue seas and skies of their brief summer season. It is no great wonder, therefore, that the Icelanders, for instance, to whom we owe the most perfect records of this belief, fancied in looking about them that the world was originally created from a strange mixture of fire and ice.

Northern mythology is grand and tragical. Its principal theme is the perpetual struggle of the beneficent forces of Nature against the injurious, and hence it is not graceful and idyllic in character like the religion of the sunny South, where the people could bask

9

in perpetual sunshine, and the fruits of the earth grew ready to their hand.

It was very natural that the dangers incurred in hunting and fishing under these inclement skies, and the suffering entailed by the long cold winters when the sun never shines, made our ancestors contemplate cold and ice as malevolent spirits; and it was with equal reason that they invoked with special fervor the beneficent influences of heat and light.

When questioned concerning the creation of the world, the Northern scalds or poets, whose songs are preserved in the Eddas and Sagas, declared that in the beginning, when there was as yet no earth, nor sea, nor air, when darkness rested over all, there existed a powerful being called Allfather, whom they dimly conceived as uncreated as well as unseen, and that whatever he willed came to pass.

Myths of creation.

In the center of space there was, in the morning of time, a great abyss called Ginnunga-gap, the cleft of clefts, the yawning gulf, whose depths no eye could fathom, as it was enveloped in perpetual twilight. North of this abode was a space or world known as Nifl-heim, the home of mist and darkness, in the center of which bubbled the exhaustless spring Hvergelmir, the seething caldron, whose waters supplied twelve great streams known as the Elivagar. As the water of these streams flowed swiftly away from its source and encountered the cold blasts from the yawning gulf, it soon hardened into huge blocks of ice, which rolled downwards into the immeasurable depths of the great abyss with a continual roar like thunder.

South of this dark chasm, and directly opposite Nifl-heim, the realm of mist, was another world called Muspells-heim, the home of elemental fire, where all was warmth and brightness, and whose frontiers were continually guarded by Surtr, the flame giant. This giant fiercely brandished his flashing sword, and continually sent forth great showers of sparks, which fell with a hissing sound upon the ice blocks in the bottom of the abyss, and partly melted them by their heat.

> " Great Surtur, with his burning sword,
>   Southward at Muspel's gate kept ward,
>   And flashes of celestial flame,
>   Life-giving, from the Fire-world came."
>   VALHALLA (J. C. Jones).

As the steam rose in clouds it again encountered the prevailing cold, and was changed into rime or hoar frost, which, layer by layer, filled up the great central space. Thus by the continual action of cold and heat, and also *Ymir and Audhumla.* probably by the will of the uncreated and unseen, a gigantic creature called Ymir or Orgelmir (seething clay), the personification of the frozen ocean, came to life amid the ice blocks in the abyss, and as he was born of rime he was called a Hrim-thurs or ice giant.

> " In early times,
>   When Ymir lived,
>   Was sand, nor sea,
>   Nor cooling wave;
>   No earth was found,
>   Nor heaven above;
>   One chaos all,
>   And nowhere grass."
>   SÆMUND'S EDDA (Henderson's tr.).

Groping about in the gloom in search of something to eat, Ymir perceived a gigantic cow called Audhumla (the nourisher), which had been created by the same agency as himself, and out of the same materials. Hastening towards her, Ymir noticed with pleasure that four great streams of milk flowed from her udder to supply him with nourishment.

All his wants were thus satisfied; but the cow, looking about her for food, began to lick the salt off a neighboring ice block with her rough tongue. There she stood patiently licking that selfsame lump until the hair of a god appeared. After she had licked some time longer the whole head emerged from its icy envelope, and by and by Buri (the producer) stepped forth entirely free.

While the cow had been thus engaged, Ymir, the giant, had fallen asleep, and as he slept a son and daughter were born from the perspiration under his armpit, and his feet produced the six-headed giant Thrudgelmir, who, shortly after his birth, brought forth in his turn the giant Bergelmir, from whom all the evil frost giants are descended.

> " Under the armpit grew,
> 'Tis said of Hrim-thurs,
> A girl and boy together;
> Foot with foot begat,
> Of that wise Jötun,
> A six-headed son."
> SÆMUND'S EDDA (Thorpe's tr.).

When these giants became aware of the existence of the god Buri, and of his son Börr (born), whom he had immediately produced, they began waging war against them, for as the gods and giants represented the opposite forces of good and evil, there was no hope of their ever coming to an agreement and living together in peace. This struggle continued evidently for ages, neither party gaining a decided advantage, until Börr married the giantess Bestla, daughter of Bolthorn (the thorn of evil), who bore him three powerful sons, Odin (spirit), Vili (will), and Ve (holy).

Odin, Vili, and Ve. These three sons immediately joined their father in his struggle against the inimical frost giants, and finally succeeded in slaying their deadliest foe, the great Ymir. As he sank down lifeless the blood gushed from his wounds in such floods that it produced a great deluge, in which all his race perished, with the exception of Bergelmir, who escaped in a boat and went with his wife to the confines of the world.

> " And all the race of Ymer thou didst drown,
> Save one, Bergelmer, — he on shipboard fled
> Thy deluge, and from him the giants sprang."
> BALDER DEAD (Matthew Arnold).

Here he took up his abode, calling the place Jötun-heim (the home of the giants), and here he begat a new race of frost giants, who inherited his dislikes, continued the feud, and were always ready to sally forth from their desolate country and make a raid into the territory of the gods.

The gods, who in Northern mythology are called Æsir (pillars and supporters of the world), having thus triumphed over all their foes, and being no longer engaged in perpetual warfare, now began to look about them, wondering how they could improve the desolate aspect of things and fashion a habitable world. After due consideration Börr's sons rolled Ymir's great corpse into the yawning abyss, and began to make the world out of its various component parts.

Out of the giant's flesh they fashioned Midgard (middle garden), as the earth was called, which was placed in the exact center of the vast space, and hedged all round with Ymir's eyebrows which formed its bulwarks or ramparts. The solid portion of Midgard was surrounded by the giant's blood or sweat, which now formed the ocean, while his bones made the hills, his flat teeth the cliffs, and his curly hair the trees and all vegetation.

Creation of the earth.

Well pleased with the result of these their first efforts at creation, the gods took the giant's unwieldy skull and poised it skillfully above earth and sea as the vaulted heavens; then scattering his brains throughout the expanse they fashioned from them the fleecy clouds.

> " Of Ymir's flesh
> Was earth created,
> Of his blood the sea,
> Of his bones the hills,
> Of his hair trees and plants,
> Of his skull the heavens,
> And of his brows
> The gentle powers
> Formed Midgard for the sons of men;
> But of his brain
> The heavy clouds are
> All created."
>
> NORSE MYTHOLOGY (R. B. Anderson).

To support the heavenly vault in place, the gods stationed the strong dwarfs, Nordri, Sudri, Austri, Westri, at its four corners, bidding them uphold it on their shoulders, and from them the four points of the compass received their present names of North, South, East, and West. To light up the world thus created, the gods began to stud the heavenly vault with sparks secured from Muspells-heim, points of light which shone steadily through the gloom like brilliant stars. The most vivid of all these sparks, however, were reserved for the manufacture of the sun and moon, which were placed in beautiful golden chariots.

> " And from the flaming world, where Muspel reigns,
>   Thou sent'st and fetched'st fire, and madest lights :
>   Sun, moon, and stars, which thou hast hung in Heaven,
>   Dividing clear the paths of night and day."
>   BALDER DEAD (Matthew Arnold).

When all these preparations had been finished, and the steeds Arvakr (the early waker) and Alsvin (the rapid goer) were harnessed to the sun chariot, the gods, fearing lest the animals should suffer from their proximity to this ardent sphere, placed under their withers great skins filled with air or with some iron refrigerant substance. They also fashioned the shield Svalin (the cooler), and placed it in front of the car to shelter them from the sun's direct rays, which would else have burned them and the earth to a crisp. The moon car was, moreover, provided with a fleet steed called Alsvider (the all-swift); but as its rays were very mild indeed, no shield was required to protect him.

The chariots were all ready, the steeds harnessed and impatient to begin their daily round, but there was no one to guide **Mani and Sol.** them along the right road. The gods, perceiving this, looked about them and soon beheld Mani (the moon) and Sol (the sun), children of giant Mundilfari, who was so inordinately proud of his beautiful offspring that he called them by the names of the newly created orbs. He gave his daughter Sol in marriage to Glaur (glow), who was probably one of Surtr's sons. The brother and sister were transferred to the sky, where, after receiving minute directions from the gods, they skillfully guided their fleet steeds along their appointed paths.

> "Know that Mundilfær is hight
> Father to the moon and sun;
> Age on age shall roll away,
> While they mark the months and days."
>
> HÁVAMÁL (W. Taylor's tr.).

Seeing how satisfactory all these arrangements were, the gods now summoned Nott (night), a daughter of one of the giants, Norvi, and intrusted to her care a dark chariot, drawn by a sable steed, Hrim-faxi (frost mane), from whose waving mane the dew and hoar frost dropped down upon the earth.

> "Hrim-faxi is the sable steed,
> From the east who brings the night,
> Fraught with the showering joys of love :
> As he champs the foamy bit,
> Drops of dew are scattered round
> To adorn the vales of earth."
>
> VAFTHRUDNI'S-MAL (W. Taylor's tr.).

The goddess of night had already thrice been married : by her first husband, Naglfari, she had had a son named Aud; by her second, Annar, a daughter Jörd (earth); and by her third, the god Dellinger (dawn), she now had a son, radiant with beauty, who was called Dag (day).

As soon as the gods became aware of this beautiful being's existence they provided a chariot for him also, drawn by the resplendent white steed Skin-faxi (shining mane), from whose mane bright beams of light shone forth in every direction, illuminating all the world, and bringing light and gladness to all.

> "Forth from the east, up the ascent of Heaven,
> Day drove his courser with the shining mane."
>
> BALDER DEAD (Matthew Arnold).

But as evil always treads close upon the footsteps of good, hoping to destroy it, the ancient inhabitants of the Northern regions imagined that both Sun and Moon were incessantly pursued by the fierce wolves Sköl (repulsion) and Hati (hatred), whose sole aim was to overtake and swallow the brilliant objects before them, so that the world might again be enveloped in its primeval darkness.

The wolves Sköll and Hati.

> " Sköll the wolf is named
> That the fair-faced goddess
> To the ocean chases;
> Another Hati hight,
> He is Hrodvitnir's son;
> He the bright maid of heaven shall precede."
>
> SÆMUND'S EDDA (Thorpe's tr.).

At times, they said, the wolves overtook and tried to swallow their prey, thus producing an eclipse of the radiant orbs. Then the terrified people raised such a deafening clamor that the wolves, frightened by the noise, hastily dropped them. Thus rescued, Sun and Moon resumed their course, fleeing more rapidly than before, the hungry monsters rushing along in their wake, anxious for the time when their efforts would prevail and the end of the world would come. For the Northern nations all believed that as their gods had sprung from an alliance between the divine element (Börr) and the mortal (Bestla), they were finite, and doomed to perish with the world they had made.

> " But even in this early morn
> Faintly foreshadowed was the dawn
> Of that fierce struggle, deadly shock,
> Which yet should end in Ragnarok;
> When Good and Evil, Death and Life,
> Beginning now, end then their strife."
>
> VALHALLA (J. C. Jones).

Mani was also accompanied by Hiuki, the waxing, and Bil, the waning moon, two children whom he had snatched from earth where a cruel father forced them to carry water all night. Our ancestors fancied they saw these children, the original " Jack and Jill," with their pail, darkly outlined upon the moon.

The gods not only appointed Sun, Moon, Day, and Night to cout it out the year, but also called Evening, Midnight, Morning, Forenoon, Noon, and Afternoon to share their duties, making Summer and Winter the rulers of the seasons. Summer, a direct descendant of Svasud (the mild and lovely), inherited his gentle disposition, and was loved by all except Winter, his deadly enemy, the son of Vindsual, himself a son of the disagreeable god Vasud, the personification of the icy wind.

> " Vindsual is the name of him
> Who begat the winter's god ;
> Summer from Suasuthur sprang :
> Both shall walk the way of years,
> Till the twilight of the gods."
> VAFTHRUDNI'S-MÁL (W. Taylor's tr.).

As the cold winds continually swept down from the north, chilling all the earth, these nations further imagined that at the extreme northern verge of the heavens sat the great giant Hræ-svelgr (the corpse swallower), all clad in eagle plumes, and that whenever he raised his arms or wings the cold blasts darted forth and swept ruthlessly over the face of the earth, blighting all things with their icy breath.

> " Hræ-svelger is the name of him
> Who sits beyond the end of heaven,
> And winnows wide his eagle-wings,
> Whence the sweeping blasts have birth."
> VAFTHRUDNI'S-MAL (W. Taylor's tr.).

While the gods were occupied in creating the earth and pro-viding for its illumination, a whole host of maggot-like creatures had been breeding in Ymir's flesh. Crawling in Dwarfs and Elves. and out, they now attracted divine attention. Summoning these uncouth beings into their presence, the gods, after giving them forms and endowing them with superhuman intelligence, divided them into two large classes. Those which

2

were dark, treacherous, and cunning by nature were banished to Svart-alfa-heim, the home of the black dwarfs, situated underground, whence they were never allowed to come forth as long as it was day, under penalty of being turned into stone. They were called Dwarfs, Trolls, Gnomes, or Kobolds, and spent all their time and energy in exploring the secret recesses of the earth. They collected gold, silver, and precious stones, which they stowed away in secret crevices, whence they could withdraw them at will. As for the remainder of these small creatures, including all that were fair, good, and useful, the gods called them Fairies and Elves, and gave them a dwelling place in the airy realm of Alf-heim (home of the light-elves), situated between heaven and earth, whence they could flit downwards whenever they pleased, to attend to the plants and flowers, sport with the birds and butterflies, or dance in the silvery moonlight on the green. Odin, who had been the leading spirit in all these undertakings, now bade the gods, his descendants, follow him to the broad plain called Idawold, far above the earth, on the other side of the great stream Ifing, whose waters never froze.

> " Ifing's deep and murky wave
>   Parts the ancient sons of earth
>   From the dwelling of the Goths:
>   Open flows the mighty flood,
>   Nor shall ice arrest its course
>   While the wheel of Ages rolls."
>   VAFTHRUDNI'S-MAL (W. Taylor's tr.).

In the very center of the sacred space, which from the beginning of the world had been reserved for their own abode and called Asgard (home of the gods), the twelve Æsir (gods) and twenty-four Asynjur (goddesses) all assembled. They decreed that no blood should ever be shed within the limits of their realm, or peace stead, but that harmony must reign there forever. Then after due consultation they established a forge where they fashioned all their weapons and the tools required to build magnificent palaces of precious metals, in which they lived for many long years in a state of such perfect happiness that this period has been called the Golden Age.

Although the gods had from the beginning designed Midgard, or Mana-heim, as the abode of man, there were at first no human beings to inhabit it. One day Odin, Vili, and Ve, according to some authorities, or Odin, Hoenir (the *Creation of man.* bright one), and Lodur, or Loki (fire), started out together and walked along the seashore, where they found either two trees, the ash, Ask, and the elm, Embla, or two blocks of wood, hewn into rude semblances of the human form. The gods gazed at first upon the inanimate wood in silent wonder, then perceiving the use it could be put to, Odin gave these logs souls, Hoenir bestowed motion and senses, and Lodur contributed blood and blooming complexions.

" There were twain and they went upon earth, and were speechless, unmighty, and wan;
They were hopeless, deathless, lifeless, and the Mighty named them Man.
Then they gave them speech and power, and they gave them color and breath;
And deeds and the hope they gave them, and they gave them Life and Death."

Sigurd the Volsung (William Morris).

This newly created man and woman were then left to rule Midgard at will. They gradually peopled it with their descendants, while the gods, remembering they had called them into life, took a special interest in all they did, watched over them, and often vouchsafed their aid and protection.

Allfather in the mean while had not been idle, but had created a huge ash called Yggdrasil, the tree of the universe, of time, or of life, which filled all the world, taking root not *The Yggdrasil tree.* only in the remotest depths of Nifl-heim, where bubbled the spring Hvergelmir, but also in Midgard, near Mimir's well (the ocean), and in Asgard, near the Urdar fountain.

These three great roots permitted the tree to attain such a marvelous height that its topmost bough, called Lerad (the peace giver), overshadowed Odin's hall, while the other wide-spreading branches towered over all the other worlds. An eagle was perched on the bough Lerad, and between his eyes sat the falcon Vedfolnir, sending his piercing glances down into heaven, earth, and Nifl-heim, and reporting all he saw.

As the tree Yggdrasil was ever green, and its leaves never withered, it served as pasturing ground not only for Odin's goat Heidrun, which supplied the heavenly mead, the drink of the gods, but also for the stags Dain, Dvalin, Duneyr, and Durathor, from whose horns the honeydew dropped down upon the earth and furnished the water for all the rivers in the world.

In the seething caldron Hvergelmir, close by the great tree, was a horrible dragon called Nidhug, which continually gnawed the roots, and was helped in his work of destruction by countless worms, whose aim it was to kill the tree, knowing that its death would be the signal for the downfall of the gods.

> " Through all our life a tempter prowls malignant,
>   The cruel Nidhug from the world below.
>   He hates that asa-light whose rays benignant
>   On th' hero's brow and glitt'ring sword bright glow."
>   VIKING TALES OF THE NORTH (R. B. Anderson).

Scampering continually up and down the branches and trunk of the tree was the squirrel Ratatosk (branch borer), the typical busybody and tale bearer, which passed up and down, reporting the eagle's remarks to the dragon, and *vice versa*, in the hope of stirring up strife between them.

To maintain the tree Yggdrasil in a perfectly healthy condition, the Norns or Fates daily sprinkled it with the holy waters from the Urdar fountain, and as this water trickled down to earth it supplied the bees with honey. From either edge of Nifl-heim, arching high above Midgard, rose the gods' bridge, Bifröst (Asabru, the rainbow), built of fire, water,

Bifröst.

and air, whose quivering and changing hues it retained, and over which none but the gods were privileged to travel to and fro, on their journey to the earth or to the Urdar well, at the foot of the ash Yggdrasil, where they daily assembled in council.

> " The gods arose
> And took their horses, and set forth to ride
> O'er the bridge Bifrost, where is Heimdall's watch,
> To the ash Igdrasil, and Ida's plain.
> Thor came on foot, the rest on horseback rode."
>
> BALDER DEAD (Matthew Arnold).

Of all the gods only Thor, the god of thunder, never passed over the bridge, for they feared that his heavy tread or the heat of his lightnings would destroy it. The gods' watchman, Heimdall, kept guard there night and day. He was armed with a very trenchant sword, and carried a trumpet called Giallar-horn, upon which he generally blew a soft note to announce the coming or going of the gods, but upon which he would blow a terrible blast when Ragnarok should come, and the frost giants and Surtr threatened to destroy the world.

> " Surt from the south comes
> With flickering flame;
> Shines from his sword
> The Val-god's sun.
> The stony hills are dashed together,
> The giantesses totter;
> Men tread the path of Hel,
> And heaven is cloven."
>
> SÆMUND'S EDDA (Thorpe's tr.).

Now although the original inhabitants of heaven were the Æsir, they were not the sole divinities of the Northern races, who also recognized the power of the sea and wind gods, the Vanas, dwelling in Vana-heim and ruling their **The Vanas.** realms as they pleased. In early times, before the golden palaces in Asgard were built, a dispute arose between the Æsir and Vanas,

and they soon resorted to arms to settle it, using rocks, mountains, and icebergs as missiles. But discovering ere long that in
unity alone lay their strength, they agreed to let the quarrel drop
and make peace, and to ratify the treaty they exchanged hostages.

It was thus that the Van, Niörd, came to dwell in Asgard with
his two children, Frey and Freya, while the Asa, Hoenir, Odin's
own brother, took up his abode in Vana-heim forever.

CHAPTER II.

ODIN.

ODIN, Wuotan, or Woden was the highest and holiest god of the Northern races. He was the all-pervading spirit of the universe, the personification of the air, the god of universal wisdom and victory, and the leader and protector of princes and heroes. As all the gods were supposed to be descended from him, he was surnamed Allfather, and as eldest and chief among them he occupied Asgard, the highest seat. Known by the name of Hlidskialf, this chair was not only an exalted throne, but also a mighty watch tower, from whence he could overlook the whole world and see at a glance all that was happening among gods, giants, elves, dwarfs, and men.

> "From the hall of Heaven he rode away
> To Lidskialf, and sate upon his throne,
> The mount, from whence his eye surveys the world.
> And far from Heaven he turn'd his shining orbs
> To look on Midgard, and the earth and men."
>
> BALDER DEAD (Matthew Arnold).

None but Odin and his wife and queen Frigga had the privilege of using this seat, and when they occupied it they generally gazed towards the south and west, the goal of all the hopes and excursions of the Northern nations. *Odin's personal appearance.*
Odin was generally represented as a tall, vigorous man, about fifty years of age, either with dark curling hair or with a long gray beard and bald head. He was clad in a suit of gray, with a blue hood, and his muscular body was enveloped in a wide blue

23

mantle all flecked with gray — an emblem of the sky with its fleecy clouds. In his hand Odin generally carried the infallible spear Gungnir, which was so sacred that an oath sworn upon its point could never be broken, and on his finger or arm he wore the marvelous ring Draupnir, the emblem of fruitfulness, precious beyond compare. When seated upon his throne or armed for the fray, in which he often took an active part, Odin wore his eagle helmet; but when he wandered about the earth in human guise, to see what men were doing, he generally donned a broad-brimmed hat, drawn down low over his forehead to conceal the fact of his having but one eye.

> " Then into the Volsungs' dwelling a mighty man there strode,
>   One-eyed and seeming ancient, yet bright his visage glowed;
>   Cloud-blue was the hood upon him, and his kirtle gleaming-gray
>   As the latter morning sun dog when the storm is on the way:
>   A bill he bore on his shoulder, whose mighty ashen beam
>   Burnt bright with the flame of the sea and the blended silver's gleam."
>   SIGURD THE VOLSUNG (William Morris).

Two ravens, Hugin (thought) and Munin (memory), perched upon his shoulders as he sat upon his throne, and these he sent out into the wide world every morning, anxiously watching for their return at nightfall, when they whispered into his ears news of all they had seen and heard, keeping him well informed about everything that was happening on earth.

> " Hugin and Munin
>   Fly each day
>   Over the spacious earth.
>   I fear for Hugin
>   That he come not back,
>   Yet more anxious am I for Munin."
>   NORSE MYTHOLOGY (R. B. Anderson).

At his feet crouched two wolves or hunting hounds, Geri and Freki, which animals were therefore considered sacred to him, and of good omen if met by the way. Odin always fed these

VALHALLA.— Hoffmann.

(*Opp. p. 25.*)

wolves with his own hands from the meat set before him, for he required no food at all, and seldom tasted anything except the sacred mead.

> " Geri and Freki
> The war-wont sates,
> The triumphant sire of hosts;
> But on wine only
> The famed in arms
> Odin, ever lives."
> LAY OF GRIMNIR (Thorpe's tr.).

When seated in state upon his throne, Odin rested his feet upon a footstool of gold, the work of the gods, whose furniture and utensils were all fashioned either of that precious metal or of silver.

Besides the magnificent hall Glads-heim, where stood the twelve seats occupied by the gods when they met in council, and Vala-skialf, where his throne, Hlidskialf, was placed, Odin had a third palace in Asgard, situated in the midst of the marvelous grove Glasir, whose leaves were all of shimmering red gold.

This palace, called Valhalla (the hall of the chosen slain), had five hundred and forty doors, wide enough to allow the passage of eight hundred warriors abreast, and above the principal gate were a boar's head and an eagle **Valhalla.** whose piercing glance looked all over the world. The walls of this marvelous building were fashioned of glittering spears, so highly polished that they illuminated all the hall. The roof was of golden shields, and the benches were decorated with fine armor, the god's gifts to his guests. Here long tables afforded ample accommodations for the warriors fallen in battle, who were called Einheriar, and were considered Odin's favorite guests.

> " Easily to be known is,
> By those who to Odin come,
> The mansion by its aspect.
> Its roof with spears is laid,
> Its hall with shields is decked,
> With corselets are its benches strewed."
> LAY OF GRIMNIR (Thorpe's tr.).

The ancient Northern nations, who deemed warfare the most honorable of occupations, and considered courage the greatest virtue, worshiped Odin principally as god of battle and victory, and believed that whenever a fight was about to occur he sent out his special attendants, the shield, battle, or wish maidens, called Valkyrs (choosers of the slain). They selected one half the dead warriors, and bore them on their fleet steeds over the quivering rainbow bridge Bifröst, into his hall, where many honors awaited them. Welcomed by Odin's sons, Hermod and Bragi, the heroes were then conducted to the foot of Odin's throne, where they received the praises due their valor. When some special favorite of the god was thus brought into Asgard, Valfather (father of the slain), as Odin was called when he presided over the warriors, sometimes rose from his throne to meet him at the door and himself bid him welcome.

Besides the hope of the glory of such a distinction, and the promise of dwelling in Odin's beloved presence day after day, other more material pleasures awaited the warriors in Valhalla.

The feast of the heroes.   They were seated around the board, where the beautiful white-armed virgins, the Valkyrs, having laid aside their armor and clad themselves in pure white robes, constantly waited upon them. These maidens, nine in number, according to some mythologists, brought the heroes great horns full of delicious mead, and set before them huge portions of boars' flesh, upon which they feasted most heartily. The usual Northern drink was beer or ale, but our ancestors fancied this beverage too coarse for the heavenly sphere. They therefore imagined that Valfather kept his table liberally supplied with mead or hydromel, which was daily furnished in great abundance by his she-goat Heidrun, continually browsing on the tender leaves and twigs on Yggdrasil's topmost branch, Lerad.

> " Rash war and perilous battle, their delight;
> And immature, and red with glorious wounds,
> Unpeaceful death their choice: deriving thence
> A right to feast and drain immortal bowls,

In Odin's hall; whose blazing roof resounds
The genial uproar of those shades who fall
In desperate fight, or by some brave attempt."
LIBERTY (James Thomson).

The meat upon which the Einheriar feasted was the flesh of the divine boar Sæhrimnir, a marvelous beast, daily slain by the cook Andhrimnir, and boiled in the great caldron Eldhrimnir; but although Odin's guests had true Northern appetites and fairly gorged themselves, there was always plenty of meat for all.

" Andhrimnir cooks
In Eldhrimnir
Sæhrimnir;
'Tis the best of flesh;
But few know
What the einherjes eat."
LAY OF GRIMNIR (Anderson's version).

Moreover the supply was exhaustless, for the boar always came to life again before the time for the next meal, when he was again slain and devoured. This miraculous renewal of supplies in the larder was not the only wonderful occurrence in Valhalla, for it is also related that the warriors, after having eaten and drunk to satiety, always called for their weapons, armed themselves, and rode out into the great courtyard, where they fought against one another, repeating the feats of arms achieved while on earth, and recklessly dealing terrible wounds, which were miraculously and completely healed as soon as the dinner horn sounded.

" All the chosen guests of Odin
Daily ply the trade of war;
From the fields of festal fight
Swift they ride in gleaming arms,
And gaily, at the board of gods,
Quaff the cup of sparkling ale
And eat Sæhrimni's vaunted flesh."
VAFTHRUDNI'S-MAL (W. Taylor's tr.).

Whole and happy once more, — for they bore one another no grudge for the cruel thrusts given and received, and lived in perfect amity together, — the Einheriar then rode gaily back to Valhalla to renew their feasts in Odin's beloved presence, while the white-armed Valkyrs, with flying hair, glided gracefully about, constantly filling their horns or their favorite drinking vessels, the skulls of their enemies, while the scalds sang of war and stirring Viking expeditions.

> " And all day long they there are hack'd and hewn
> 'Mid dust, and groans, and limbs lopp'd off, and blood;
> But all at night return to Odin's hall
> Woundless and fresh; such lot is theirs in Heaven."
> BALDER DEAD (Matthew Arnold).

Thus fighting and feasting, the heroes were said to spend day after day in perfect bliss, while Odin delighted in their strength and number, which, however, he foresaw would not long avail to ward off his downfall when the day of the last battle had dawned.

As such pleasures were the highest a Northern warrior's fancy could paint, it was very natural that all fighting men should love Odin, and early in life should dedicate themselves to his service. They vowed to die arms in hand, if possible, and even wounded themselves with their own spears when death drew near, if they had been unfortunate enough to escape death on the battlefield and were threatened with " straw death," as they called decease from old age or sickness.

> " To Odin then true-fast
> Carves he fair runics, —
> Death-runes cut deep on his arm and his breast."
> VIKING TALES OF THE NORTH (R. B. Anderson).

In reward for this devotion Odin watched with special care over his favorites, giving them a magic sword, spear, or horse, and making them invincible until their last hour had come, when he himself appeared to claim or destroy the gift he had bestowed, and the Valkyrs bore them off to Valhalla.

> "He gave to Hermod
> A helm and corselet,
> And from him Sigmund
> A sword received."
>
> LAY OF HYNDLA (Thorpe's tr.).

Whenever Odin took an active part in war, he generally rode his eight-footed gray steed, Sleipnir, brandished his white shield, and flung his glittering spear over the heads of the combatants, who only awaited this signal to fall Sleipnir. upon one another, while the god dashed into their midst shouting his warcry: "Odin has you all!"

> "And Odin donn'd
> His dazzling corselet and his helm of gold,
> And led the way on Sleipnir."
>
> BALDER DEAD (Matthew Arnold).

At times he also used his magic bow, from which he shot ten arrows at once, every one invariably bringing down a foe. Odin was also supposed to inspire his favorite warriors with the renowned "Berserker rage" (bare sark or shirt), which enabled them, although naked, weaponless, and sore beset, to perform unheard-of feats of valor and strength, and go about as with charmed lives.

As Odin's characteristics, like the all-pervading elements, were multitudinous, so were also his names, of which he had no less than two hundred, almost all of which were descriptive of some phase of his being. He was considered the ancient god of seamen and of the wind:

> "Mighty Odin,
> Norsemen hearts we bend to thee!
> Steer our barks, all-potent Woden,
> O'er the surging Baltic Sea."
>
> VAIL.

Odin, as wind god, generally rode about on his eight-footed steed Sleipnir, a habit which gave rise to the oldest Northern riddle, which runs as follows: "Who are the two who ride to the Thing? Three eyes have they together, ten feet, and one tail; and thus they travel through the lands." And as the souls of the dead were supposed to be wafted away on the wings of the storm, Odin was worshiped as the leader of all disembodied spirits. In this character he was most generally known as the Wild Huntsman, and when people heard the rush and roar of the wind they cried aloud in superstitious fear, fancying they heard and saw him ride past with his train, all mounted on snorting steeds, and accompanied by baying hounds. And the passing of the

The Wild Hunt. panied by baying hounds. And the passing of the Wild Hunt, known as Woden's Hunt, the Raging Host, Gabriel's Hounds, or Asgardreia, was also considered a presage of misfortune of some kind, such as pestilence or war.

> "The Rhine flows bright; but its waves ere long
>   Must hear a voice of war,
> And a clash of spears our hills among,
>   And a trumpet from afar;
> And the brave on a bloody turf must lie,
> For the Huntsman hath gone by!"
>
> THE WILD HUNTSMAN (Mrs. Hemans).

People further fancied that if any were so sacrilegious as to join in the wild halloo in mockery, they were immediately snatched up and whirled away with the vanishing host, while those who joined in the halloo with implicit good faith were rewarded for their credulity by the sudden gift of a horse's leg, hurled at them from above, which, if they carefully kept until the morrow, was changed into a solid lump of gold.

Even after the introduction of Christianity the ignorant Northern people still dreaded the on-coming storm, declaring that it was the Wild Hunt sweeping across the sky.

> "And ofttimes will start,
> For overhead are sweeping Gabriel's hounds,
>   Doomed with their impious lord the flying hart
> To chase forever on aëreal grounds."
>
> SONNET (Wordsworth).

Sometimes it left behind it a small black dog, which, cowering and whining upon a neighboring hearth, had to be kept for a whole year and carefully tended unless the people succeeded in exorcising it or frightening it away. The usual recipe, the same as for the riddance of changelings, was to brew beer in egg-shells, which performance so startled the spectral dog that he fled with his tail between his legs, exclaiming that, although as old as the Behmer, or Bohemian forest, he had never yet seen such an uncanny sight.

> " I am as old
> As the Behmer wold,
> And have in my life
> Such a brewing not seen."
> OLD SAYING (Thorpe's tr.).

The object of this phantom hunt varied greatly, and was either a visionary boar or wild horse, white-breasted maidens who were caught and borne away bound only once in seven years, or the wood nymphs, called Moss Maidens, who were thought to represent the autumn leaves torn from the trees and whirled away by the wintry gale.

In the middle ages, when the belief in the old heathen deities was partly forgotten, the leader of the Wild Hunt was no longer Odin, but Charlemagne, Frederick Barbarossa, King Arthur, or some Sabbath breaker, like the squire of Rodenstein or Hans von Hackelberg, who, in punishment for his sins, was condemned to hunt forever through the realms of air.

As the winds blew fiercest in autumn and winter, Odin was supposed to hunt in preference during that season, especially during the time between Christmas and Twelfth-night, and the peasants were always careful to leave the last sheaf or measure of grain out in the fields to serve as food for his horse.

This hunt was of course known by various names in the different countries of northern Europe; but as the tales told about it are all alike, they evidently originated in the same old heathen belief, and to this day ignorant people of the North still fancy that the baying of a hound on a stormy night is an infallible presage of death.

> "Still, still shall last th dreadful chase,
> Till time itself sha ave an end;
> By day, they scour e s cavern'd space,
> At midnight's wi hour, ascend.

> "This is the horn, and hound, and horse
> That oft the lated ant hears;
> Appall'd, he sig requent cross,
> When the wild invades his ears.

> "The wakeful pries t drops a tear
> For human pri for human woe,
> When, at his mi ight mass, he hears
> The infernal cry of 'Holla, ho!'"
>
> Sir Walter Scott.

The Wild Hunt, or Raging Host of Germany, was called Herlathing in England, from the mythical king Herla, its supposed leader; in northern France it bore the name of Mesnée d'Hellequin, from Hel, goddess of death; and in the middle ages it was known as Cain's Hunt or Herod's Hunt, these latter names being given because the leaders were supposed to be unable to find rest on account of the iniquitous murders of Abel, of John the Baptist and of the Holy Innocents.

In central France the Wild Huntsman, whom we have already seen in other countries as Odin, Charlemagne, Barbarossa, Rodenstein, von Hackelberg, King Arthur, Hel, one of the Swedish kings, Gabriel, Cain, or Herod, is also called the Great Huntsman of Fontainebleau (*le Grand Veneur de Fontainebleau*), and people declare that on the eve of Henry IV.'s murder, and also just before the outbreak of the great French Revolution, his shouts were distinctly heard as he swept across the sky.

It was generally believed among the Northern nations that the soul escaped from the body in the shape of a mouse, which crept out of a corpse's mouth and ran away, and it was also said to creep

(*Opp.* p. 32.)

THE PIED PIPER OF HAMELIN.—H. Kaulbach.

in and out of the mouths of people in a trance. While the soul was absent, no effort or remedy could recall the patient to life; but as soon as it had come back animation returned.

As Odin was the leader of all disembodied spirits, he was identified in the middle ages with the Pied Piper of Hamelin. According to mediæval legends, Hamelin was so infested by rats (the souls of the dead) that life became unbearable, and a large reward was offered to the person who would **The Pied** rid the town of these rodents. A piper, in party- **Piper.** colored garments, undertook the job, and piped so gaily that the rats were one and all beguiled out of their holes, along the street, and down to the river Weser, where they were drowned.

> " And ere three shrill notes the pipe uttered,
>   You heard as if an army muttered;
>   And the muttering grew to a grumbling;
>   And the grumbling grew to a mighty rumbling;
>   And out of the houses the rats came tumbling.
>   Great rats, small rats, lean rats, brawny rats,
>   Brown rats, black rats, gray rats, tawny rats,
>   Grave old plodders, gay young friskers,
>   Fathers, mothers, uncles, cousins,
>   Cocking tails and pricking whiskers,
>   Families by tens and dozens,
>   Brothers, sisters, husbands, wives —
>   Followed the Piper for their lives.
>   From street to street he piped advancing,
>   And step for step they followed dancing,
>   Until they came to the river Weser,
>   Wherein all plunged and perished ! "
>   ROBERT BROWNING.

As the rats were all dead, and there was no chance of their returning to plague them, the people of Hamelin refused to pay the promised reward, and braving the piper's anger bade him do his worst. A few moments later the magic flute again began to play, and the astonished parents saw all their children gaily swarm out of the houses and merrily follow the piper.

3

" There was a rustling that seemed like a bustling
    Of merry crowds justling at pitching and hustling;
    Small feet were pattering, wooden shoes clattering,
    Little hands clapping and little tongues chattering,
    And, like fowls in a farmyard when barley is scattering,
    Out came all the children running.
    All the little boys and girls,
    With rosy cheeks and flaxen curls,
    And sparkling eyes and teeth like pearls,
    Tripping and skipping, ran merrily after
    The wonderful music with shouting and laughter."
                                        ROBERT BROWNING.

While the parents stood there helpless and spellbound, the piper
led the children out of the town to the Koppelberg, a hill, which
miraculously opened to receive them, and only closed again
when the last child had passed out of sight. The children were
never seen in Hamelin again, and in commemoration of this
public calamity all official decrees have since been dated so
many years after the Pied Piper's visit.

" They made a decree that lawyers never
        Should think their records dated duly
    If, after the day of the month and year,
    These words did not as well appear,
    ' And so long after what happened here
        On the Twenty-second of July,
    Thirteen hundred and seventy-six.'
    And the better in memory to fix
    The place of the children's last retreat,
    They called it the Pied Piper street —
    Where any one playing on pipe or tabor
    Was sure for the future to lose his labor."
                                        ROBERT BROWNING.

In this myth Odin is the piper, the shrill tones of the flute are
emblematic of the whistling wind, the rats represent the souls of
the dead, which cheerfully follow him, and he even leads the
children into the hollow mountain, which is typical of the grave.

Another German legend, which owes its existence to this belief, is the story of Bishop Hatto, the miserly prelate, who, annoyed by the clamors of the poor during a time of famine, had them all burned alive in a deserted barn, like **Bishop Hatto.** the rats whom he declared they resembled, rather than give them some of the precious grain which he had laid up for himself.

> " ' I' faith, 'tis an excellent bonfire ! ' quoth he,
> ' And the country is greatly obliged to me
> For ridding it in these times forlorn
> Of rats that only consume the corn.' "
>
> ROBERT SOUTHEY.

No sooner had this terrible crime been accomplished than the souls of the poor murdered wretches, assuming the forms of the rats to which he had likened them, came rushing towards the wicked bishop, whom they pursued even into the middle of the Rhine, where he took refuge in a stone tower to escape from their fangs. But the rats swam to the tower, gnawed their way through the stone walls, and pouring in on all sides at once, they pounced upon the bishop and devoured him.

> " And in at the windows, and in at the door,
> And through the walls, helter-skelter they pour,
> And down from the ceiling, and up through the floor,
> From the right and the left, from behind and before,
> From within and without, from above and below,
> And all at once to the Bishop they go.
> They have whetted their teeth against the stones ;
> And now they pick the Bishop's bones ;
> They gnaw'd the flesh from every limb,
> For they were sent to do judgment on him ! "
>
> ROBERT SOUTHEY.

The red glow of the sunset above the Rat Tower near Bingen on the Rhine is supposed to be the reflection of the hell fire in which the wicked bishop is slowly roasting in punishment for this heinous crime.

In some parts of Germany Odin was considered identical with

the Saxon god Irmin, whose statue, the Irminsul, near Paderborn, was destroyed by Charlemagne in 772. Irmin was said to possess a ponderous brazen chariot, in which he rode across the sky along the path which we know as the Milky Way, but which the ancient Germans designated as Irmin's Way. This chariot, whose rumbling sound occasionally became perceptible to mortal ears as thunder, never left the sky, where it can still be seen in the constellation of the Great Bear, which is also known in the North as Odin's, or Charles's Wain.

Irmin.

> " The Wain, who wheels on high
> His circling course, and on Orion waits;
> Sole star that never bathes in the Ocean wave."
> HOMER'S ILIAD (Derby's tr.).

To obtain the great wisdom for which he is so famous, Odin, in the morn of time, wandered off to Mimir's (Memor, memory) spring, "the fountain of all wit and wisdom," in whose liquid depths even the future was clearly mirrored, and besought the old man who guarded it to let him have a draught. But Mimir, who well knew the value of such a favor (for his spring was considered the source or headwater of memory), refused to grant it unless Odin would consent to give one of his eyes in exchange.

Mimir's well.

The god did not hesitate, but immediately plucked out one of his eyes, which Mimir kept in pledge, sinking it deep down into his fountain, where it shone with mild luster, leaving Odin with but one eye, which is considered emblematic of the sun.

> " Through our whole lives we strive towards the sun;
> That burning forehead is the eye of Odin.
> His second eye, the moon, shines not so bright;
> It has he placed in pledge in Mimer's fountain,
> That he may fetch the healing waters thence,
> Each morning, for the strengthening of this eye."
> OEHLENSCHLÄGER (Howitt's tr.).

Drinking deeply of Mimir's fount, Odin gained the knowledge he coveted, and such was the benefit received that he never regretted the sacrifice he had made, but as further memorial of that day broke off a branch of the sacred tree Yggdrasil, which overshadowed the spring, and fashioned from it his beloved spear Gungnir.

> " A dauntless god
> Drew for drink to its gleam,
> Where he left in endless
> Payment the light of an eye.
> From the world-ash
> Ere Wotan went he broke a bough;
> For a spear the staff
> He split with strength from the stem."
> DUSK OF THE GODS, WAGNER (Forman's tr.).

But although Odin had won all knowledge, he was sad and oppressed, for he had also won an insight into futurity, and had become aware of the transitory nature of all things, and even of the fate of the gods, who were doomed to pass away. This knowledge so affected his spirits that he ever after wore a melancholy and contemplative expression.

To test the value of the wisdom he had thus obtained, Odin soon went to visit the most learned of all the giants, Vafthrudnir, and entered with him into a contest of wit, in which the stake was nothing less than the loser's head.

> " Odin rose with speed, and went
> To contend in runic lore
> With the wise and crafty Jute.
> To Vafthrudni's royal hall
> Came the mighty king of spells."
> VAFTHRUDNI'S-MAL (W. Taylor's tr.).

On this occasion Odin had disguised himself as a Wanderer, by Frigga's advice, and when asked his name declared it was Gangrad. The contest of wit immediately began, **Odin and** Vafthrudnir questioning his guest concerning the **Vafthrudnir.** horses which carried Day and Night across the sky, the river

Ifing separating Jötun-heim from Asgard, and also about Vigrid, the field where the last battle was to be fought.

All these questions were minutely answered by Odin, who, when Vafthrudnir had ended, began the interrogatory in his turn, and received equally explicit answers about the origin of heaven and earth, the creation of the gods, their quarrel with the Vanas, the occupations of the heroes in Valhalla, the offices of the Norns, and the rulers who were to replace the Æsir when they had all perished with the world they had created. But, when in conclusion, Odin bent near the giant and softly inquired what words Allfather whispered to his dead son Balder as he lay upon his funeral pyre, Vafthrudnir suddenly recognized his divine visitor. Starting back in dismay he declared that no one but Odin himself could answer that question, and that it was now quite plain to him that he had madly striven in a contest of wisdom and wit with the king of the gods, and fully deserved the penalty of failure, the loss of his head.

> " Not the man of mortal race
> Knows the words which thou hast spoken
> To thy son in days of yore.
> I hear the coming tread of death ;
> He soon shall raze the runic lore,
> And knowledge of the rise of gods,
> From his ill-fated soul who strove
> With Odin's self the strife of wit,
> Wisest of the wise that breathe :
> Our stake was life, and thou hast won."
> VAFTHRUDNI'S-MAL (W. Taylor's tr.).

As is the case with so many of the Northern myths, which are often fragmentary and obscure, this one ends here, and none of the scalds inform us whether Odin really slew his rival, nor what was the answer to his last question ; but mythologists have haz-arded the suggestion that the word whispered by Odin in Balder's ear, to console him for his untimely death, must have been the hopeful term " resurrection."

Besides being god of wisdom, Odin was god and inventor of runes, the earliest alphabet used by Northern nations, which characters, meaning mystery, were at first used for divination, although in later times they served for inscriptions and records. Just as wisdom could only be obtained at the cost of sacrifice, Odin himself relates that he hung nine days and nights from the sacred tree Yggdrasil, gazing down into the immeasurable depths of Nifl-heim, plunged in deep thought, ere, after wounding himself with his spear, he won the knowledge he sought.

Invention of runes.

> " I know that I hung
> On a wind-rocked tree
> Nine whole nights,
> With a spear wounded,
> And to Odin offered
> Myself to myself;
> On that tree
> Of which no one knows
> From what root it springs."
> ODIN'S RUNE-SONG (Thorpe's tr.).

When he had fully mastered this knowledge, Odin cut magic runes upon his spear Gungnir, upon the teeth of his horse Sleipnir, upon the claws of the bear, and upon countless other animate and inanimate things. And because he had thus hung over the abyss for such a long space of time, he was ever after considered the patron divinity of all who were condemned to be hanged or who perished by the noose.

After obtaining the gift of wisdom and runes, which gave him power over all things, Odin also coveted the gift of eloquence and poetry, which became his in a manner which we shall relate in a subsequent chapter.

Odin, as has already been stated, took great interest in the affairs of mortals, and, we are told, was specially fond of watching King Hrauding's handsome little sons, Geirrod and Agnar, when they were about eight and ten years of age. One day these little lads went fishing, and when

Geirrod and Agnar.

a storm suddenly arose their boat drifted far out to sea, and was finally stranded upon an island, where dwelt an old couple, Odin and Frigga, in disguise. The lads were warmly welcomed and kindly treated, Odin choosing Geirrod as his favorite, and teaching him the use of arms, while Frigga petted and made much of little Agnar. The boys tarried on the island with their kind protectors during the long, cold winter season; but when spring came, the skies were blue, and the sea calm, they embarked in a boat which Odin provided, and set out for their native shores. Favored by gentle breezes, they were soon wafted thither; but as the boat neared the shore Geirrod quickly sprang out and shoved it far into the water, bidding his brother sail away into the evil spirit's power. At that selfsame moment the wind veered, and Agnar was carried away, while his brother hastened back to his father's palace, where he was joyfully received, and where, in due time, he succeeded his father upon the throne.

Years had passed since Odin and Frigga had spent that winter in human form on the desert island, when one day, while the royal couple were seated on the throne Hlidskialf, Odin bade his wife notice how powerful his pupil had become, and taunted her because her favorite Agnar had married a giantess and had remained poor and of no importance in the world. Frigga quietly replied that it was better to be poor than hard hearted, and accused Geirrod of lack of hospitality — one of the most heinous crimes in the eyes of a Northerner. She even went so far as to declare that in spite of all his wealth he often ill treated his guests.

When Odin heard this accusation he declared that he would prove the falsity of her charge by assuming the guise of a Wanderer and testing Geirrod's generosity. Wrapped in his cloud-hued raiment, with slouch hat and pilgrim staff, —

> ' Wanderer calls me the world,
> Far have I carried my feet,
> On the back of the earth
> I have boundlessly been," —
>
> WAGNER (Forman's tr.).

Odin immediately set out by a roundabout way, while Frigga, to outwit him, sent Geirrod a secret warning to beware of a man in wide mantle and broad-brimmed hat, as he was a wicked enchanter who would work him ill.

As soon, therefore, as Odin presented himself before the king's palace he was dragged into Geirrod's presence, where, when he had given his name as Grimnir, and had refused to tell whence he came or what he wanted, he was bound between two fires, whose flames played around him without quite touching him. There he remained eight days and nights, in obstinate silence, without a morsel of food, and had it not been that Agnar, who had returned to his brother's palace and occupied a menial position there, once secretly brought him a horn of ale, he would have had nothing to drink.

At the end of the eighth day, while Geirrod, seated upon his throne, was gloating over his prisoner's sufferings, Odin began to sing — softly at first, then louder and louder, until the hall reëchoed with his triumphant notes — a prophecy that the king, who had so long enjoyed the god's favor, would soon perish by his own sword.

> " The fallen by the sword
> Ygg shall now have;
> Thy life is now run out:
> Wroth with thee are the Dîsir:
> Odin thou now shalt see:
> Draw near to me if thou canst."
> SÆMUND'S EDDA (Thorpe's tr.).

As the last notes died away the chains dropped from his hands, the flames flickered and went out, and Odin stood in the midst of the hall, no longer in human form, but in all the power and beauty of a god.

On hearing the ominous prophecy Geirrod hastily drew his sword, intending to slay the insolent singer; but when he beheld the sudden transformation he started in dismay, tripped, fell upon the sharp blade, and perished as Odin had just foretold.

Turning to Agnar, who, according to some accounts, was the king's son and not his brother, Odin then bade him ascend the throne in reward for his humanity and, further to repay him for the timely draught of ale, the king of the gods blessed him with all manner of prosperity.

On another occasion Odin wandered off to earth, and was absent so long that no one ever expected to see him in Asgard again. His brothers Vili and Ve, who by some mythologists are considered as other personifications of himself, then usurped his power, occupied his throne, and even, we are told, married his wife Frigga.

> "Be thou silent, Frigg!
> Thou art Fiörgyn's daughter
> And ever hast been fond of men,
> Since Ve and Vili, it is said,
> Thou, Vidrir's wife, didst
> Both to thy bosom take."
>
> SÆMUND'S EDDA (Thorpe's tr.).

But upon his return they vanished forever; and in commemoration of the disappearance of the false Odin, who had ruled seven months and had brought nothing but unhappiness to the world, and of the return of the benevolent deity, the heathen Northerners formerly celebrated yearly festivals and processions, which were long continued as May-day rejoicings. Until very lately there was always, on that day, a grand procession in Sweden, known as the May Ride, in which a flower-decked May king (Odin) pelted with blossoms the fur-enveloped Winter (his supplanter), until he put him to ignominious flight. In England the first of May was also a festive occasion, in which May-pole dances, May queens, Maid Marian, and Jack in the Green played prominent parts.

May-day festivals.

As personification of heaven, Odin, of course, was the lover and spouse of the earth, and as it appeared under a threefold aspect, the Northerners, although a chaste race, depicted him as a polygamist, and allotted to him several wives. The first among these was Jörd (Erda), the primitive earth, daughter of Night or of the giantess Fiorgyn. She bore him his famous son Thor, the god of thunder. The second and principal wife was Frigga, a personification of the civilized world. She gave him Balder, the gentle god of spring, Hermod, and, according to some authorities, Tyr. The third wife was Rinda, a personification of the hard and frozen earth, who reluctantly yields to his warm embrace, but finally gives birth to Vali, the emblem of vegetation. Odin is also said to have married Saga or Laga, the goddess of history (hence our verb "to say"), and to have daily visited her in the crystal hall of Sokvabek, beneath a cool, ever-flowing river, to drink its waters and listen to her songs about olden times and vanished races.

> "Sokvabek hight the fourth dwelling;
> Over it flow the cool billows;
> Glad drink there Odin and Saga
> Every day from golden cups."
>
> NORSE MYTHOLOGY (R. B. Anderson).

His other wives were Grid, the mother of Vidar; Gunlod, the mother of Bragi; Skadi; and the nine giantesses who simultaneously bore Heimdall—all of whom play more or less important parts in the various myths of the North.

Besides this ancient Odin, there was a more modern, semi-historical personage of the same name, to whom all the virtues, powers, and adventures of his predecessor have been attributed. He was the chief of the Æsir, *Historical Odin.* inhabitants of Asia Minor, who, sore pressed by the Romans, and threatened with destruction or slavery, left their native land about 70 B.C., and migrated into Europe. This Odin is said to have conquered Russia, Germany, Denmark, Norway, and Sweden, leaving a son on the throne of each conquered country. He also built the town of Odensö. He was welcomed in Sweden by Gylfi, the king, who made him associate ruler, and allowed him to found the city of Sigtuna, where he built a temple and introduced a new system of worship. Tradition further relates that as his end drew near, this mythical Odin assembled his followers, publicly cut himself nine times in the breast with his spear, — a ceremony called "carving Geir odds," — and told them he was about to return to his native land Asgard, his old home, where he would await their coming, to share with him a life of feasting, drinking, and fighting.

According to another account, Gylfi, having heard of the power of the Æsir, the inhabitants of Asgard, and wishing to ascertain whether these reports were true, journeyed off to the south. He soon came to Odin's palace, where he was expected, and where he was deluded by the vision of three divinities, enthroned one above the other, and called Har, Iafn-har, and Thridi. The gatekeeper, Gangler, answered all his questions, gave him a long explanation of Northern mythology, which is recorded in the Younger Edda, and having finished his instructions, suddenly vanished with the palace amid a deafening noise.

According to other very ancient poems, Odin's sons, Weldegg, Beldegg, Sigi, Skiold, Sæming, and Yngvi, became kings of East Saxony, West Saxony, Franconia, Denmark, Norway, and Sweden, and from them are descended the Saxons, Hengist and Horsa, and the royal families of the Northern lands. Still another version relates that Odin and Frigga had seven sons, who founded the Anglo-Saxon heptarchy. In the course of time this mysterious king was confounded with the Odin whose worship he introduced, and all his deeds were attributed to the god.

Odin was worshiped in numerous temples, but especially in the great fane at Upsala, where the most solemn festivals were held, and where sacrifices were offered. The victim was generally a horse, but in times of pressing need human offerings were made, even the king being once offered up to avert a famine.

> " Upsal's temple, where the North
> Saw Valhal's halls fair imag'd here on earth."
> VIKING TALES OF THE NORTH (R. B. Anderson).

The first toast at every festival here was drunk in his honor, and, besides the first of May, one day in every week was held sacred to him, and, from his Saxon name, Woden, was called Woden's day, whence the English word "Wednesday" has been derived. It was customary for the people to assemble at his shrine on festive occasions, to hear the songs of the scalds, who were rewarded for their minstrelsy by the gift of golden bracelets or armlets, which curled up at the ends and were called "Odin's serpents."

There are but few remains of ancient Northern art now extant, and although rude statues of Odin were once quite common they have all disappeared, as they were made of wood — a perishable substance, which in the hands of the missionaries and especially of Olaf the Saint, the Northern iconoclast, was soon reduced to ashes.

> "There in the Temple, carved in wood,
> The image of great Odin stood."
> SAGA OF KING OLAF (Longfellow)

Odin himself is supposed to have given his people a code of laws whereby to govern their conduct, in a poem called Hávamal, or the High Song, which forms part of the Edda. In this lay he taught the fallibility of man, the necessity for courage, temperance, independence, and truthfulness, respect for old age, hospitality, charity, and contentment, and gave instructions for the burial of the dead.

> "At home let a man be cheerful,
> And toward a guest liberal;
> Of wise conduct he should be,
> Of good memory and ready speech;
> If much knowledge he desires,
> He must often talk on what is good."
> HÁVAMÁL (Thorpe's tr.).

CHAPTER III.

FRIGGA.

FRIGGA or Frigg, daughter of Fiorgyn and sister of Jörd, according to some mythologists, is considered by others as a daughter of Jörd and Odin, whom she eventually married. This wedding caused such general rejoicing in Asgard, where the goddess was greatly beloved, that ever after it was customary to celebrate its anniversary with feast and song, and the goddess being declared patroness of marriage, her health was always proposed with that of Odin and Thor at wedding feasts.

The queen of the gods.

Frigga was goddess of the atmosphere, or rather of the clouds, and as such was represented as wearing either snow-white or dark garments, according to her somewhat variable moods. She was queen of the gods, and she alone had the privilege of sitting on the throne Hlidskialf, beside her august husband. From thence she, too, could look over all the world and see what was happening, and, according to our ancestors' declarations, she possessed the knowledge of the future, which, however, no one could ever prevail upon her to reveal, thus proving that Northern women could keep a secret inviolate.

> " Of me the gods are sprung;
> And all that is to come I know, but lock
> In my own breast, and have to none reveal'd."
> BALDER DEAD (Matthew Arnold).

She was generally represented as a tall, beautiful, and stately woman, crowned with heron plumes, the symbol of silence or

46

forgetfulness, and clothed in pure-white robes, secured at the waist by a golden girdle, from which hung a bunch of keys, the distinctive sign of the Northern housewife, whose special patroness she was said to be. Although she often appeared beside her husband, Frigga preferred to remain in her own palace, called Fensalir, the hall of mists or of the sea, where she diligently twirled her wheel or distaff, spinning golden thread or weaving long webs of bright-colored clouds.

In order to perform this work she owned a marvelous jeweled spinning wheel or distaff, which at night shone brightly in the sky in the shape of a constellation, known in the North as Frigga's Spinning Wheel, while the inhabitants of the South called the same stars Orion's Girdle.

To her hall Fensalir the gracious goddess invited all husbands and wives who had led virtuous lives on earth, so that they might enjoy each other's companionship even after death, and never be called upon to part again.

> " There in the glen, Fensalir stands, the house
> Of Frea, honor'd mother of the gods,
> And shows its lighted windows and the open doors."
> BALDER DEAD (Matthew Arnold).

Frigga was therefore considered the goddess of conjugal and motherly love, and was specially worshiped by married lovers and tender parents. This exalted office did not so entirely absorb all her thoughts, however, that she had no time for other matters ; for we are told that she was very fond of dress, and whenever she appeared before the assembled gods her attire was rich and becoming, and her jewels always chosen with much taste. This love of adornment once led her sadly astray, for, in her longing to possess some new jewel, she secretly purloined a piece of gold from a statue representing her husband, The stolen which had just been placed in his temple. The gold. stolen metal was intrusted to the dwarfs, with instructions to fashion a marvelous necklace for her use. This jewel, once finished, was so resplendent that it greatly enhanced her charms and even increased Odin's love for her. But when he discovered the theft of the gold he angrily summoned the dwarfs and bade them reveal who had dared to touch his statue. Unwilling to betray the queen of the gods, the dwarfs remained obstinately silent, and, seeing that no information could be elicited from them, Odin commanded that the statue should be placed above the temple gate, and set to work to devise runes which should endow it with the power of speech and enable it to denounce the thief. When Frigga heard these tidings she trembled with fear, and implored her favorite attendant, Fulla, to invent some means of protecting her from Allfather's wrath. Fulla, who was always ready to serve her mistress, immediately departed, and soon returned, accompanied by a hideous dwarf, who promised to prevent the statue from speaking if Frigga would only deign to smile graciously upon him. This boon having been granted, the dwarf hastened off to the temple, caused a deep sleep to fall upon the guards, and while they were thus unconscious, pulled the statue down from its perch and broke it to pieces, so that it could never betray Frigga's theft in spite of all Odin's efforts to give it the power of speech.

Odin, discovering this sacrilege on the morrow, was very angry indeed; so angry that he left Asgard and utterly disappeared, carrying away with him all the blessings which he had been wont to shower upon gods and men. According to some authorities, his brothers, as we have already seen, took advantage of his absence to assume his form and secure possession of his throne and wife; but although they looked exactly like him they could not restore the lost blessings, and allowed the ice giants, or Jotuns, to invade the earth and bind it fast in their cold fetters. These wicked giants also pinched the leaves and buds till they all shriveled up, stripped the trees bare, shrouded the earth in a great white coverlet, and veiled it in impenetrable mists.

But at the end of seven weary months the true Odin relented and returned, and when he saw all the evil that had been done

(*Opp. p.* 48.)

FRIGGA.

he drove the usurpers away, forced the frost giants to beat a hasty retreat, released the earth from her icy bonds, and again showered all his blessings down upon her, cheering her with the light of his smile.

As has already been seen, Odin, although god of wit and wisdom, was sometimes outwitted by his wife Frigga, who, womanlike, was sure to obtain her will by some means. On one occasion the divine pair were seated upon **Odin outwitted.** Hlidskialf, gazing with interest upon the Winilers and Vandals, who were preparing for a battle which was to decide which people should henceforth have the supremacy. Odin gazed with satisfaction upon the Vandals, who were loudly praying to him for victory; but Frigga watched the movements of the Winilers with more attention, because they had entreated her aid. She therefore turned to Odin and coaxingly inquired whom he meant to favor on the morrow; he, wishing to evade her question, declared he would not yet decide, as it was time for bed, but would give the victory to those upon whom his eyes first rested in the morning.

This answer was shrewdly calculated, for Odin knew that his bed was so turned that upon waking he would face the Vandals, and he intended looking out from thence, instead of waiting until he had mounted his throne. But, although so cunningly contrived, this plan was entirely frustrated by Frigga, who, divining his purpose, waited until he was sound asleep and then noiselessly turned his bed around so that he should face her favorites instead of his. Then she sent word to the Winilers to dress their women in armor and send them out in battle array at dawn, with their long hair carefully combed down over their cheeks and breasts.

> " Take thou thy women-folk,
>   Maidens and wives:
>   Over your ankles
>   Lace on the white war-hose;
>   Over your bosoms
>   Link up the hard mail-nets;

Over your lips
Plait long tresses with cunning ; —
So war beasts full-bearded
King Odin shall deem you,
When off the gray sea-beach
At sunrise ye greet him."

THE LONGBEARDS' SAGA (Charles Kingsley).

These instructions were carried out with scrupulous exactness by the Winiler women, and when Odin awoke and sat up in bed early the next morning, his first conscious glance fell upon their armed host, and he exclaimed in surprise, " What Longbeards are those ? " (In German the ancient word for long beards was Langobarden, which was the name used to designate the Lombards.) Frigga, upon hearing this exclamation, which she had foreseen, immediately cried out in triumph that Allfather had given them a new name, and was in honor bound to follow the usual Northern custom and give them also a baptismal gift.

" ' A name thou hast given them,
Shames neither thee nor them,
Well can they wear it.
Give them the victory,
First have they greeted thee ;
Give them the victory,
Yoke-fellow mine ! ' "

THE LONGBEARDS' SAGA (Charles Kingsley).

Odin, seeing he had been so cleverly outwitted, gave them the victory, and in memory of this auspicious day the Winilers retained the name given by the king of the gods, who ever after watched over them with special care, and vouchsafed them many blessings, among others a home in the sunny South, on the fruitful plains of Lombardy.

Frigga had, as her own special attendants, a number of beautiful maidens, among whom were Fulla (Volla), her sister, according to some authorities, to whom she intrusted her jewel casket. Fulla always presided over her mistress's toilet, was privileged to put on her golden shoes, attended her everywhere, was her confidante and adviser, and often told her how best to help the mortals who implored her aid. Fulla was very beautiful in-deed, and had long golden hair, which she wore **Fulla.** flowing loose over her shoulders, restrained only by a golden circlet or snood. As her hair was emblematic of the golden grain, this circlet represented the binding of the sheaf. Fulla was also known as Abundia, or Abundantia, in some parts of Germany, where she was considered the symbol of the fullness of the earth.

Hlin, Frigga's second attendant, was the goddess of consola-tion, sent out to kiss away the tears of mourners and pour balm into hearts wrung by grief. She also listened with ever-open ears to the prayers of mortals, repeated them to her mistress, and advised her at times how best to answer them and give the desired relief.

Gna was Frigga's swift messenger, who, mounted upon her fleet steed Hofvarpnir (hoof thrower), traveled with marvelous rapidity through fire and air, over land and sea, and was therefore considered the personification of the **Gna.** refreshing breeze. Darting thus to and fro, Gna saw all that was happening upon earth, and told her mistress all she knew. On one occasion, as she was passing over Hunaland, she saw King Rerir, a lineal descendant of Odin, sitting mournfully by the shore, bewailing his childlessness. The queen of heaven, who was also goddess of childbirth, upon hearing this took an apple (the emblem of fruitfulness) from her private store, gave it to Gna, and bade her carry it to the king. With the rapidity of the element she personified, Gna darted away, passed over Rerir's head, and dropped her apple into his lap with a radiant smile.

> " ' What flies up there, so quickly driving past ? '
> Her answer from the clouds, as rushing by :
> ' I fly not, nor do drive, but hurry fast,
> Hoof flinger swift through cloud and mist and sky.' "
> ASGARD AND THE GODS (Wägner-Macdowall).

The king, after pondering for a moment upon the meaning of this sudden apparition and gift, returned home, his heart beating high with hope, gave the apple to his wife to eat, and to his intense joy was soon no longer childless, for his wife bore him a son, Volsung, the great Northern hero, who became so famous that he gave his name to all his race.

Besides the three above-mentioned attendants, Frigga also had in her train the mild and gracious maiden Lofn (praise or love), whose duty it was to remove all obstacles from the path of lovers.

Lofn.

> " My lily tall, from her saddle bearing,
>   I led then forth through the temple, faring
>   To th' altar-circle where, priests among,
>   Lofn's vows she took with unfalt'ring tongue."
>   VIKING TALES OF THE NORTH (R. B. Anderson).

Vjofn's duty was to incline obdurate hearts to love, to maintain peace and concord among mankind, and to reconcile quarreling husbands and wives. Syn (truth) guarded the door of Frigga's palace, refusing to open it to those who were not allowed to come in. When she had once shut the door upon a would-be intruder there was no appeal which would avail to change her decision. She therefore presided over all tribunals and trials, and whenever a thing was to be vetoed the usual formula was to declare that Syn was against it.

Gefjon was also one of the maidens in Frigga's palace, and to her were intrusted all those who died virgins, whom she received and made happy forever. According to some mythologists, Gefjon did not always remain a virgin herself, but married one of the giants, by whom she had four sons. This same tradition goes on to declare that Odin sent her ahead of him to visit Gylfi, King of Sweden, and beg for some land which she might call her own. The king, amused at her request, promised her as much land as she could plow around in one day and night. Gefjon, nothing daunted, changed her four

Gefjon.

sons into oxen, harnessed them to a plow, and began to cut a furrow so wide and deep that the king and his courtiers were amazed. But Gefjon continued her work without giving any signs of fatigue, and when she had plowed all around a large piece of land forcibly wrenched it away, and made her oxen drag it down into the sea, where she made it fast and called it Seeland.

> " Gefjun drew from Gylfi,
> Rich in stored up treasure, .
> The land she joined to Denmark.
> Four heads and eight eyes bearing,
> While hot sweat trickled down them,
> The oxen dragged the reft mass
> That formed this winsome island."
>
> NORSE MYTHOLOGY (R. B. Anderson).

As for the hollow she left behind her, it was quickly filled with water and formed a lake, at first called Logrum (the sea), but now known as Mälar, whose every indentation corresponds with the headlands of Seeland. Gefjon then married Skiold, one of Odin's sons, and became the ancestress of the royal Danish race of Skioldungs, dwelling in the city of Hleidra or Lethra, which she founded, and which became the principal place of sacrifice for the heathen Danes.

Eira, also Frigga's attendant, was considered a most skillful physician. She gathered simples all over the earth to cure both wounds and diseases, and it was her province to teach her science to women, who were the only ones to practice medicine among the ancient nations of the North.

Eira.

> " Gaping wounds are bound by Eyra."
>
> VALHALLA (J. C. Jones).

Vara heard all oaths and punished perjurers, while she rewarded those who faithfully kept their word. Then there were also Vör (faith), who knew all that was to occur throughout the world, and Snotra, goddess of virtue, who had mastered every kind of study.

With such a band of followers it is no wonder that Frigga was considered an influential goddess; but in spite of the prominent place she occupied in Northern religion, she had no special temple or shrine, and was but little worshiped except in company with Odin.

While Frigga was not known by this name in southern Ger-. many, there were other goddesses worshiped there, whose attributes were so exactly like hers, that they were evidently the same, although they bore very different names in the various provinces. Among them was the fair goddess Holda (Hulda or Frau Holle)

Holda. who graciously dispensed many rich gifts, and as she presided over the weather, the people were wont to declare when the snowflakes fell that Frau Holle was shaking her bed, and when it rained, that she was washing her clothes, often pointing to the white clouds as her linen which she had put out to bleach. When long gray strips of clouds drifted across the sky they said she was weaving, for she too was supposed to be a very diligent weaver, spinner, and housekeeper. It is said she gave flax to mankind and taught them how to use it, and in Tyrol the following story is told about the way in which she bestowed this invaluable gift:

There was once a peasant who daily left his wife and children down in the valley to take his sheep up the mountain to pasture;

Discovery of flax. and as he watched his flock graze on the mountain side, he often had the opportunity to use his cross-bow and bring down a chamois, whose flesh furnished his larder with food for many a day.

While pursuing some fine game one day he saw it disappear behind a bowlder, and when he came to the spot, he was amazed to see a doorway in the neighboring glacier, for in the excitement of the pursuit he had climbed higher and higher until he was now on top of the mountain, where glittered the everlasting snow.

The shepherd boldly passed through the open door, and soon found himself in a wonderful jeweled and stalactite-hung cave, in the center of which stood a beautiful woman, clad in silvery robes, and attended by a host of lovely maidens crowned with Alpine roses. In his surprise, the shepherd sank to his knees, and as in a dream heard the queenly central figure bid him choose anything he saw to carry away with him. Although dazzled by the glow of the precious stones around him, the shepherd's eyes constantly reverted to a little nosegay of blue flowers which the gracious apparition held in her hand, and he now timidly proffered a request that it might become his. Smiling with pleasure, Holda, for it was she, gave it to him, telling him he had chosen wisely and would live as long as the flowers did not droop and fade. Then giving the shepherd a measure of seed which she told him to sow in his field, the goddess bade him begone; and as the thunder pealed and the earth shook, the poor man found himself out upon the mountain side once more, and slowly wended his way home to tell his adventure to his wife and show her the lovely blue flowers and the measure of seed.

The woman reproached her husband bitterly for not having brought some of the precious stones which he so glowingly described, instead of the blossoms and seed; nevertheless the man sowed the latter, and often lingered near the field at nightfall to see his new crop grow, for to his surprise the measure had supplied seed enough for several acres.

Soon the little green shoots began to appear, and one moonlight night, while the peasant was gazing upon them, wondering what kind of grain they would produce, he saw a mistlike form hover above the field, with hands outstretched as if in blessing. At last the field blossomed, and countless little blue flowers opened their calyxes to the golden sun. When the flowers had withered and the seed was ripe, Holda came once more to teach the peasant and his wife how to harvest the flax stalks and spin, weave, and bleach the linen they produced. Of course all the people of the neighborhood were anxious to purchase both linen and flaxseed, and the peasant and his wife soon grew very rich indeed, for while he plowed, sowed, and harvested, she spun, wove, and bleached her linen. When the man had lived to a good old age and seen his grandchildren and great grandchildren grow up around him, he noticed that his carefully treasured bouquet, whose flowers had remained fresh for many a year, had wilted and died.

Knowing that his time had come and that he too must soon die, the peasant climbed the mountain once more, came to the glacier, and found the doorway which he had long vainly sought. He vanished within, and was never seen or heard of again, for the legend states that the goddess took him under her care, and bade him live in her cave, where his every wish was gratified.

According to a mediæval tradition, Holda dwelt in a cave in the Hörselberg, in Thuringia, where she was known as Frau Venus, and was considered as an enchantress who lured mortals into her realm, where she detained them forever, steeping their senses in all manner of sensual pleasures. The most famous of her victims is doubtless Tannhäuser, who, anxious to save his soul, escaped from her power and hastened to Rome to confess his sins and seek absolution. But the pope, hearing that he had been in the company of one of the heathen goddesses, whom the priests taught were nothing but demons, declared that the knight could no more hope for pardon than to see his staff bear buds and bloom.

Tannhäuser.

> "Hast thou within the nets of Satan lain?
> Hast thou thy soul to her perdition pledged?
> Hast thou thy lip to Hell's Enchantress lent,
> To drain damnation from her reeking cup?
> Then know that sooner from the withered staff
> That in my hand I hold green leaves shall spring,
> Than from the brand in hell-fire scorched rebloom
> The blossoms of salvation."
>
> TANNHÄUSER (Owen Meredith).

Crushed with grief at this sentence, Tannhäuser fled, and finding no rest, returned to the Hörselberg, where he reëntered the cave in spite of the entreaties of the German mentor, the faithful Eckhardt. He had no sooner disappeared, however, than the

(Opp. p. 57.)

EASTRE or OSTARA.

pope's messengers arrived, proclaiming that he was pardoned, for the withered staff had miraculously bloomed, proving to all that there was no sin too heinous to be pardoned, providing repentance were sincere.

> " Dashed to the hip with travel, dewed with haste,
> A flying post, and in his hand he bore
> A withered staff o'erflourished with green leaves;
> Who, — followed by a crowd of youth and eld,
> That sang to stun with sound the lark in heaven,
> 'A miracle! a miracle from Rome!
> Glory to God that makes the bare bough green!'—
> Sprang in the midst, and, hot for answer, asked
> News of the Knight Tannhäuser."
>
> TANNHÄUSER (Owen Meredith).

This same Holda was also considered the owner of a magic fountain called Quickborn, which rivaled the famed fountain of youth, and of a chariot in which she rode from place to place, inspecting her domain. This wagon having once suffered damage, the goddess bade a wheelwright repair it, and when he had finished told him to keep the chips as his pay. The man, indignant at such a meager reward, kept only a very few; but to his surprise found them on the morrow changed to solid gold.

> " Fricka, thy wife —
> This way she reins her harness of rams.
> Hey! how she whirls
> The golden whip;
> The luckless beasts
> Unboundedly bleat;
> Her wheels wildly she rattles;
> Wrath is lit in her look."
>
> WAGNER (Forman's tr.).

The Saxon goddess Eástre, or Ostara, goddess of spring, whose name has survived in the English word Easter, is also identical with Frigga, for she too is considered goddess of the earth, or rather of Nature's resurrection after the long death of winter.

This gracious goddess was so dearly loved by the old Teutons, that even after Christianity had been introduced they still retained a pleasant recollection of her, utterly refused to have her degraded to the rank of a demon, like many of their other divinities, and transferred her name to their great Christian feast. It had long been customary to celebrate this day by the exchange of presents of colored eggs, for the egg is the type of the beginning of life; so the early Christians continued to observe this rule, declaring, however, that the egg is also symbolical of the resurrection. In various parts of Germany, stone altars can still be seen, which are known as Easter-stones, because they were dedicated to the fair goddess Ostara. They were crowned with flowers by the young people, who danced gaily around them by the light of great bonfires,—a species of popular games kept up until the middle of the present century, in spite of the priests' denunciations and of the repeatedly published edicts against them.

Eástre, the goddess of spring.

In other parts of Germany, Frigga, Holda, or Ostara is known by the name of Brechta, Bertha, or the White Lady. She is best known under this title in Thuringia, where she was supposed to dwell in a hollow mountain, keeping watch over the Heimchen, the souls of unborn children, and of those who died unbaptized. Here Bertha watched over agriculture, caring for the plants, which her infant troop watered carefully, for each babe was supposed to carry a little jar for that express purpose. As long as the goddess was duly respected and her retreat unmolested, she remained where she was; but tradition relates that she once left the country with her infant train dragging her plow, and settled elsewhere to continue her kind ministrations. Bertha is the legendary ancestress of several noble families, and she is supposed to be the same as the industrious queen of the same name, the mythical mother of Charlemagne, whose era has become proverbial, for in speaking of the golden age in France and Germany it is customary to say, "in the days when Bertha spun."

Bertha, the White Lady

As this Bertha is supposed to have developed a very large and flat foot, from continually pressing the treadle of her wheel, she is often represented in mediæval art as a woman with a splay foot, and hence known as *la reine pédauque.*

As ancestress of the imperial house of Germany, the White Lady is supposed to appear in the palace before a death or misfortune in the family, and this superstition is still so rife in Germany, that the newspapers in 1884 contained the official report of a sentinel, who declared that he had seen her flit past him in one of the palace corridors.

As Bertha was so renowned for her spinning, she naturally was regarded as the special patroness of that branch of female industry, and was said to flit through the streets of every village, at nightfall, during the twelve nights between Christmas and January 6th, peering into every window to ascertain whether the work were all done.

The maidens whose work had all been carefully performed were rewarded by a present of one of her own golden threads or a distaff full of extra-fine flax; but wherever a careless spinner was found, her wheel was broken, her flax soiled, and if she had failed to honor the goddess by eating plenty of the cakes baked at that epoch of the year, she was cruelly punished.

In Mecklenburg, this same goddess is known as Frau Gode, or Wode, the female form of Wuotan or Odin, and her appearance is always considered the harbinger of great prosperity. She is also supposed to be a great huntress, and to lead the Wild Hunt, mounted upon a white horse, her attendants being changed into hounds and all manner of wild beasts.

In Holland she was called Vrou-elde, and from her the Milky Way is known by the Dutch as Vrou-elden-straat; while in parts of northern Germany she was called Nerthus (Mother Earth). Her sacred car was kept on an island, presumably Rügen, where the priests guarded it carefully until she appeared to take a yearly journey throughout her realm and bless the land. The goddess then sat in this car, which was drawn by two cows, her face completely hidden by a thick veil, respectfully escorted by her priests. The people seeing her pass did her homage by ceasing all warfare, laid aside their weapons, donned festive attire, and began no quarrel until the goddess had again retired to her sanctuary. Then both car and goddess were bathed in a secret lake (the Schwartze See in Rügen), which swallowed up the slaves who had assisted at the bathing, and once more the priests resumed their watch over the sanctuary and grove of Nerthus or Hlodyn, to await her next apparition.

In Scandinavia, this goddess was also known as Huldra, and boasted of a train of attendant wood nymphs, who sometimes sought the society of mortals, to enjoy a dance upon the village green. They could always be detected, however, by the tip of a cow's tail which trailed from beneath their long snow-white garments. These Huldra folk were the special protectors of the herds of cattle on the mountain sides, and were said to surprise the lonely traveler, at times, by the marvelous beauty of the melodies they sang to beguile their labors.

CHAPTER IV.

THOR.

ACCORDING to some mythologists, Thor, or Donar, is the son of Jörd (Erda), and of Odin, but others state that his mother was Frigga, queen of the gods. This child was very remarkable for his great size and strength, and very soon after his birth amazed the assembled gods by playfully lifting and throwing about ten loads of bear skins. Although generally good tempered, Thor occasionally flew into a terrible rage, and as he was very dangerous under these circumstances, his mother, unable to control him, sent him away from home and intrusted him to the care of Vingnir (the winged), and of Hlora (heat). These foster parents, who are also considered as the personification of sheet lightning, soon managed to control their trouble-some charge, and brought him up so wisely, that all the gods were duly grateful for their kind offices. Thor himself, recognizing all he owed them, assumed the names of Vingthor and Hlorridi, by which he is also known.

Thor's foster parents.

"Cry on, Vingi-Thor,
With the dancing of the ring-mail and the smitten shields of war."
SIGURD THE VOLSUNG (William Morris).

Having attained his full growth and the age of reason, Thor was admitted in Asgard among the other gods, where he occupied one of the twelve seats in the great judgment hall. He was also given the realm of Thrud-vang or Thrud-heim, where he built a wonderful palace called Bilskirnir (lightning), the most spacious in all Asgard. It contained five hundred and forty halls for the accommodation of the thralls, who after death were welcomed to his home, where they were treated as well as their masters in Valhalla, for Thor was the patron god of the peasants and lower classes.

> " Five hundred halls
> And forty more,
> Methinketh, hath
> Bowed Bilskirnir.
> Of houses roofed
> There's none I know
> My son's surpassing."
> SÆMUND'S EDDA (Percy's tr.).

As he was god of thunder, Thor alone was never allowed to pass over the wonderful bridge Bifröst, lest he should set it aflame by the heat of his presence; and when he daily wished to join his fellow gods by the Urdar fountain, under the shade of the sacred tree Yggdrasil, he was forced to make his way thither on foot, wading through the rivers Kormt and Ormt, and the two streams Kerlaug, to the trysting place.

Thor, who was honored as the highest god in Norway, came second in the trilogy of all the other countries, and was called " old Thor," because he is supposed by some mythologists to have belonged to an older dynasty of gods, and not on account of his actual age, for he was represented and described as a man in his prime, tall and well formed, with muscular limbs and bristling red hair and beard, from which, in moments of anger, the sparks fairly flew.

> " First, Thor with the bent brow,
> In red beard muttering low,
> Darting fierce lightnings from eyeballs that glow,
> Comes, while each chariot wheel
> Echoes in thunder peal,
> As his dread hammer shock
> Makes Earth and Heaven rock,
> Clouds rifting above, while Earth quakes below."
> VALHALLA (J. C. Jones).

The Northern races further adorned him with a crown, on each point of which was either a glittering star, or a steadily burning flame, so that his head was ever surrounded by a kind of halo of fire, his own element.

Thor was the proud possessor of a magic hammer called Miöl-nir (the crusher) which he hurled at his enemies, the frost giants, with destructive power, and which possessed the wonderful property of always returning to his hand, however far away he might hurl it.

Thor's hammer.

> "I am the Thunderer!
> Here in my Northland,
> My fastness and fortress,
> Reign I forever!
>
> "Here amid icebergs
> Rule I the nations;
> This is my hammer,
> Miölnir the mighty;
> Giants and sorcerers
> Cannot withstand it!"
> SAGA OF KING OLAF (Longfellow).

As this huge hammer, the emblem of the thunderbolts, was generally red hot, the god had an iron gauntlet called Iarn-greiper, which enabled him to grasp it firmly and hurl it very far, his strength, which was already remarkable, being always doubled when he wore his magic belt called Megin-giörd.

> "This is my girdle:
> Whenever I brace it,
> Strength is redoubled!"
> SAGA OF KING OLAF (Longfellow).

Thor's hammer was considered so very sacred by the ancient Northern people, that they were wont to make the sign of the hammer, as the Christians later taught them to make the sign of the cross, to ward off all evil influences, and to secure many blessings. The same sign was also made over the newly born

infant when water was poured over its head and a name given
it. The hammer was used to drive in boundary stakes, which it
was considered sacrilegious to remove, to hallow the threshold of
a new house, to solemnize a marriage, and, lastly, to consecrate
the funeral pyre upon which the bodies of heroes were burned,
together with their weapons and steeds, and, in some cases, with
their wives and dependents.

In Sweden, Thor, like Odin, was supposed to wear a broad-
brimmed hat, and hence the storm clouds in that country are
known as Thor's hat, a name also given to one of the principal
mountains in Norway. The rumble and roar of the thunder were
called the roll of his chariot, for he alone among the gods never rode
on horseback, but walked, or drove in a brazen chariot drawn by
two goats, Tanngniostr (tooth cracker), and Tanngrisnr (tooth
gnasher), from whose teeth and hoofs the sparks constantly flew.

> " Thou camest near the next, O warrior Thor !
> Shouldering thy hammer, in thy chariot drawn,
> Swaying the long-hair'd goats with silver'd rein."
> BALDER DEAD (Matthew Arnold).

When the god thus drove about from place to place, he was
called Aku-thor, or Thor the charioteer, and in southern Germany
the people, fancying a brazen chariot alone inadequate to furnish
all the noise they heard, declared it was loaded with copper kettles,
which rattled and clashed, and therefore often called him, with
disrespectful familiarity, the kettle vender.

Thor was twice married; first to the giantess Iarnsaxa (iron
stone), who bore him two sons, Magni (strength) and Modi
(courage), both destined to survive their father and
the twilight of the gods, and rule over the new
world which was to rise like a phenix from the ashes of the first.
His second wife was Sif, the golden-haired, who also bore him
two children, Lorride, and a daughter named Thrud, a young
giantess renowned for her size and strength. By the well-known
affinity of contrast, Thrud was wooed by the dwarf Alvis, whom

Thor's family.

she rather favored; and one evening, when this suitor, who, being a dwarf, could not face the light of day, presented himself in Asgard to sue for her hand, the assembled gods did not refuse their consent. They had scarcely signified their approbation, however, when Thor, who had been absent, suddenly appeared, and casting a glance of contempt upon the puny lover, declared he would have to prove that his knowledge atoned for his small stature, before he could win his bride.

To test Alvis's mental powers, Thor then questioned him in the language of the gods, Vanas, elves, and dwarfs, artfully prolonging his examination until sunrise, when the first beam of light, falling upon the unhappy dwarf, petrified him. There he stood, an enduring example of the gods' power, and served as a warning to all other dwarfs who would fain have tested it.

> " Ne'er in human bosom
> Have I found so many
> Words of the old time.
> Thee with subtlest cunning
> Have I yet befooled.
> Above ground standeth thou, dwarf,
> By day art overtaken,
> Bright sunshine fills the hall."
> SÆMUND'S EDDA (Howitt's version).

Sif, Thor's wife, was very vain of a magnificent head of long golden hair which covered her from head to foot like a brilliant veil; and as she too was a symbol of the earth, her hair was said to represent the long grass, or the golden grain covering the Northern harvest fields. Thor was very proud of his wife's beautiful hair; imagine his dismay, therefore, upon waking one morning, to find her all shorn, and as bald and denuded of ornament as the earth when the grain has all been garnered, and nothing but the stubble remains! In his anger, Thor sprang to his feet, vowing he would punish the perpetrator of this outrage, whom he immediately and rightly conjectured to be Loki, the arch plotter, ever on the lookout for some evil deed to

Sif, the golden-haired.

5

perform. Seizing his hammer, Thor soon overtook Loki in spite of his attempting to evade him by changing form, caught him by the throat, and almost strangled him ere he yielded to his imploring signs, and slightly loosed his powerful grasp. As soon as Loki could catch his breath, he implored forgiveness, but all his entreaties were vain, until he promised to procure for Sif a new head of hair, as beautiful as the first, and as luxuriant in growth.

> "And thence for Sif new tresses I'll bring
>   Of gold, ere the daylight's gone,
> So that she shall liken a field in spring,
>   With its yellow-flowered garment on."
>   THE DWARFS, OEHLENSCHLÄGER (Pigott's tr.).

Thor, hearing this, consented to let the traitor go; so Loki rapidly crept down into the bowels of the earth, where Svart-alfaheim was situated, to beg the dwarf Dvalin to fashion not only the precious hair, but a present for Odin and Frey, whose anger he wished to disarm.

The dwarf soon made the spear Gungnir, which never failed in its aim, and the ship Skidbladnir, which, always wafted by favorable winds, could sail through the air as well as on the water, and was so elastic, that although it could contain the gods and all their steeds, it could be folded up into the very smallest compass and thrust in one's pocket. Lastly, he spun the very finest golden thread, from which he fashioned the required hair for Sif, declaring that as soon as it touched her head it would grow fast there and become alive.

> " Though they now seem dead, let them touch but her head,
>   Each hair shall the life-moisture fill;
> Nor shall malice nor spell henceforward prevail
>   Sif's tresses to work aught of ill."
>   THE DWARFS, OEHLENSCHLÄGER (Pigott's tr.).

Loki was so pleased with these proofs of the dwarfs' skill that he declared the son of Ivald was the most clever of smiths — words which were overheard by Brock, another dwarf, who exclaimed that he was sure his brother Sindri could produce three objects which would surpass those which Loki held, not only in intrinsic value, but also in magical properties. Loki immediately challenged the dwarf to show his skill, wagering his head against Brock's on the result of the undertaking.

Sindri, apprised of the wager, accepted Brock's offer to blow the bellows, warning him, however, that he must work persistently if he wished to succeed; then he threw some gold in the fire, and went out to bespeak the favor of the hidden powers. During his absence Brock diligently plied the bellows, while Loki, hoping to make him fail, changed himself into a gadfly and cruelly stung his hand. In spite of the pain, the dwarf did not let go, and when Sindri returned, he drew out of the fire an enormous wild boar, called Gullin-bursti, on account of its golden bristles, which had the power of radiating light as he flitted across the sky, for he could travel through the air with marvelous velocity.

> " And now, strange to tell, from the roaring fire
> Came the golden-haired Gullinbörst,
> To serve as a charger the sun-god Frey,
> Sure, of all wild boars this the first."
> THE DWARFS, OEHLENSCHLÄGER (Pigott's tr.).

This first piece of work successfully completed, Sindri flung some more gold on the fire and bade his brother blow, ere he again went out to secure magic assistance. This time Loki, still disguised as a gadfly, stung the dwarf on his cheek; but in spite of the pain Brock worked on, and when Sindri returned, he triumphantly drew out of the flames the magic ring Draupnir, the emblem of fertility, from which eight similar rings dropped every ninth night.

> " They worked it and turned it with wondrous skill,
> Till they gave it the virtue rare,
> That each thrice third night from its rim there fell
> Eight rings, as their parent fair."
> THE DWARFS, OEHLENSCHLÄGER (Pigott's tr.).

Now a lump of iron was cast in the flames, and with a new caution not to forfeit their success by inattention, Sindri passed out, leaving Brock to ply the bellows and wrestle with the gadfly, which this time stung him above the eye until the blood began to flow in such a stream, that it prevented his seeing what he was doing. Hastily raising his hand for a second, Brock dashed aside the stream of blood; but short as was the interruption, Sindri uttered an exclamation of disappointment when he drew his work out of the fire, for the hammer he had fashioned had too short a handle.

> " Then the dwarf raised his hand to his brow for the smart,
>   Ere the iron well out was beat,
> And they found that the haft by an inch was too short,
>   But to alter it then 'twas too late."
>
> THE DWARFS, OEHLENSCHLÄGER (Pigott's tr.).

Notwithstanding this mishap, Brock was so sure of winning the wager that he did not hesitate to present himself before the gods in Asgard, gave Odin the ring Draupnir, Frey the boar Gullin-bursti, and Thor the hammer Miölnir, whose power none could resist.

Loki immediately gave the spear Gungnir to Odin, the ship Skidbladnir to Frey, and the golden hair to Thor; but although the latter immediately grew upon Sif's head and was unanimously declared more beautiful than her own locks had ever been, the gods decreed that Brock had won the wager, for the hammer Miölnir, in Thor's hands, would prove invaluable against the frost giants on the last day.

> " And at their head came Thor,
> Shouldering his hammer, which the giants know."
>
> BALDER DEAD (Matthew Arnold).

Wishing to save his head, Loki fled, but was soon overtaken by Thor, who brought him back and handed him over to Brock, telling him, however, that although Loki's head was rightfully his, he must not touch his neck. Thus hindered from obtaining

Jacques Reich
d'après
Joh. Gehrts

(Opp. p. 69.)

THOR.

full vengeance, the dwarf tried to sew Loki's lips together, but, as his sword would not pierce them, he was obliged to borrow his brother's awl. However, Loki, after enduring the gods' gibes in silence for a little while, managed to cut the string and was soon as loquacious as ever.

In spite of his redoubtable hammer, Thor was never considered as the injurious god of the storm, who destroyed peaceful homesteads and ruined the harvest by sudden hail storms and cloud bursts, for the Northerners fancied he hurled it only against ice giants and rocky walls, reducing the latter to powder to fertilize the earth and make it yield plentiful fruit to the tillers of the soil.

In Germany, where the eastern storms are always cold and blighting, while the western bring warm rains and mild weather, Thor was supposed to journey always from west to east, to wage war against the evil spirits which would fain have enveloped the country in impenetrable veils of mist and have bound it in icy fetters.

As the giants from Jötun-heim were continually sending out cold blasts of wind to nip the tender buds and hinder the growth of the flowers, Thor once made up his mind to go and force them to better behavior. Accompanied Journey to Jötun-heim. by Loki he therefore set out in his chariot. After riding for a whole day the gods came at nightfall to the confines of the giant-world, where, seeing a peasant's hut, they resolved to spend the night and refresh themselves.

Their host was hospitable but very poor, and Thor seeing that he would scarcely be able to supply the necessary food to satisfy his by no means small appetite, slew both his goats, which he cooked and began to eat, inviting his host and family to partake freely of the food thus provided, but cautioning them to throw all the bones, without breaking them, into the skins spread out on the floor.

The peasant and his family ate heartily, but a youth called Thialfi, encouraged by Loki, ventured to break one of the bones and suck out the marrow, thinking his disobedience would never be detected. On the morrow, however, Thor, ready to depart, struck the goat skins with his hammer Miölnir, and immediately the goats sprang up as lively as before, except that one seemed somewhat lame. Perceiving in a second that his commands had been disregarded, Thor would have slain the whole family in his wrath. The culprit acknowledged his fault, however, and the peasant offered to compensate for the loss by giving the irate god not only his son Thialfi, but also his daughter Roskva, to serve him forever.

Charging the man to take good care of the goats, which he left there until he should return, and bidding the young peasants accompany him, Thor now set out on foot with Loki, and after walking all day found himself at nightfall in a bleak and barren country, which was enveloped in an almost impenetrable gray mist. After seeking for some time, Thor saw through the fog the uncertain outline of what looked like a peculiar-shaped house. Its open portal was so wide and high that it seemed to take up all one side of the house. Entering and finding neither fire nor light, Thor and his companions flung themselves wearily down on the floor to sleep, but were soon disturbed by a peculiar noise, and a prolonged trembling of the ground beneath them. Fearing lest the main roof should fall during this earthquake, Thor and his companions took refuge in a wing of the building, where they soon fell sound asleep. At dawn, the god and his companions passed out, but they had not gone very far ere they saw the recumbent form of a sleeping giant, and perceived that the peculiar sounds which had disturbed their rest were produced by his snores. At that moment the giant awoke, arose, stretched himself, looked about him for his missing property, and a second later he picked up the object which Thor and his companions had mistaken in the darkness for a house. They then perceived with amazement that the wing in which they had all slept was the separate place in a mitten for the giant's great thumb! Learning that Thor and his companions were on their way to

Utgard, as the giants' realm was also called, Skrymir, the giant, proposed to be their guide; and after walking with them all day, he offered them the provisions in his wallet ere he dropped asleep. But, in spite of strenuous efforts, neither Thor nor his companions could unfasten the knots which Skrymir had tied.

> " Skrymir's thongs
> Seemed to thee hard,
> When at the food thou couldst not get,
> When, in full health, of hunger dying."
>
> SÆMUND'S EDDA (Thorpe's tr.).

Angry because of his snoring, which kept them awake, Thor thrice dealt him fearful blows with his hammer. These strokes, instead of annihilating the monster, merely evoked sleepy comments to the effect that a leaf, a bit   Utgard-loki. of bark, or a twig from a bird's nest overhead had fallen upon his face. Early on the morrow, Skrymir left Thor and his companions, pointing out the shortest road to Utgard-loki's castle, which was built of great ice blocks, with huge glittering icicles as pillars. The gods, slipping between the bars of the great gate, presented themselves boldly before the king of the giants, Utgard-loki, who, recognizing them, immediately pretended to be greatly surprised at their small size, and expressed a wish to see for himself what they could do, as he had often heard their prowess vaunted.

Loki, who had fasted longer than he wished, immediately declared he was ready to eat for a wager with any one. So the king ordered a great wooden trough full of meat to be brought into the hall, and placing Loki at one end and his cook Logi at the other, he bade them see which would win. Although Loki did wonders, and soon reached the middle of the trough, he still found himself beaten, for whereas he had picked the bones clean, his opponent had devoured both them and the trough.

Smiling contemptuously, Utgard-loki said that it was evident they could not do much in the eating line, and so nettled Thor thereby, that he declared if Loki could not eat more than the voracious cook, he felt confident he could drain the biggest vessel in the house, such was his unquenchable thirst. Immediately a horn was brought in, and, Utgard-loki declaring that good drinkers emptied it at one draught, moderately thirsty persons at two, and small drinkers at three, Thor applied his lips to the rim. But, although he drank so deep that he thought he would burst, the liquid still came almost up to the rim when he raised his head. A second and third attempt to empty this horn proved equally unsuccessful. Thialfi then offered to run a race, and a young fellow named Hugi soon outstripped him, although he made remarkably good time.

Thor next proposed to show his strength by lifting great weights, but when challenged to pick up the giant's cat, he tugged and strained, only to succeed in raising one paw from the floor, although he had taken the precaution to enhance his strength as much as possible by tightening his belt Megin-giörd.

> " Strong is great Thor, no doubt, when Megingarder
> He braces tightly o'er his rock-firm loins."
> VIKING TALES OF THE NORTH (R. B. Anderson).

An attempt on his part to wrestle with Utgard-loki's old nurse Elli, the only opponent deemed worthy of such a puny fellow, ended equally disastrously, and the gods, acknowledging they were beaten, were hospitably entertained. On the morrow they were escorted to the confines of Utgard, where the giant politely informed them that he hoped they would never call upon him again, as he had been forced to employ magic against them. He then went on to explain that he was the giant Skrymir, and that had he not taken the precaution to interpose a mountain between his head and Thor's blows, he would have been slain, as deep clefts in the mountain side testified to the god's strength. Next he informed them that Loki's opponent was Logi (wild fire); that Thialfi had run a race with Hugi (thought), than which no swifter runner exists; that Thor's drinking horn was connected

with the ocean, where his deep draughts had produced a perceptible ebb; that the cat was in reality the terrible Midgard snake
encircling the world, which Thor had nearly pulled out of the
sea; and that Elli, his nurse, was old age, whom none can resist.
Having finished these explanations and cautioned them never to
return or he would defend himself by similar delusions, Utgard-
loki vanished, and although Thor angrily brandished his hammer to destroy his castle, such a mist enveloped it that it could
not be seen, and the thunder god was obliged to return to Thrud-
vang without having accomplished his purpose, the extermination
of the race of giants.

> " The strong-armed Thor
> Full oft against giant Jotunheim did wend,
> But spite his belt celestial, spite his gauntlets,
> Utgard-Loki still his throne retains;
> Evil, itself a force, to force yields never."
>
> VIKING TALES OF THE NORTH (R. B. Anderson).

As Odin was once dashing through the air on his eight-footed
steed Sleipnir, he attracted the attention of the giant Hrungnir,
who proposed a race, declaring he was sure his own   Thor and
steed Gullfaxi could rival Sleipnir in speed.   In   Hrungnir.
the heat of the race, Hrungnir did not even notice in what direction they were going, and, in the vain hope of overtaking Odin,
urged his steed on to the very gates of Valhalla.   Discovering
where he was, the giant then grew pale with fear, for he knew he
had jeopardized his life by venturing into the stronghold of the
gods, his hereditary foes.

The Æsir, however, were too honorable to take even an enemy
at such a disadvantage, and, instead of doing him any harm,
asked him into their banqueting halls, where he proceeded to indulge in liberal potations of the heavenly mead set before him.
He soon grew so excited that he began to boast of his power, declaring he would come some day and take possession of Asgard,
which he would destroy, as well as all the gods, excepting only

Freya and Sif, upon whom he gazed with an admiring, drunken leer.

The gods, knowing he was not responsible, let him talk unmolested; but Thor, coming home just then from one of his journeys, and hearing him propose to carry away his beloved Sif, flew into a terrible rage. He furiously brandished his hammer, intending to annihilate the boaster. This the gods would not permit, however, and they quickly threw themselves between the irate Thunderer and their guest, imploring the former to respect the sacred rights of hospitality, and not desecrate their peace-stead by shedding blood.

Thor at last consented to bridle his wrath, providing the giant Hrungnir would appoint a time and place for a holmgang, as a Northern duel was generally called. Thus challenged, Hrungnir promised to meet Thor at Griottunagard, the confines of his realm, three days later, and departed somewhat sobered by the fright he had experienced. When his fellow giants heard how rash he had been, they chided him sorely; but hearing he was to have the privilege of being accompanied by a squire, whom Thialfi would engage in fight, they proceeded to construct a creature of clay, nine miles long, and proportionately wide, whom they called Mokerkialfi (mist wader). As they could find no human heart big enough to put in this monster's breast, they secured that of a mare, which, however, kept fluttering and quivering with apprehension. The day of the duel arrived. Hrungnir and his squire were on the ground awaiting the arrival of their respective opponents. The giant had not only a flint heart and skull, but also a shield and club of the same substance, and therefore deemed himself well-nigh invincible. But when he heard a terrible noise, and Thialfi came running up to announce his master's coming, he gladly followed the herald's advice and stood upon his shield, lest the thunder god should come up from the ground and attack him unprotected.

A moment later, however, he saw his mistake, for, while Thialfi attacked Mokerkialfi with a spade, Thor came rushing up and flung his hammer full at his opponent's head. Hrungnir, to ward off the blow, interposed his stone club, which was shivered into pieces, that flew all over the earth, supplying all the flint stones to be found, and one fragment sank deep in Thor's forehead. As the god dropped fainting to the ground, his hammer crashed against the head of Hrungnir, who fell down dead beside him, in such a position that one of his ponderous legs was thrown over the recumbent god.

> " Thou now remindest me
>   How I with Hrungnir fought,
>   That stout-hearted Jotun,
>   Whose head was all of stone;
>   Yet I made him fall
>   And sink before me."
>   SÆMUND'S EDDA (Thorpe's tr.).

Thialfi, who, in the mean while, had disposed of the great clay giant with its cowardly mare's heart, now rushed to his master's rescue; but all his efforts and those of the assembled gods, whom he quickly summoned, could not raise the pinioning leg. While they were standing there, helplessly wondering what they should do next, Thor's little son Magni came up. According to varying accounts, he was then only three days or three years old, but he quickly seized the giant's foot, and, unaided, set his father free, declaring that had he only been summoned sooner he would easily have disposed of both giant and squire. This exhibition of strength upon his part made the gods wonder greatly, and helped them to recognize the truth of the various predictions, which one and all declared that their descendants would be mightier than they, would survive them, and would rule in their turn over the new heaven and earth.

To reward his son for his timely aid, Thor gave him the steed Gullfaxi (golden-maned), to which he had fallen heir by right of conquest, and Magni ever after rode this marvelous horse, which almost equaled the renowned Sleipnir in speed and endurance.

After vainly trying to remove the stone splinter from his forehead, Thor sadly returned home to Thrudvang, where Sif's loving efforts were equally unsuccessful. She therefore resolved to send for Groa (green-making), a sorceress, noted for her skill in medicine and for the efficacy of her spells and incantations. Groa immediately signified her readiness to render every service in her power to the god who had so often benefited her, and solemnly began to recite powerful runes, under whose influence Thor felt the stone grow looser and looser. In his delight at the prospect of a speedy deliverance, Thor wished to reward the enchantress. Knowing that nothing could give greater pleasure to a mother than the prospect of seeing a long-lost child, he therefore told her he had recently crossed the Elivagar, or ice streams, to rescue her little son Orvandil (germ) from the frost giants' cruel power, and had succeeded in carrying him off in a basket. But, as the little rogue would persist in sticking one of his bare toes through a hole in the basket, it had been frost bitten, and Thor, accidentally breaking it off, had flung it up into the sky, where it shone as a star, known in the North as "Orvandil's Toe."

Groa, the sorceress.

Delighted with these tidings, the prophetess paused in her incantations to express her joy, but, having forgotten just where she left off, she was never able to continue her spell, and the flint stone remained imbedded in Thor's forehead, whence it could never be dislodged.

Of course, as Thor's hammer always did him such good service, it was the most prized of all his possessions, and his dismay was very great when he awoke one morning and found it gone. His cry of anger and disappointment soon brought Loki to his side, and to him Thor confided the secret of his loss, declaring that were the giants to hear of it, they would soon attempt to storm Asgard and destroy the gods.

> "Wroth waxed Thor, when his sleep was flown,
> And he found his trusty hammer gone;

He smote his brow, his beard he shook,
The son of earth 'gan round him look;
And this the first word that he spoke:
'Now listen what I tell thee, Loke;
Which neither on earth below is known,
Nor in heaven above: my hammer's gone.'"
THRYM'S QUIDA (Herbert's tr.).

Loki declared he would try to discover the thief and recover the hammer, if Freya would only lend him her falcon plumes, and immediately hastened off to Folkvang to borrow them. In the form of a bird he then winged his flight across the river Ifing, and over the barren stretches of Jötun-heim, where he shrewdly suspected the thief was to be found. There he saw Thrym, prince of the frost giants and god of the destructive thunder storm, sitting alone on a hillside, and, artfully questioning him, soon learned that he had stolen the hammer, had buried it deep underground, and would never give it up unless Freya were brought to him, in bridal array, ready to become his wife.

Thor and Thrym.

"I have the Thunderer's hammer bound
Fathoms eight beneath the ground;
With it shall no one homeward tread
Till he bring me Freya to share my bed."
THRYM'S QUIDA (Herbert's tr.).

Indignant at the giant's presumption, Loki returned to Thrud-vang, where Thor, hearing what he had learned, declared it would be well to visit Freya and try to prevail upon her to sacrifice herself for the general good. But when the Æsir told the goddess of beauty what they wished her to do, she flew into such a passion that even her necklace burst. She told them that she would never leave her beloved husband for any god, and much less to marry an ugly old giant and dwell in Jötun-heim, where all was dreary in the extreme, and where she would soon die of longing for the green fields and flowery meadows, in which she loved to roam. Seeing that further persuasions would be useless, Loki and Thor returned home and there devised another plan for recovering the hammer. By Heimdall's advice, Thor borrowed and reluctantly put on all Freya's clothes and her necklace, and enveloped himself in a thick veil. Loki, having attired himself as a handmaiden, then mounted with him in the goat-drawn chariot, to ride to Jötun-heim, where they intended to play the respective parts of the goddess of beauty and of her attendant.

> " Home were driven
> Then the goats,
> And hitched to the car;
> Hasten they must —
> The mountains crashed,
> The earth stood in flames:
> Odin's son
> Rode to Jotun-heim."
> NORSE MYTHOLOGY (R. B. Anderson).

Thrym welcomed his guests at the palace door, overjoyed at the thought that he was about to secure undisputed possession of the goddess of beauty, for whom he had long sighed in vain. He quickly led them to the banquet hall, where Thor, the bride elect, almost disgraced himself by eating an ox, eight huge salmon, and all the cakes and sweets provided for the women, washing down these miscellaneous viands with two whole barrels of mead.

The giant bridegroom watched these gastronomic feats with amazement, and was not even reassured when Loki confidentially whispered to him that the bride was so deeply in love with him that she had not been able to taste a morsel of food for more than eight days. Thrym then sought to kiss the bride, but drew back appalled at the fire of her glance, which Loki explained as a burning glance of love. The giant's sister, claiming the usual gifts, was not even noticed; so Loki again whispered to the wondering Thrym that love made people absent-minded. Intoxicated with passion and mead, which he, too, had drunk in liberal quantities, the bridegroom now bade his servants produce the sacred hammer to consecrate the marriage, and as soon as it was brought he himself laid it in the pretended Freya's lap. The next moment a powerful hand closed over the short handle, and the weapon, rapidly hurled by Thor, soon slew the giant, his sister, and all the invited guests.

> " ' Bear in the hammer to plight the maid;
> Upon her lap the bruiser lay,
> And firmly plight our hands and fay.'
> The Thunderer's soul smiled in his breast;
> When the hammer hard on his lap was placed,
> Thrym first, the king of the Thursi, he slew,
> And slaughtered all the giant crew."
> THRYM'S QUIDA (Herbert's tr.).

Leaving a smoking heap of ruins behind them, the gods then drove rapidly back to Asgard, where the borrowed garments were given back to Freya, and the Æsir all rejoiced at the recovery of the precious hammer. When next Odin glanced towards that part of Jötun-heim from the top of his throne Hlidskialf, he saw the ruins covered with tender green shoots, for Thor, having conquered his enemy, had taken possession of his land, which no longer remained barren and desolate as before, but brought forth fruit in abundance.

Loki, in search of adventures, once borrowed Freya's falcon garb and flew off to another part of Jötun-heim, where he perched on top of the gables of Geirrod's house, and, gazing about him, soon attracted the attention of this giant, who bade one of his servants catch the bird. Amused at the fellow's clumsy attempts to secure him, Loki flitted about from place to place, only moving just as the giant was about to lay hands upon him, until, miscalculating his distance, he suddenly found himself a captive.

Geirrod, gazing upon the bird's bright eyes, shrewdly suspected that it was a god in disguise, and to force him to speak, locked him up in a cage, where he kept him for three whole months without food or drink. Conquered at last by hunger and thirst,

Loki revealed his identity, and obtained his release by promising that he would induce Thor to visit Geirrod without his hammer, belt, or magic gauntlet. Loki then flew back to Asgard, and told Thor that he had been royally entertained, and that his host had expressed a strong desire to see the powerful thunder-god, of whom Loki had told him such marvelous tales. Flat-tered by this artful speech, Thor was soon brought to consent to a journey to Jötun-heim, and immediately set out, leaving his three marvelous weapons at home. He and Loki had not gone very far, however, ere they came to the house of the giantess Grid, one of Odin's many wives, who, seeing Thor disarmed, lent him her own girdle, staff, and glove, warning him to beware of treachery. Some time after leaving her, Thor and Loki came to the river Veimer, which the thunder-god, accustomed to wad-ing, coolly prepared to ford, bidding Loki and Thialfi cling fast to his belt if they would come safe across.

In the middle of the stream, however, a sudden cloudburst and freshet overtook them; the waters began to rise and roar, and although Thor leaned heavily upon his staff, he was almost swept away by the force of the raging current.

> " Wax not, Veimer,
> Since to wade I desire
> To the realm of the giants!
> Know, if thou waxest,
> Then waxes my asamight
> As high as the heavens."
> NORSE MYTHOLOGY (R. B. Anderson).

Looking up the stream, Thor now became aware of the presence of Geirrod's daughter Gialp, and rightly suspected that she was the cause of the storm. He picked up a huge bowlder, which he flung at her, muttering that the best place to dam a river was at its source. The rock had the desired effect, for the giantess fled, the waters abated, and Thor, exhausted but safe, pulled himself up on the opposite bank by a little shrub, the mountain-ash or sorb, which has since been known as "Thor's salvation," and considered gifted with occult powers. After resting awhile the god resumed his journey; but upon arriving at Geirrod's house he was so exhausted that he sank wearily down upon the only chair in sight. To his surprise, however, he felt it rise beneath him, and fearing lest he should be crushed against the rafters, he braced the borrowed staff against the ceiling and forced the chair downward with all his might. A terrible cracking, sudden cries, and moans of pain proved that he had broken the backs of the giant's daughters, Gialp and Greip, who had slipped under his chair and had treacherously tried to slay him.

> " Once I employed
> My asamight
> In the realm of giants,
> When Gialp and Greip,
> Geirrod's daughters,
> Wanted to lift me to heaven."
> NORSE MYTHOLOGY (R. B. Anderson).

Geirrod now challenged Thor to show his strength and skill, and without waiting for the preconcerted signal, flung a red-hot wedge at him. Thor, quick of eye and a practiced catcher, caught the missile with the giantess's iron glove, and hurled it back at his opponent. Such was the force of the god, that the missile passed, not only through the pillar behind which the giant had taken refuge, but through him and the wall of the house, and buried itself deep in the earth without.

Thor then marched up to the giant's corpse, which at the blow from his weapon had been changed into stone, and set it up in a conspicuous place, as a monument of his strength and of the victory he had won over his redoubtable foes, the mountain giants.

Thor's name has been given to many of the places he was wont to frequent, such as the principal harbor of the Faroe Islands, and to families which claim to be de- **Worship of** scended from him. It is still extant in such names **Thor.** as Thunderhill in Surrey, and in the family names of Thorburn

6

and Thorwaldsen, but is most conspicuous in the name of one of the days of the week, Thor's day or Thursday.

> " Over the whole earth
> Still is it Thor's day ! "
> SAGA OF KING OLAF (Longfellow).

Thor was considered a preëminently benevolent deity, and it was for that reason that he was so widely worshiped and that his temples arose at Moeri, Hlader, Godey, Gothland, Upsala, and other places, where the people never failed to invoke him for a favorable year at Yule-tide, his principal festival. It was customary on this occasion to burn a great log of oak, his sacred tree, as an emblem of the warmth and light of summer, which would soon come to drive away the darkness and cold of winter.

Brides invariably wore red, Thor's favorite color, which was considered emblematical of love, and for the same reason betrothal rings in the North were almost always set with a red stone.

Thor's temples and statues, like Odin's, were fashioned of wood, and the greater number of them were destroyed during the reign of King Olaf the Saint. According to ancient chronicles, this monarch forcibly converted his subjects. He was specially incensed against the inhabitants of a certain province, because they worshiped a rude image of Thor, which they decked with golden ornaments, and before which they set food every evening, declaring the god ate it, as no trace of it was left in the morning.

The people, being called upon in 1030 to renounce this idol in favor of the true God, promised to consent if the morrow were cloudy ; but when after a whole night spent in ardent prayer, Olaf rapturously beheld a cloudy day, the obstinate people declared they were not yet convinced of his God's power, and would only believe if the sun shone on the following day.

Once more Olaf spent the night in prayer, but at dawn his chagrin was great to see the sky overcast. Nevertheless, determined to gain his end he assembled the people near Thor's statue, and after secretly bidding his principal attendant smash the idol with his battle ax if the people turned their eyes away but for a moment, he began to address them. Suddenly, while all were listening to him, Olaf pointed to the horizon, where the sun was slowly breaking its way through the clouds, and exclaimed, "Behold our God!" While the people one and all turned to see what he meant, the attendant broke the idol, and a host of mice and other vermin scattered on all sides. Seeing now that the statue was hollow, and that the food placed before their god had been devoured by noxious animals only, the people ceased to revere Thor, and definitely accepted the faith which King Olaf had so long and vainly pressed upon them.

CHAPTER V.

TYR.

TYR, Tiu, or Ziu was the son of Odin, and, according to different mythologists, his mother was either Frigga, queen of the gods, or a beautiful giantess whose name is unknown, but who was a personification of the raging sea. He is the god of martial honor, and one of the twelve principal deities of Asgard. Although he appears to have had no special dwelling there, he was always welcome to Vingolf or Valhalla, and occupied one of the twelve thrones in the great council hall of Glads-heim.

> " The hall Glads-heim, which is built of gold ;
> Where are in circle ranged twelve golden chairs,
> And in the midst one higher, Odin's throne."
> BALDER DEAD (Matthew Arnold).

Tyr was regarded also as the god of courage and of war, and therefore frequently invoked by the various nations of the North, who cried to him as well as to Odin to obtain victory. That he ranked next to Odin and Thor is proved by his name, Tiu, having been given to one of the days of the week, Tiu's day, which in modern English has become Tuesday. Under the name of Ziu, Tyr was the principal divinity of the Suabians, who originally called their capital, the modern Augsburg, Ziusburg. This people, venerating the god as they did, were wont to worship him under the emblem of a sword, his distinctive attribute, and in his honor held great sword dances, where various figures were carried out. Sometimes the participants forming two long lines, crossed their swords, point upwards, and

The god of war.

challenged the boldest among their number to take a flying leap over them. At other times the warriors joined their sword points closely together in the shape of a rose or wheel, and when this figure was complete invited their chief to stand on the navel thus formed of flat, shining steel blades, and then they bore him upon it through the camp in triumph. The sword point was further considered so sacred that it became customary to register oaths upon it.

> " . . . Come hither, gentlemen,
> And lay your hands again upon my sword;
> Never to speak of this that you have heard,
> Swear by my sword."
> HAMLET (Shakespeare).

A distinctive feature of the worship of this god among the Franks and some other Northern nations was that the priests called Druids or Godi offered up human sacrifices upon his altars, generally cutting the bloody or spread eagle upon their victims, that is to say, making a deep incision on either side of the backbone, turning the ribs thus loosened inside out, and tearing out the viscera through the opening thus made. Of course only prisoners of war were treated thus, and it was considered a point of honor with north European races to endure this torture without a moan. These sacrifices were made upon rude stone altars called dolmens, which can still be seen in Northern Europe. As Tyr was considered the patron god of the sword, it was deemed indispensable to engrave the sign or rune representing him upon the blade of every sword—an observance which the Edda enjoined upon all those who were desirous of obtaining victory.

> " Sig-runes thou must know,
> If victory (*sigr*) thou wilt have,
> And on thy sword's hilt rist them;
> Some on the chapes,
> Some on the guard,
> And twice name the name of Tyr."
> LAY OF SIGDRIFA (Thorpe's tr.).

Tyr was identical with the Saxon god Saxnot (from *sax*, a sword), and with Er, Heru, or Cheru, the chief divinity of the Cheruski, who also considered him god of the sun, and deemed his shining sword blade an emblem of its rays.

> " This very sword a ray of light
> Snatched from the Sun ! "
> VALHALLA (J. C. Jones).

According to an ancient legend, Cheru's sword, which had been fashioned by the dwarfs, sons of Ivald — the same who had also made Odin's spear — was held very sacred by his people, to whose care he had intrusted it, declaring that those who possessed it were sure to have the victory over their foes. But although carefully guarded in the temple, where it was hung so that it reflected the first beams of the morning sun, it suddenly and mysteriously disappeared one night. A Vala, druidess, or prophetess, consulted by the priests, revealed that the Norns had decreed that whoever wielded it would conquer the world and come to his death by it ; but in spite of all entreaties she refused to tell who had taken it or where it might be found. Some time after this occurrence a tall and dignified stranger came to Cologne, where Vitellius, the Roman prefect, was feasting, called him away from his beloved dainties, gave him the sword, telling him it would bring him glory and renown, and hailed him as emperor. This cry was taken up by the assembled legions, and Vitellius, without making any personal effort to secure the honor, found himself elected Emperor of Rome.

Tyr's sword.

The new ruler, however, was so absorbed in indulging his taste for food and drink that he paid but little heed to the divine weapon. One day while leisurely making his way towards Rome he carelessly left it hanging in the antechamber to his apartments. A German soldier seized this opportunity to substitute in its stead his own rusty blade. The besotted emperor went on, and was so busily engaged in feasting that he did not notice the exchange. When he arrived at Rome, he learned that the Eastern legions had named Vespasian emperor, and that he was even then on his way home to claim the throne.

Searching for the sacred weapon to defend his rights, Vitellius now discovered the theft, and, overcome by superstitious fears, did not even attempt to fight. He crawled away into a dark corner of his palace, whence he was ignominiously dragged by the enraged populace to the foot of the Capitoline Hill. There the prophecy was duly fulfilled, for the German soldier, who had joined the opposite faction, coming along at that moment, cut off Vitellius' head with the sacred sword.

The German soldier now changed from one legion to another, and traveled over many lands; but wherever he and his sword were found, victory was assured. After winning great honor and distinction, this man, having grown old, retired from active service to the banks of the Danube, where he secretly buried his treasured weapon, building his hut over its resting place to guard it as long as he lived. But although implored, when he lay on his deathbed, to reveal where he had hidden it, he persistently refused to do so, saying that it would be found by the man who was destined to conquer the world, but that he would not be able to escape the curse. Years passed by. Wave after wave the tide of barbarian invasion swept over that part of the country, and last of all came the terrible Huns under the leadership of Attila, the "Scourge of God." As he passed along the river, he saw a peasant mournfully examining his cow's foot, which had been wounded by some sharp instrument hidden in the long grass, and when search was made the point of a buried sword was found sticking out of the soil.

Attila, seeing the beautiful workmanship and the fine state of preservation of this weapon, immediately exclaimed that it was Cheru's sword, and brandishing it above his head announced that he was about to conquer the world. Battle after battle was fought by the Huns, who, according to the Saga, were everywhere victorious, until Attila, weary of warfare, settled down in Hungary, taking to wife the beautiful Burgundian princess Ildico, whose father he had slain. This princess, resenting the murder of her kin and wishing to avenge it, took advantage of the king's state of intoxication upon his wedding night to secure possession of the divine sword, with which she slew him in his bed, once more fulfilling the prophecy uttered so many years before.

The magic sword again disappeared for a long time, only to be unearthed once more and wielded by the Duke of Alva, Charles V.'s general, who shortly after won the victory of Mühlberg (1547). Since then nothing more has been heard of the sword of the god Cheru, in whose honor the Franks were wont to celebrate yearly martial games; but it is said that when the heathen gods were renounced in favor of Christianity, the priests transferred many of their attributes to the saints, and that this sword became the property of the Archangel St. Michael, who has wielded it ever since.

Tyr, whose name was synonymous with bravery and wisdom, was also considered by the ancient Northern people to have the white-armed Valkyrs, Odin's attendants, at his beck and call, and to designate the warriors whom they had best transfer to Valhalla to aid the gods on the last day.

> "The god Tyr sent
> Gondul and Skogul
> To choose a king
> Of the race of Ingve,
> To dwell with Odin
> In roomy Valhal."
> NORSE MYTHOLOGY (R. B. Anderson).

Tyr was generally spoken of and represented as one-armed, just as Odin was called one-eyed. This fact is explained in

Story of the wolf Fenris. various ways by different authorities; some claim that it was because he could give the victory only to one side; others, because a sword has but one blade. However this may be, these explanations did not satisfy the ancients, who preferred to account for the fact by the following myth:

Loki, the arch deceiver, went to Jötun-heim and secretly married the hideous giantess Angur-boda (anguish boding), who bore him three monstrous children—the wolf Fenris, Hel, the party-colored goddess of death, and Iörmungandr, a terrible serpent. He kept the existence of these monsters secret as long as he could ; but they speedily grew so large that they could no longer remain confined in the cave where they had come to light. Odin, from the top of his throne Hlidskialf, soon became aware of their existence, and also of the frightful rapidity with which they increased in size. Fearing lest the monsters, when they had gained a little more strength, should invade Asgard and destroy the gods, All-father determined to get rid of them, and, striding off to Jötun-heim, flung Hel down into the depths of Nifl-heim, where he told her she could reign over the nine dismal worlds of the dead. He threw Iörmungandr into the sea, where he stretched himself and grew until he encircled all the earth and could bite his own tail.

> " Into mid-ocean's dark depths hurled,
>   Grown with each day to giant size,
> The serpent soon inclosed the world,
>   With tail in mouth, in circle-wise ;
>   Held harmless still
>   By Odin's will."
> VALHALLA (J. C. Jones).

None too well pleased that the serpent should have attained such fearful dimensions in his new element, Odin resolved to lead Fenris to Asgard, where he hoped, by kindly treatment, to make him gentle and tractable. But the gods one and all shrank back in dismay when they saw the wolf, and none dared approach to give him food except Tyr, whom nothing ever daunted. Seeing that Fenris daily increased in size, strength, voracity, and fierce-ness, the gods assembled in council to deliberate how they might best dispose of him. They unanimously decided that it would desecrate their peace-steads to slay him, and resolved to bind him fast so that he could work them no harm.

With that purpose in view, they ordered a strong chain named

Læding, and, going out into the yard with it, playfully proposed to Fenris to bind it about him, to see whether his vaunted strength could burst it asunder. Confident in his ability to release himself, Fenris patiently allowed them to bind him fast, but when all stood aside, he shook and stretched himself and easily broke the chain to pieces.

Concealing their chagrin, the gods praised his strength, but soon left him to order a much stronger fetter, Droma, which, after some persuasion, the wolf allowed them to fasten around him also. A short, sharp struggle sufficed, however, to burst this bond too; so it has become proverbial in the North to use the figurative expressions," to get loose out of Læding," and " to dash out of Droma," whenever great difficulties have to be surmounted.

> " Twice did the Æsir strive to bind,
> Twice did they fetters powerless find;
> Iron or brass of no avail,
> Naught, save through magic, could prevail."
> VALHALLA (J. C. Jones).

The gods, perceiving now that ordinary bonds, however strong, would never prevail against the Fenris wolf's great strength, bade Skirnir, Frey's servant, go down to Svart-alfa-heim and bid the dwarfs fashion a bond which nothing could sever.

By magic arts the dark elves manufactured a slender silken rope out of such impalpable materials as the sound of a cat's footsteps, a woman's beard, the roots of a mountain, the longings of the bear, the voice of fishes, and the spittle of birds, and when it was finished they gave it to Skirnir, assuring him that no strength would avail to break it, and that the more it was strained the stronger it would become.

> " Gleipnir, at last,
> By Dark Elves cast,
> In Svart-alf-heim, with strong spells wrought,
> To Odin was by Skirnir brought :

As soft as silk, as light as air,
Yet still of magic power most rare."
VALHALLA (J. C. Jones).

Armed with this bond, called Gleipnir, the gods went with Fenris to the Island of Lyngvi, in the middle of Lake Amsvartnir, and again proposed to test his strength. But although Fenris had grown still stronger, he mistrusted the bond which looked so slight. He therefore refused to allow himself to be bound, unless one of the Æsir would consent to put his hand in his mouth, and leave it there, as a pledge of good faith, and that no magic arts were to be used against him.

The gods heard this condition with dismay, and all drew back except Tyr, who, seeing that the others would not venture to comply with this request, boldly stepped forward and thrust his hand between the monster's jaws. The gods now fastened Gleipnir around Fenris's neck and paws, shouting and laughing with glee when they saw that his utmost efforts to free himself were fruitless. Tyr, however, could not share their joy, for the wolf, finding himself captive, snapped his teeth together for rage, biting off the god's hand at the wrist, which since then has been known as the wolf's joint.

LOKI.

" Be silent, Tyr !
Thou couldst never settle
A strife 'twixt two ;
Of thy right hand also
I must mention make,
Which Fenris from thee took.

TYR.

I óf a hand am wanting
But thou of honest fame ;
Sad is the lack of either.
Nor is the wolf at ease :
He in bonds must bide
Until the gods' destruction."
SÆMUND'S EDDA (Thorpe's tr.).

Deprived of his right hand, Tyr was now forced to use the maimed arm for his shield, and to wield his sword with his left hand; but such was his dexterity that he slew just as many enemies as before.

The gods, in spite of all the wolf's struggles, now drew the end of the fetter Gelgia through the rock Gioll, and fastened it to the bowlder Thviti, which was sunk deep in the ground. Opening wide his fearful jaws, Fenris uttered such terrible howls that the gods, to silence him, thrust a sword into his mouth, the hilt resting upon his lower jaw and the point against his palate. The blood then began to pour out in such streams that it formed a great river, called Von. The wolf was condemned to remain thus chained fast until the last day, when his bonds would burst and he would find himself free to avenge his wrongs.

> "The wolf Fenrir,
> Freed from the chain,
> Shall range the earth."
> DEATH-SONG OF HÂKON (W. Taylor's tr.).

While some mythologists see in this myth an emblem of crime restrained and made innocuous by the power of the law, others see the underground fire, which kept within bounds can injure no one, but which unfettered fills the world with destruction and woe. Just as Odin's second eye is said to rest in Mimir's well, so Tyr's second hand (sword) is found in Fenris's jaws, as he has no more use for two weapons than the sky for two suns.

Tyr's worship is commemorated in sundry places (such as Tübingen, in Germany), which bear more or less modified forms of his name. It has also been given to the aconite, a plant known in Northern countries as "Tyr's helm."

CHAPTER VI.

BRAGI.

At the time of the dispute between the Æsir and Vanas, when the peace articles had all been agreed upon, a vase was brought into the assembly into which both parties solemnly spat. From this saliva the gods created Kvasir, *Origin of poetry.* a being renowned for his wisdom and goodness, who went about the world answering all questions asked him, thus teaching and benefiting all mankind. The dwarfs, hearing about Kvasir's great wisdom, coveted it, and finding him asleep one day, two of their number, Fialar and Galar, treacherously slew him, and drained every drop of his blood into three vessels — the kettle Od-hroerir (inspiration) and the bowls Son (expiation) and Boden (offering). After duly mixing this blood with honey, they manufactured from it a sort of beverage so inspiring that any one who tasted it immediately became a poet, and could sing with a charm which was certain to win all hearts.

Now, although the dwarfs had brewed this marvelous mead for their own consumption, they did not even taste it, but hid it away in a secret place, while they went out in search of further adventures. They had not gone very far ere they found the giant Gilling also sound asleep lying on a steep bank, and maliciously rolled him into the water, where he perished. Then hastening to his dwelling, some climbed on the roof, carrying a huge millstone, while the others, entering, told the giantess that her husband was dead. This news caused the poor woman great grief; but just as she was rushing out of the house to view Gilling's remains, the wicked dwarfs rolled the millstone down upon her head, and killed her. According to another account, the dwarfs invited the giant to go fishing with them, and succeeded in slaying him by sending him out in a leaky vessel, which sank beneath his weight.

The crime thus committed did not long remain unpunished, for although Gilling's wife was dead, he had left a brother, Suttung, who determined to avenge him. Seizing the dwarfs in his mighty grasp, this giant placed them on a shoal far out at sea, where they would surely have perished at the next high tide had they not succeeded in redeeming their lives by relinquishing their recently brewed mead. As soon as Suttung set them ashore, they therefore gave him the precious compound, which he intrusted to his daughter Gunlod, bidding her guard it night and day, and allow neither gods nor mortals to have even a taste. To fulfill this command, Gunlod carried the three vessels into the hollow mountain, where she kept watch over them with the most scrupulous care, little suspecting that Odin had discovered their place of concealment, thanks to the sharp eyes of his ever-vigilant ravens Hugin and Munin.

As Odin had mastered the runic lore and had tasted the waters of Mimir's fountain, he was already the wisest of gods; but hearing of the power of the draught of inspiration manufactured out of Kvasir's blood, he became very anxious to obtain possession of it also. With this purpose in view he therefore donned his broad-brimmed hat, wrapped himself in his cloud-hued cloak, and journeyed off to Jötun-heim. On his way to the giant's dwelling he passed by a field where nine ugly thralls were busy making hay. Odin paused for a moment, watched them work, and then proposed to whet their scythes, which seemed very dull indeed—an offer which the thralls eagerly accepted.

Drawing a whetstone from his bosom, Odin proceeded to sharpen the nine scythes, skillfully giving them such a keen edge that the thralls, finding their labor much lightened, asked for his whetstone. With good-humored acquiescence, Odin tossed the whetstone over the wall; but as the nine thralls simultaneously sprang forward to catch it, they wounded one another with their keen scythes. In anger at their respective carelessness, they now began to fight, and did not pause until they were all either mortally wounded or dead.

Quite undismayed by this tragedy, Odin continued on his way, and soon came to the house of the giant Baugi, a brother of Suttung, who received him very hospitably, and in the course of the conversation informed him that he was greatly embarrassed, as it was harvest time and all his workmen had just been found dead in the hayfield.

Odin, who on this occasion had given his name as Bolwerk (evil doer), promptly offered his services to the giant, promising to accomplish as much work as the nine thralls, and to labor diligently all summer in exchange for one single draught of Suttung's magic mead when the busy season was ended. This bargain was immediately concluded, and Baugi's new servant, Bolwerk, worked incessantly all summer long, more than fulfilling his part of the contract, and safely garnering all the grain before the autumn rains began to fall. When the first days of winter came, Bolwerk presented himself before his master, claiming his reward. But Baugi hesitated and demurred, saying he dared not openly ask his brother Suttung for a draught of inspiration, but would try to obtain it by cunning. Together, Bolwerk and Baugi then proceeded to the mountain where Gunlod dwelt, and as they could find no other mode of entering the secret cave, Odin produced his trusty auger, called Rati, and bade the giant bore with all his might to make a hole through which he might crawl into the mountain.

Baugi silently obeyed, and after a few moments' work withdrew the tool, saying that he had pierced through the mountain side, and that Odin would have no difficulty in slipping through. But the god, mistrusting this statement, merely blew into the hole, and when the dust and chips came flying into his face, he sternly bade Baugi resume his boring and never attempt to deceive him again.

The giant bored on, and when he withdrew his tool again, Odin ascertained that the hole was really finished. Changing himself into a worm, he wriggled through with such remarkable rapidity that he managed to escape, although Baugi treacherously thrust the sharp auger into the hole after him, intending to kill him.

> "Rati's mouth I caused
> To make a space,
> And to gnaw the rock;
> Over and under me
> Were the Jötun's ways:
> Thus I my head did peril."
> HÁVAMÁL (Thorpe's tr.).

Having reached the stalactite-hung cave, Odin reassumed his usual godlike form and starry mantle, and then presented himself before the beautiful Gunlod to exert all his fascinations to win her love, and coax her to grant him a sip from each of the vessels confided to her care.

Won by his passionate wooing, Gunlod consented to become his wife, and after he had spent three whole days with her in this retreat, she brought out the vessels from their secret hiding place, and told him he might take a sip from each.

> "And a draught obtained
> Of the precious mead,
> Drawn from Od-hroerir."
> ODIN'S RUNE-SONG (Thorpe's tr.).

Odin made use of this permission to drink so deeply that he completely drained all three vessels, and then, having obtained all he wanted, and being intoxicated with love, poetry, and inspiration, he donned his eagle plumes, rose higher and higher up into the blue, and, after hovering for a moment over the mountain top, winged his heavy flight towards Asgard.

He was still very far from the gods' realm, however, when he suddenly became aware of a pursuer, and, turning his head, ascertained that Suttung, having also assumed the form of an eagle, was coming rapidly after him to compel him to surrender the stolen mead. Odin therefore flew faster and faster, straining every nerve to reach Asgard before the foe should overtake him, while the gods anxiously watched the race.

Seeing that Odin was greatly handicapped and would scarcely be able to escape, the Æsir hastily gathered all the combustible materials they could find, and as soon as he had flown over the ramparts of their dwelling, they set fire to the mass of fuel, so that the flames, rising high, singed the wings of Suttung, who, bewildered with pain, fell into the very midst of the fire, where he was burned to death.

As for Odin, he flew on to the spot where the gods had prepared vessels for the stolen mead, and disgorged the draught of inspiration in such breathless haste that a few drops were scattered over the earth. There they became the portion of rhymsters and poetasters, the gods reserving the divine beverage for their own consumption, and only occasionally vouchsafing a taste to some favored mortal, who, immediately after, won world-wide renown by his inspired songs.

> "Of a well-assumed form
> I made good use:
> Few things fail the wise;
> For Od-hroerir
> Is now come up
> To men's earthly dwellings."
>
> HÁVAMÁL (Thorpe's tr.).

As men and gods owed this priceless gift to Odin, they were ever ready to show him their gratitude, and not only called it by his name, but also worshiped him as god of eloquence, poetry, and song, and made him the patron of all scalds.

Although Odin had thus won the gift of poetry, he seldom made use of it himself. It was reserved for his son Bragi, the child of Gunlod, to become the god of poetry and music and to charm the world with his songs.

The god of music.

7

> " White-bearded bard, ag'd
> Bragi, his gold harp
> Sweeps — and yet softer
> Stealeth the day."
>
> VIKING TALES OF THE NORTH (R. B. Anderson).

As soon as Bragi was born in the stalactite-hung cave where Odin had won Gunlod's affections, the dwarfs presented him with a magic golden harp, and, setting him on board of one of their own vessels, sent him out into the wide world. As the boat gently passed out of subterranean darkness, and floated over the threshold of Nain, the realm of the dwarf of death, Bragi, the fair and immaculate young god, who until then had shown no signs of life, suddenly sat up, and, seizing the golden harp beside him, began to sing the wondrous song of life, which at times rose up to heaven, and then sank down to the underground realm of Hel, the goddess of death.

> " Yggdrasil's ash is
> Of all trees most excellent,
> And of all ships, Skidbladnir;
> Of the Æsir, Odin,
> And of horses, Sleipnir;
> Bifröst of bridges,
> And of scalds, Bragi."
>
> LAY OF GRIMNIR (Thorpe's tr.).

While he played the vessel was gently wafted over sunlit waters, and soon touched the shore. The god Bragi then proceeded on foot, threading his way through the bare and silent forest, playing as he walked. At the sound of his tender music the trees began to bud and bloom, and the grass underfoot was gemmed with countless flowers.

Here he met Idun, daughter of Ivald, the fair goddess of immortal youth, whom the dwarfs allowed to visit the earth from time to time, and at her approach nature invariably assumed its loveliest and gentlest aspect.

Bragi having secured this fair goddess for his wife hastened with her to Asgard, where both were warmly welcomed and where Odin, after tracing runes on Bragi's tongue, decreed that he should be the heavenly minstrel and compose songs in honor of the gods and of the heroes whom he received in Valhalla.

As Bragi was god of poetry, eloquence, and song, the Northern races also called poetry by his name, and scalds of either sex were frequently designated as Braga-men or Braga-wo- **Worship of** men. Bragi was greatly honored by all the North- **Bragi.** ern races, and hence his health was always drunk on solemn or festive occasions, but especially at funeral feasts and at Yule-tide celebrations.

When it was time to drink this toast, which was served in cups shaped like a ship, and was called the Bragaful, the sacred sign of the hammer was first made over it. Then the new ruler or head of the family solemnly pledged himself to some great deed of valor, which he was bound to execute within the year, unless he wished to be considered destitute of honor. Following his example, all the guests were then wont to make similar vows and declare what they would do; and as some of them, owing to previous potations, talked rather too freely of their intentions on these occasions, this custom seems to connect the god's name with the vulgar but very expressive English verb "to brag."

In art, Bragi is generally represented as an elderly man, with long white hair and beard, and holding the golden harp from which his fingers could draw such magic tones.

CHAPTER VII.

IDUN.

IDUN, the personification of spring or immortal youth, who, according to some mythologists, had no birth and was never to taste death, was also warmly welcomed by the gods when she made her appearance in Asgard with Bragi. To win their affections she promised them a daily taste of the marvelous apples which she bore in her casket, which had the power of conferring immortal youth and loveliness upon all who partook of them.

The apples of youth.

> " The golden apples
> Out of her garden
> Have yielded you dower of youth,
> Ate you them every day."
>
> WAGNER (Forman's tr.).

Thanks to this magic fruit, the Scandinavian gods, who, because they sprang from a mixed race, were not all immortal, warded off the approach of old age and disease, and remained vigorous, beautiful, and young through countless ages. These apples were therefore considered very precious indeed, and Idun carefully treasured them in her magic casket. But no matter how many she drew out, the same number always remained for distribution at the feast of the gods, to whom alone she vouchsafed a taste, although dwarfs and giants were eager to obtain possession of this fruit.

> " Bright Iduna, Maid immortal!
> Standing at Valhalla's portal,

100

In her casket has rich store
Of rare apples, gilded o'er ;
Those rare apples, not of Earth,
Ageing Æsir give fresh birth."

VALHALLA (J. C. Jones).

One day, Odin, Hoenir, and Loki started out upon one of their usual excursions to earth, and, after wandering for a long while, found themselves in a deserted region, where they could discover no hospitable dwelling. Weary and very hungry, the gods perceiving a herd of oxen, slew one, kindled a fire, and sat down beside it to rest while waiting for their meat to cook.

To their surprise, however, in spite of the roaring flames the meat remained quite raw. Realizing that some magic must be at work, they looked about them to discover what could hinder their cookery. They finally perceived an eagle perched upon a tree above them. The bird addressed them and declared that the spell would be removed and the meat done to a turn in a very short time if they would only give him as much food as he could eat. The gods agreed to do this, and the eagle, swooping downwards, fanned the flames with his huge wings, and soon the meat was cooked. But as he was about to carry off three quarters of the ox as his share, Loki seized a great stake lying near at hand, and began to belabor the voracious bird, forgetting that it was versed in magic arts. To his great dismay one end of the stake stuck fast to the eagle's back, the other to his hands, and he found himself dragged over stones and through briers, flying through the air, his arms almost torn out of their sockets. In vain he cried for mercy and implored the eagle to let him go ; the bird flew on, until he promised any ransom his ravisher could ask in exchange for his release.

The bird, who was the storm giant Thiassi in eagle guise, let him go only upon one condition. He made him **Thiassi, the** promise upon the most solemn of oaths that he **storm giant.** would lure Idun out of Asgard, so that the giant might obtain possession of her and of her magic fruit.

Released at last, Loki returned to join Odin and Hoenir, to whom, however, he was very careful not to confide the condition upon which he had obtained his freedom; and when they had returned to Asgard he began to plan how he might entice Idun outside of the gods' abode. A few days later, Bragi being absent on one of his minstrel tours, Loki sought Idun in the groves of Brunnaker, where she had taken up her abode, and by artfully describing some apples which grew at a short distance from there, and which he mendaciously declared were exactly like hers, he lured her away from home with a crystal dish full of fruit, which she intended to compare with that which he extolled. No sooner had Idun left Asgard, however, than the deceiver Loki forsook her, and ere she could return home the storm giant Thiassi swept down from the north on his eagle wings, caught her up in his cruel talons, and bore her swiftly away to his barren and desolate home of Thrym-heim.

> "Thrymheim the sixth is named,
> Where Thiassi dwelt,
> That all-powerful Jötun."
> LAY OF GRIMNIR (Thorpe's tr.).

There she pined, grew pale and sad, but persistently refused to give him the smallest bite of her magic fruit, which, as he well knew, would make him beautiful and renew his strength and youth.

> "All woes that fall
> On Odin's hall
> Can be traced to Loki base.
> From out Valhalla's portal
> 'Twas he who pure Iduna lured, —
> Whose casket fair
> Held apples rare
> That render gods immortal, —
> And in Thiassi's tower immured."
> VALHALLA (J. C. Jones).

Time passed. The gods, thinking that Idun had accompanied her husband and would soon return, at first paid no heed to her departure, but little by little the beneficial effect of their last apple feast passed away. They gradually felt themselves grow old and stiff, and saw their youth and beauty disappear; so they became alarmed and began to search for the missing goddess of perpetual youth.

Close investigation very soon revealed the fact that she had last been seen in Loki's company, and when Odin sternly called him to account, this god was forced to reveal that he had betrayed her into the storm giant's power.

> "By his mocking, scornful mien,
> Soon in Valhal it was seen
> 'Twas the traitor Loki's art
> Which had led Idun apart
> To gloomy tower
> And Jotun power."
>
> VALHALLA (J. C. Jones).

The gods now indignantly bade Loki undo the harm he had done and immediately bring the goddess back, warning him that unless he complied with this command he would forfeit his life.

Thus adjured, Loki promised to do all he could, and, borrowing Freya's falcon plumage, flew off to Thrym-heim, where he found Idun alone, sadly mourning her exile from Asgard and her beloved Bragi. Changing the fair goddess into a nut according to some mythologists, or according to others, into a swallow, Loki held her tightly between his claws, and rapidly winged his way back to Asgard, hoping he would reach the shelter of its high walls ere Thiassi returned from his fishing excursion in the Northern seas.

The gods, assembled on the ramparts of the heavenly city, were watching for his return with far more anxiety than they had for Odin when he went in search of Od-hroerir, and, remembering the success of their ruse on that occasion, they had gathered great piles of fuel, which they were ready to set on fire at any moment.

Suddenly they saw Loki coming, but descried in his wake the

giant Thiassi, who, in eagle plumes, was striving to overtake him and claim his prey. Loki, knowing his life depended upon the success of his venture, made such great efforts to reach the goal ere Thiassi overtook him that he cleared the wall and sank exhausted in the midst of the gods, who, setting fire to the accumulated fuel, singed Thiassi's wings, blinded him with smoke, and, when he dropped stunned in their midst, ruthlessly fell upon and slew him.

Return of Idun.

The Æsir were overjoyed at the recovery of Idun,—who hastened to deal out her apples to them all. Feeling their wonted strength and good looks return with every mouthful they ate, they good-naturedly declared that it was no wonder even the giants longed to taste the apples of perpetual youth. They therefore vowed they would place Thiassi's eyes as constellations in the heavens, in order to soften any feeling of anger which his relatives might experience upon learning how he had been slain.

> " Up I cast the eyes
> Of Allvaldi's son
> Into the heaven serene :
> They are signs the greatest
> Of my deeds."
>
> LAY OF HARBARD (Thorpe's tr.).

The physical explanation of this myth is obvious. Idun, the emblem of vegetation, is forcibly carried away in autumn, when Bragi is absent and the singing of the birds has ceased. The cold wintry wind, Thiassi, detains her in the frozen, barren north, where she cannot thrive, until Loki, the south wind, brings back the seed or the swallow, which are both precursors of the returning spring. The youth, beauty, and strength conferred by Idun are symbolical of Nature's resurrection in spring after winter's sleep, when color and vigor return to the earth, which has grown wrinkled and gray.

The goddess of spring.

As the disappearance of Idun (vegetation) was a yearly occurrence, the old scalds were not content with this one myth, but also invented another, which, unfortunately, has come down to us only in a fragmentary and very incomplete form. According to this account, Idun was once sitting upon the branches of the sacred ash Yggdrasil, when, growing suddenly faint, she loosed her hold and dropped down on the ground beneath, to the lowest depths of Nifl-heim. There she lay, pale and motionless, gazing with fixed and horror-struck eyes upon the grewsome sights of Hel's realm, trembling violently all the while, as if overcome by the penetrating cold.

> "In the dales dwells
> The prescient Dîs,
> From Yggdrasil's
> Ash sunk down,
> Of alfen race,
> Idun by name,
> The youngest of Ivaldi's
> Elder children.
> She ill brooked
> Her descent
> Under the hoar tree's
> Trunk confined.
> She would not happy be
> With Norvi's daughter,
> Accustomed to a pleasanter
> Abode at home."
> ODIN'S RAVENS' SONG (Thorpe's tr.).

Seeing that she did not rouse herself and return, Odin finally bade Bragi, Heimdall, and another of the gods go in search of her, giving them a white wolfskin to envelop her in, so that she should not suffer from the cold, and bidding them make every effort to rouse her from her stupor.

> "A wolf's skin they gave her,
> In which herself she clad."
> ODIN'S RAVENS' SONG (Thorpe's tr.).

But although Idun passively allowed them to wrap her up in the warm wolfskin, she persistently refused to speak or move, and the gods sadly suspected she foresaw great ills, for the tears continually rolled down her pallid cheeks. Bragi, seeing her unhappiness, bade the other gods return to Asgard without him, vowing that he would remain beside her until she was ready to leave Hel's dismal realm. But the sight of her woe oppressed him so sorely that he had no heart for his usual merry songs, and the strings of his harp remained entirely mute.

> "That voice-like zephyr o'er flow'r meads creeping,
> Like Bragi's music his harp strings sweeping."
> VIKING TALES OF THE NORTH (R. B. Anderson).

In this myth Idun's fall from Yggdrasil is symbolical of the autumnal falling of the leaves, which lie limp and helpless on the cold bare ground until they are hidden from sight under the snow, represented by the wolfskin, which Odin, the sky, sends down to keep them warm; and the cessation of the birds' songs is further typified by Bragi's silent harp.

CHAPTER VIII.

NIÖRD.

WE have already seen how the Æsir and Vanas exchanged hostages after the terrible war they had waged against each other, and that while Hoenir, Odin's brother, went to live in Vana-heim, Niörd, with his two children, Frey and Freya, definitely took up his abode in Asgard.

> "In Vana-heim
> Wise powers him created,
> And to the gods a hostage gave."
> LAY OF VAFTHRUDNIR (Thorpe's tr.).

As ruler of the winds, and of the sea near the shore, Niörd was given the palace of Nôatûn, near the seashore, where we are told he stilled the terrible tempests stirred up by Ægir, god of the deep sea.

> "Niörd, the god of storms, whom fishers know;
> Not born in Heaven — he was in Van-heim rear'd,
> With men, but lives a hostage with the gods;
> He knows each frith, and every rocky creek
> Fringed with dark pines, and sands where sea fowl scream."
> BALDER DEAD (Matthew Arnold).

He also extended his special protection over commerce and fishing, which two occupations could be pursued with advantage only during the short summer months, of which he was in a measure considered the personification.

Niörd is represented in art as a very handsome god, in the prime of life, clad in a short green tunic, with a crown of shells

107

and seaweed upon his head, or a broad-brimmed hat adorned with eagle or heron plumes. As personification of the summer, he was invoked to still the raging storms which desolated the coasts during the winter months. He was also implored to hasten the vernal warmth and thereby extinguish the winter fires.

God of summer.

As agriculture was practiced only during the summer months, and principally along the fiords or sea inlets, Niörd was also invoked for favorable harvests, for he was said to delight in prospering those who placed their trust in him.

Niörd's first wife, according to some authorities, was his sister Nerthus, Mother Earth, who in Germany was identified with Frigga, as we have seen, but in Scandinavia was considered a separate divinity. He was, however, obliged to part with her when summoned to Asgard, where he occupied one of the twelve seats in the great council hall, and was present at all the assemblies of the gods, withdrawing to Nôatûn only when his services were not required by the Æsir.

> "Nôatûn is the eleventh;
> There Niörd has
> Himself a dwelling made,
> Prince of men;
> Guiltless of sin,
> He rules o'er the high-built fane."
> LAY OF GRIMNIR (Thorpe's tr.).

In his own home by the seashore, Niörd delighted in watching the gulls fly to and fro, and in observing the graceful movements of the swans, his favorite birds, which were held sacred to him. He spent many an hour, too, considering the gambols of the gentle seals, which came to bask in the sunshine at his feet.

Shortly after Idun's recovery from Thrym-heim, and Thiassi's death within the bounds of Asgard, the assembled gods were greatly surprised and dismayed to see Skadi, the giant's daughter, appear one day in their midst, demanding satisfaction for her father's death. Although the

Skadi, goddess of winter.

daughter of an ugly old Hrim-thurs, Skadi, the goddess of winter, was very beautiful indeed, in her silvery armor, with her glittering spear, sharp-pointed arrows, short white hunting dress, white fur leggings, and broad snowshoes, and as she confronted the gods they could not but recognize the justice of her claim, and offered the usual fine in atonement. Skadi, however, was so very angry that she at first refused this compromise, and sternly demanded a life for a life, until Loki, wishing to appease her wrath, and thinking that if he could only make those proud lips unbend enough to smile the rest would be easy, began to play all manner of pranks. Fastening a goat to himself by an invisible cord, he went through a series of antics, grotesquely reproduced by the goat; and this sight was so very comical that all the gods fairly shouted with merriment, and even Skadi was seen to smile.

Taking advantage of this softened mood, the gods pointed to the firmament where her father's eyes glowed like radiant stars in the northern hemisphere. They told her they had placed them there to show him all honor, and finally added that she might select as husband any of the gods present at the assembly, providing she were content to judge of their attractions by their naked feet.

Blindfolded, so that she could see only the feet of the gods standing in a circle around her, Skadi looked about her until she saw a pair of beautifully formed feet. She felt sure they must belong to Balder, the god of light, whose bright face had charmed her, and she designated their owner as her choice.

But when the bandage was removed, she discovered to her secret chagrin that she had chosen Niörd, to whom her troth was plighted, and with whom she nevertheless spent a very happy honeymoon in Asgard, where all seemed to delight in doing her honor. This time passed, however; Niörd took his bride home to Nôatûn, where the monotonous sound of the waves, the shrieking of the gulls, and the cries of the seals so disturbed Skadi's slumbers that she finally declared it was quite impossible for her to remain there any longer, and implored her husband to take her back to her native Thrym-heim.

> " Sleep could I not
> On my sea-strand couch,
> For screams of the sea fowl.
> There wakes me,
> When from the wave he comes,
> Every morning the mew (gull)."
> NORSE MYTHOLOGY (R. B. Anderson).

Niörd, anxious to please his new wife, consented to take her to Thrym-heim and dwell there with her nine nights out of every twelve, providing she would spend the remaining three with him at Nôatûn; but when he reached the mountain region, the sough-ing of the wind in the pines, the thunder of the avalanches, the cracking of the ice, the roar of the waterfalls, and the howling of the wolves appeared to him as unbearable as the sound of the sea had seemed to his wife, and he could not but rejoice when his time of exile was ended, and he once more found him-self domiciled at Nôatûn.

> " Am weary of the mountains;
> Not long was I there,
> Only nine nights;
> The howl of the wolves
> Methought sounded ill
> To the song of the swans."
> NORSE MYTHOLOGY (R. B. Anderson).

For some time, Niörd and Skadi, who are the personifications of summer and winter, alternated thus, the wife spending the three short summer months by the sea, and he re-luctantly remaining with her in Thrym-heim dur-ing the nine long winter months. But, finding at last that their tastes would never agree, they decided to part forever, and re-turned to their respective homes, where each could follow the occupations which custom had endeared.

Parting of Niörd and Skadi.

> "Thrym-heim it's called,
> Where Thjasse dwelled,
> That stream-mighty giant;
> But Skade now dwells,
> Pure bride of the gods,
> In her father's old mansion."
> NORSE MYTHOLOGY (R. B. Anderson).

Skadi now resumed her wonted pastime of hunting, leaving her realm again only to marry the semi-historical Odin, to whom she bore a son called Sæming, the first king of Norway, and the supposed founder of the royal race which long ruled that country.

According to other accounts, however, Skadi eventually married Uller, the winter-god. As Skadi was a skillful markswoman, she is represented with bow and arrow, and, as goddess of the chase, she is generally accompanied by one of the wolf-like Eskimo dogs so common in the North. Skadi was invoked by hunters and by winter travelers, whose sleighs she guided over the snow and ice, thus helping them to reach their destination in safety.

Skadi's anger against the gods, who had slain her father, the storm giant, is an emblem of the unbending rigidity of the ice-enveloped earth, which, softened at last by the frolicsome play of Loki (the heat lightning), smiles, and permits the embrace of Niörd (summer). His love, however, cannot hold her for more than three months of the year (typified in the myth by nights), as she is always secretly longing for the wintry storms and her wonted mountain amusements.

As Niörd was supposed to bless the vessels passing in and out of port, his temples were situated by the seashore; it was there that the oaths in his name were commonly sworn, and his health was drunk at every banquet, where he was invariably named with his son Frey.

Worship of Niörd.

As all aquatic plants were supposed to belong to him, the marine sponge was known in the North as "Niörd's glove," a name which was retained until lately, when the same plant has been popularly called the "Virgin's hand."

CHAPTER IX.

FREY.

FREY, or Fro, as he was called in Germany, was the son of Niörd and Nerthus, or of Niörd and Skadi, and was born in Vana-heim. He therefore belonged to the race of the Vanas, the divinities of water and air, but was warmly welcomed in Asgard when he came thither as hostage with his father. As it was customary among the Northern nations to bestow some valuable gift upon a child when he cut his first tooth, the Æsir gave the infant Frey the beautiful realm of Alf-heim or Fairyland, the home of all the Light Elves.

> " Alf-heim the gods to Frey
> Gave in days of yore
> For a tooth gift."
> SÆMUND'S EDDA (Thorpe's tr.).

Here Frey, the god of the golden sunshine and the warm summer showers, took up his abode, charmed with the company of
The god of fairyland. the elves and fairies, who implicitly obeyed his every order, and at a sign from him flitted to and fro, doing all the good in their power, for they were preëminently beneficent spirits.

Frey received from the gods a marvelous sword (an emblem of the sunbeams), which had the power of fighting successfully, and of its own accord, as soon as it was drawn from its sheath. Because he carried this glittering weapon, Frey has sometimes been confounded with the sword-god Tyr or Saxnot, although

112

(*Opp.* p. 112.)

FREY.

he wielded it principally against the frost giants, whom he hated
almost as much as did Thor.

> "With a short-shafted hammer fights conquering Thor;
> Frey's own sword but an ell long is made."
> VIKING TALES OF THE NORTH (R. B. Anderson).

The dwarfs from Svart-alfa-heim gave Frey the golden-bristled
boar Gullin-bursti (the golden-bristled), a personification of the
sun. The radiant bristles of this animal were considered symbolical either of the solar rays, of the golden grain, which at his
bidding waved over the harvest fields of Midgard, or of agriculture, for the boar (by tearing up the ground with his sharp tusk)
was supposed to have first taught mankind how to plow.

> "There was Frey, and sat
> On the gold-bristled boar, who first, they say,
> Plowed the brown earth, and made it green for Frey."
> LOVERS OF GUDRUN (William Morris).

Frey sometimes rode astride of this marvelous boar, whose celerity was very great, and at other times harnessed him to his golden
chariot, which was said to contain the fruits and flowers which
he lavishly scattered abroad over the face of the earth.

Frey was, moreover, the proud possessor, not only of the dauntless steed Blodug-hofi, which dashed through fire and water at
his command, but also of the magic ship Skidbladnir, a personification of the clouds. This vessel, navigating over land and sea,
was always wafted along by favorable winds, and was so elastic
that, while it could assume large enough proportions to carry the
gods, their steeds, and all their equipments, it could also be folded
up like a napkin and thrust out of sight.

> "Ivaldi's sons
> Went in days of old
> Skidbladnir to form,
> Of ships the best,
> For the bright Frey,
> Niörd's benign son."
> LAY OF GRIMNIR (Thorpe's tr.).

8

It is related in one of the lays of the Edda that Frey once ventured to ascend Odin's throne Hlidskialf, and from this exalted seat cast a glance over all the wide earth. Gazing towards the frozen North, he saw a beautiful young maiden enter the house of the frost giant Gymir, and as she raised her hand to lift the latch her radiant beauty illuminated sea and sky.

A moment later, this lovely creature, whose name was Gerda, and who is considered as a personification of the flashing Northern lights, vanished within her father's house, and Frey pensively wended his way back to Alfheim, his heart oppressed with longing to make this fair maiden his wife. Being deeply in love, he was melancholy and absentminded in the extreme, and began to behave so strangely that his father, Niörd, became greatly alarmed about his health, and bade his favorite servant, Skirnir, discover the cause of this sudden change. After much persuasion, Skirnir finally won from Frey an account of his ascent of Hlidskialf, and of the fair vision he had seen. He confessed his love and especially his utter despair, for as Gerda was the daughter of Gymir and Angur-boda, and a relative of the murdered giant Thiassi, he feared she would never view his suit with favor.

The wooing of Gerda.

> "In Gymer's court I saw her move,
> The maid who fires my breast with love;
> Her snow-white arms and bosom fair
> Shone lovely, kindling sea and air.
> Dear is she to my wishes, more
> Than e'er was maid to youth before;
> But gods and elves, I wot it well,
> Forbid that we together dwell."
> SKIRNER'S LAY (Herbert's tr.).

Skirnir, however, consolingly replied that he could see no reason why his master should take such a despondent view of the matter, and proposed to go and woo the maiden in his name, providing Frey would lend him his steed for the journey, and give him his glittering sword in reward.

Overjoyed at the mere prospect of winning the beautiful Gerda, Frey handed Skirnir the flashing sword, and bade him use his horse, ere he resumed his interrupted day-dream; for ever since he had fallen in love he had frequently indulged in revery. In his absorption he did not even notice that Skirnir was still hovering near him, and did not perceive him cunningly steal the reflection of his face from the surface of the brook near which he was seated, and imprison it in his drinking horn, intending "to pour it out in Gerda's cup, and by its beauty win the heart of the giantess for the lord" for whom he was about to go a-wooing. Provided with this portrait, with eleven golden apples, and with the magic ring Draupnir, Skirnir now rode off to Jötun-heim, to fulfill his embassy. As soon as he came near Gymir's dwelling he heard the loud and persistent howling of his watch dogs, which were personifications of the wintry winds. A shepherd, guarding his flock in the vicinity, told him, in answer to his inquiry, that it would be impossible for him to approach the house, on account of the flaming barrier which surrounded it; but Skirnir, knowing that Blodug-hofi would dash through any fire, merely set spurs to his steed, and, riding up to the giant's door, soon found himself ushered into the presence of the lovely Gerda.

To induce this fair maiden to lend a favorable ear to his master's proposals, Skirnir showed her the purloined portrait, and proffered the golden apples and magic ring, which she haughtily refused to accept, declaring that her father had gold enough and to spare.

> "I take not, I, that wondrous ring,
>   Though it from Balder's pile you bring.
>   Gold lack not I, in Gymer's bower;
>   Enough for me my father's dower."
>   SKIRNER'S LAY (Herbert's tr.).

Indignant at her scorn, Skirnir now threatened to use his magic sword to cut off her head; but as this threat did not in the least frighten the maiden, and she calmly defied him, he had recourse to magic arts. Cutting runes in his stick, he told her that unless she yielded ere the spell was ended, she would be condemned either to eternal celibacy, or to marry some hideous old frost giant whom she could never love.

Terrified into submission by the frightful description he gave of her cheerless future in case she persisted in her refusal, Gerda finally consented to become Frey's wife, and dismissed Skirnir, promising to meet her future spouse on the ninth night, in the land of Buri, the green grove, where she would dispel his sadness and make him happy.

> "Burri is hight the seat of love;
> Nine nights elapsed, in that known grove
> Shall brave Niorder's gallant boy
> From Gerda take the kiss of joy."
> SKIRNER'S LAY (Herbert's tr.).

Delighted with his success, Skirnir hurried back to Alf-heim, where Frey eagerly came to meet him, and insisted upon knowing the result of his journey. When he learned that Gerda had consented to become his wife, his face grew radiant with joy; but when Skirnir further informed him that he would have to wait nine nights ere he could behold his promised bride, he turned sadly away, declaring the time would appear interminable.

> "Long is one night, and longer twain;
> But how for three endure my pain?
> A month of rapture sooner flies
> Than half one night of wishful sighs."
> SKIRNER'S LAY (Herbert's tr.).

In spite of this loverlike despondency, however, the time of waiting came to an end, and Frey joyfully hastened to the green grove, where he met Gerda, who became his happy wife, and proudly sat upon his throne beside him.

> "Frey to wife had Gerd;
> She was Gymir's daughter,
> From Jötuns sprung."
> SÆMUND'S EDDA (Thorpe's tr.).

According to some mythologists, Gerda is not a personification of the aurora borealis, but of the earth, which, hard, cold, and unyielding, resists the spring-god's proffers of adornment and fruitfulness (the apples and ring), defies the flashing sunbeams (Frey's sword), and only consents to receive his kiss when it learns that it will else be doomed to perpetual barrenness, or given over entirely into the power of the giants (ice and snow). The nine nights of waiting are typical of the nine winter months, at the end of which the earth becomes the bride of the sun, in the groves where the trees are budding forth into leaf and blossom.

Frey and Gerda, we are told, became the parents of a son called Fiolnir, whose birth consoled Gerda for the loss of her brother Beli. The latter had attacked Frey and had been slain by him, although the sun-god, deprived of his matchless sword, had been obliged to defend himself with a stag horn which he hastily snatched from the wall of his dwelling.

Besides the faithful Skirnir, Frey had two other attendants, a married couple, Beyggvir and Beyla, the personifications of mill refuse and manure, which two ingredients, being used in agriculture for fertilizing purposes, were therefore considered Frey's faithful servants, in spite of their unpleasing qualities.

Snorro-Sturleson, in his "Heimskringla," or chronicle of the ancient kings of Norway, states that Frey was an historical personage who bore the name of Ingvi-Frey, and ruled in Upsala after the death of the semi-historical Odin and Niörd. The historical Frey. Under his reign the people enjoyed such prosperity and peace that they declared their king must be a god. They therefore began to invoke him as such, carrying their enthusiastic admiration for him to such lengths that when he died the priests, not daring to reveal the fact, laid him in a great mound instead of burning his body, as had been customary until then. They then informed the people that Frey — whose name was the Northern synonym for "master"—had "gone into the mound," an expression which eventually became the Northern phrase for death.

Only three years later the people, who had continued paying their taxes to the king by pouring the gold, silver, and copper coin into the mound by three different openings, discovered that Frey was dead. As their peace and prosperity had remained undisturbed, they decreed that his corpse should never be burned, and thus inaugurated the custom of mound burial, which in due time supplanted the funeral pyre in many places. One of the three mounds near Gamla Upsala still bears this god's name. His statues were placed in the great temple there, and his name was duly mentioned in all solemn oaths, of which the usual formula was, "So help me Frey, Niörd, and the Almighty Asa" (Odin).

No weapons were ever admitted in Frey's temples, the most celebrated of which were at Throndhjeim, and at Thvera in Ice-

Worship of Frey.

land, where oxen or horses were offered up in sacrifice to him, and where a heavy gold ring was dipped in the victim's blood ere the above-mentioned oath was solemnly taken upon it.

Frey's statues, like those of all the other Northern divinities, were roughly hewn blocks of wood, and the last of these sacred images seems to have been destroyed by Olaf the Saint, who forcibly converted many of his subjects. Besides being god of sunshine, fruitfulness, peace, and prosperity, Frey was considered the patron of horses and horsemen, and the deliverer of all captives.

> "Frey is the best
> Of all the chiefs
> Among the gods.
> He causes not tears
> To maids or mothers:
> His desire is to loosen the fetters
> Of those enchained."
>
> NORSE MYTHOLOGY (R. B. Anderson).

One month of every year, the Yule month, or Thor's month, was considered sacred to Frey as well as to Thor, and began on the longest night of the year, which bore the name of Mother

Night. This month was a time of feasting and rejoicing, for it heralded the return of the sun. The festival was called Yule (wheel) because the sun was supposed to resemble a wheel rapidly revolving across the sky. This re- *The Yule feast.* semblance gave rise to a singular custom in England, Germany, and along the banks of the Moselle. Until within late years, the people were wont to assemble yearly upon a mountain, to set fire to a huge wooden wheel, twined with straw, which, all ablaze, was then sent rolling down the hill and plunged with a hiss into the water.

"Some others get a rotten Wheele, all worn and cast aside,
Which, covered round about with strawe and tow, they closely hide;
And caryed to some mountaines top, being all with fire light,
They hurle it down with violence, when darke appears the night;
Resembling much the sunne, that from the Heavens down should fal,
A strange and monstrous sight it seemes, and fearful to them all;
But they suppose their mischiefs are all likewise throwne to hell,
And that, from harmes and dangers now, in safetie here they dwell."
NAOGEORGUS.

All the Northern races considered the Yule feast the greatest of the year, and were wont to celebrate it with dance, feasting, and drinking, each god being pledged by name. The missionaries, perceiving the extreme popularity of this feast, thought best to encourage drinking to the health of the Lord and his twelve apostles when they first began to convert the Northern heathens. In honor of Frey, boar's flesh was eaten on this occasion. Crowned with laurel and rosemary, the animal's head was brought into the banquet hall with much ceremony—a custom long after observed at Oxford, where the following lines were sung:

"Caput apri defero
Reddens laude Domino.
The boar's head in hand bring I,
With garlands gay and rosemary.
I pray you all sing merrily
Qui estis in convivio."
QUEEN'S COLLEGE CAROL, OXFORD.

The father of the family then laid his hand on this dish, which was called "the boar of atonement," swearing he would be faithful to his family, and would fulfill all his obligations — an example which was followed by all present, from the highest to the lowest. This dish could be carved only by a man of unblemished reputation and tried courage, for the boar's head was a sacred emblem which was supposed to inspire every one with fear. For that reason a boar's head was frequently used as ornament for the helmets of Northern kings and heroes whose bravery was unquestioned.

As Frey's name of Fro is phonetically the same as the word used in German for gladness, he was considered the patron of

God of conjugal happiness. every joy, and was invariably invoked by married couples who wished to live in harmony. Those who succeeded in doing so for a certain length of time were publicly rewarded by the gift of a piece of boar's flesh, for which, in later times, the English and Viennese substituted a flitch of bacon or a ham.

> "You shall swear, by custom of confession,
> If ever you made nuptial transgression,
> Be you either married man or wife:
> If you have brawls or contentious strife;
> Or otherwise, at bed or at board,
> Offended each other in deed or word;
> Or, since the parish clerk said Amen,
> You wish'd yourselves unmarried again;
> Or, in a twelvemonth and a day
> Repented not in thought any way,
> But continued true in thought and desire
> As when you join'd hands in the quire.
> If to these conditions, with all feare,
> Of your own accord you will freely sweare,
> A whole gammon of bacon you shall receive,
> And bear it hence with love and good leave:
> For this our custom at Dunmow well known —
> Though the pleasure be ours, the bacon's your own."
>
> BRAND'S POPULAR ANTIQUITIES

At Dunmow, England, and in Vienna, Austria, this custom was kept up very long indeed, the ham or flitch of bacon being hung over the city gate, whence the successful candidate was expected to bring it down, after he had satisfied the judges that he lived in peace with his wife, but was not under petticoat rule. It is said that in Vienna this ham once remained for a long time unclaimed until at last a worthy burgher presented himself before the judges, bearing his wife's written affidavit that they had been married twelve years and had never disagreed — a statement which was confirmed by all their neighbors. The judges, satisfied with the proofs laid before them, told the candidate that the prize was his, and that he only need climb the ladder placed beneath it and bring it down. Rejoicing at having secured such a fine ham, the man obeyed; but as he was about to reach upwards, he noticed that the ham, exposed to the noonday sun, was beginning to melt, and that a drop of fat threatened to fall upon and stain his Sunday coat. Hastily beating a retreat, he pulled off his coat, jocosely remarking that his wife would scold him roundly were he to stain it, a confession which made the bystanders roar with laughter, and which cost him his ham.

Another Yule-tide custom was the burning of a huge log, which had to last all night or it was considered of very bad omen indeed. The charred remains of this log were carefully collected, and treasured up to set fire to the log of the following year.

> " With the last yeeres brand
> Light the new block, and
> For good successe in his spending,
> On your psaltries play,
> That sweet luck may
> Come while the log is a-tending."
> HESPERIDES (Herrick).

This festival was so popular in Scandinavia, where it was celebrated in January, that King Olaf, seeing how dear it was to the Northern heart, transferred most of its observances to Christmas day, thereby doing much to reconcile the ignorant people to their change of religion.

As god of peace and prosperity, Frey is supposed to have re-appeared upon earth many times, and to have ruled the Swedes under the name of Ingvi-Frey, whence his descendants were called Inglings. He also governed the Danes under the name of Frid-leef. In Denmark he is said to have married the beautiful maiden Freygerda, whom he had rescued from a dragon. By her he had a son named Frodi, who, in due time, succeeded him as king.

This Frodi ruled Denmark in the days when there was "peace throughout all the world," that is to say, just at the time when Christ was born in Bethlehem of Judea; and because all his sub-jects lived in amity, he was generally known as Peace Frodi.

This king once received from Hengi-kiaptr a pair of magic millstones, called Grotti, which were so ponderous that none of his servants nor even his strongest warriors could turn them. As Peace Frodi knew that the mill was enchanted and would grind anything he wished, he was very anxious indeed to set it to work, and, during a visit to Sweden, saw and purchased as slaves the two giantesses Menia and Fenia, whose powerful muscles and frames had attracted his attention.

How the sea became salt.

On his return home, Peace Frodi led these women to the mill, and bade them turn the grindstones and grind out gold, peace, and prosperity — a wish which was immediately fulfilled. Cheerfully the women worked on, hour after hour, until the king's coffers were overflowing with gold and his land with prosperity and peace.

> "Let us grind riches to Frothi!
> Let us grind him, happy
> In plenty of substance,
> On our gladdening Quern."
>
> GROTTA-SAVNGR (Longfellow's tr.).

But when Menia and Fenia would fain have rested awhile, the king, whose greed had been excited, bade them work on. In spite of their cries and entreaties he forced them to labor hour after hour, allowing them only as much time to rest as was required for the singing of a verse in a song, until, exasperated by his cruelty, the giantesses resolved to have their revenge. Once while Frodi slept they changed their song, and grimly began to grind an armed host, instead of prosperity and peace. By their spells they induced the Viking Mysinger to land with his troops, surprise the Danes, who were wrapped in slumber, and slay them all.

> "An army must come
> Hither forthwith,
> And burn the town
> For the prince."
> GROTTA-SAVNGR (Longfellow's tr.).

This Viking then placed the magic millstones Grotti and the two slaves on board his vessel, and bade the women grind for him, saying that he wanted salt, as it was a very valuable staple of commerce at that time. The women obeyed; the millstones went round, grinding salt in abundance; but the Viking, as cruel as Frodi, kept the women persistently at work, until they ground such an immense quantity of salt that its weight sunk the ship and all on board.

The ponderous millstones sank straight down into the sea in the Pentland Firth, or off the northwestern coast of Norway, making a deep round hole. The waters, rushing into the vortex and gurgling in the holes in the center of the stones, produced the great whirlpool, which is known as the Maelstrom. As for the salt, it soon melted; but such was the quantity ground by the giantesses that it tainted all the waters of the sea, which have ever since been very salt indeed.

CHAPTER X.

FREYA.

FREYA, the fair Northern goddess of beauty and love, was the sister of Frey and the daughter of Niörd and Nerthus, or Skadi. She was the most beautiful and best beloved of all the goddesses, and while in Germany she was identified with Frigga, in Norway, Sweden, Denmark, and Iceland she was considered a separate divinity. Freya, having been born in Vana-heim, was also known as Vanadis, the goddess of the Vanas, or as Vanabride.

As soon as she reached Asgard, the gods were so charmed by her beauty and grace that they bestowed upon her the realm of Folkvang and the great hall Sessrymnir (the roomy-seated), where they assured her she could easily accommodate all her guests.

> "Folkvang 'tis called,
> Where Freyja has right
> To dispose of the hall-seats.
> Every day of the slain
> She chooses the half,
> And leaves half to Odin."
> NORSE MYTHOLOGY (R. B. Anderson).

Although goddess of love, Freya was not soft and pleasure-loving only, for the ancient Northern races said that she had very martial tastes, and that as Valfreya she often led the Valkyrs down to the battlefields, choosing and claiming one half the heroes slain. She was therefore often represented with corselet and helmet, shield and spear, only

Queen of the Valkyrs.

(Opp. p. 124.)

FREYA.

the lower part of her body being clad in the usual flowing feminine garb.

Freya transported the chosen slain to Folkvang, where they were duly entertained, and where she also welcomed all pure maidens and faithful wives, that they might enjoy the company of their lovers and husbands even after death. The joys of her abode were so enticing to the heroic Northern women that they often rushed into battle when their loved ones were slain, hoping to meet with the same fate; or they fell upon their swords, or were voluntarily burned on the same funeral pyre as the beloved remains.

As Freya was inclined to lend a favorable ear to lovers' prayers, she was often invoked by them, and it was customary to indite love songs in her honor, which were sung on all festive occasions, her very name in Germany being used as the verb "to woo."

Freya, the golden-haired and blue-eyed goddess, was also, at times, considered a personification of the earth. She therefore married Odur, a symbol of the summer sun, whom she dearly loved, and by whom she had two *Freya and Odur.* daughters, Hnoss and Gersemi, so beautiful that all things lovely and precious were called by their names.

So long as Odur lingered contentedly at her side, Freya was smiling and perfectly happy; but, alas! this god was a rover, and, wearying of his wife's company, he suddenly left home and wandered far out into the wide world. Freya, sad and forsaken, wept abundantly, and her tears fell down upon the hard rocks, which softened at their contact. We are even told that they trickled down to the very center of the stones, where they were transformed to drops of gold. The tears which fell into the sea, however, were changed into translucent amber.

Weary of her widowed condition, and longing to clasp her beloved in her arms once more, Freya finally started out in search of him, passing through many lands, where she was called by different names, such as Mardel, Horn, Gefn, Syr, Skialf, and Thrung, inquiring of all she met whether her husband had passed that way, and shedding so many tears that gold can be found in all parts of the earth.

> " And Freya next came nigh, with golden tears;
> The loveliest Goddess she in Heaven, by all
> Most honor'd after Frea, Odin's wife.
> Her long ago the wandering Oder took
> To mate, but left her to roam distant lands;
> Since then she seeks him, and weeps tears of gold.
> Names hath she many; Vanadis on earth
> They call her, Freya is her name in Heaven."
>
> BALDER DEAD (Matthew Arnold).

Far away in the sunny South, under the flowering myrtle trees, Freya found Odur at last, and her love being restored to her, she grew happy and smiling once more, and as radiant as a bride. It is perhaps because Freya found her husband beneath the flowering myrtle, that Northern brides, to this day, wear myrtle in preference to the conventional orange wreath.

Hand in hand, Odur and Freya now gently wended their way home once more, and in the light of their happiness the grass grew green, the flowers bloomed, and the birds sang, for all Nature sympathized as heartily with Freya's joy as it had mourned with her when she was in sorrow.

> " Out of the morning land,
> Over the snowdrifts,
> Beautiful Freya came
> Tripping to Scoring.
> White were the moorlands,
> And frozen before her;
> Green were the moorlands,
> And blooming behind her.
> Out of her gold locks
> Shaking the spring flowers,
> Out of her garments
> Shaking the south wind,
> Around in the birches
> Awaking the throstles,

And making chaste housewives all
Long for their heroes home,
Loving and love-giving,
Came she to Scoring."
THE LONGBEARDS' SAGA (Charles Kingsley).

The prettiest plants and flowers in the North were called Freya's hair or Freya's eye dew, while the butterfly was called Freya's hen. This goddess was also supposed to have a special affection for the fairies, whom she loved to watch dancing in the moonbeams, and for whom she reserved her daintiest flowers and sweetest honey. Odur, Freya's husband, besides being considered a personification of the sun, was also regarded as an emblem of passion, or of the intoxicating pleasures of love; so the ancients declared that it was no wonder his wife could not be happy without him.

As goddess of beauty, Freya was very fond of the toilet, of glittering adornments, and of precious jewels. One day, while she was in Svart-alfa-heim, the underground kingdom, she saw four dwarfs carefully fashioning the most wonderful necklace she had ever seen. Almost beside herself with longing to possess this treasure, which was called Brisinga-men, and was an emblem of the stars, or of the fruitfulness of the earth, Freya implored the dwarfs to give it to her; but they obstinately refused to do so unless she would promise to grant them her favor. Having secured the necklace at this price, Freya hastened to put it on, and its beauty so enhanced her charms that the goddess wore it night and day, and only occasionally could be persuaded to loan it to the other divinities. Thor, however, wore this necklace when he personated Freya in Jötun-heim, and Loki coveted and would have stolen it, had it not been for the watchfulness of Heimdall.

Freya was also the proud possessor of a falcon garb, or falcon plumes, which enabled the wearer to flit through the air like a bird; and this garment was so invaluable that it was twice borrowed by Loki, and was used by Freya herself when in search of the missing Odur.

> " Freya one day
> Falcon wings took, and through space hied away ;
> Northward and southward she sought her
> Dearly-loved Odur."
>
> FRIDTHIOF'S SAGA, TEGNÉR (Stephens's tr.).

As Freya was also considered goddess of fecundity, she was sometimes represented as riding about with her brother Frey in the chariot drawn by the golden-bristled boar, scattering, with lavish hands, fruits and flowers to gladden the hearts of all mankind. She also had a chariot of her own, however, in which she generally traveled, which was drawn by cats, her favorite animals, the emblems of caressing fondness and sensuality, or the personifications of fecundity.

> " Then came dark-bearded Niörd, and after him
> Freyia, thin robed, about her ankles slim
> The gray cats playing."
>
> LOVERS OF GUDRUN (William Morris).

Frey and Freya were held in such high honor throughout the North that their names, in modified forms, are still used for " master " and " mistress," and one day of the week is called Freya's day, or Friday, even by the English-speaking race. Freya's temples were very numerous indeed, and were long maintained by her votaries, the last in Magdeburg, Germany, being destroyed by order of Charlemagne.

The Northern people were wont to invoke her not only for success in love, prosperity, and increase, but also at times for
Story of Ottar and Angantyr. aid and protection. This she vouchsafed to all who served her truly, as is proved by the story of Ottar and Angantyr, two men who, after disputing for some time concerning their rights to a certain piece of property, laid their quarrel before the Thing. In that popular assembly it was soon decreed that the man who could prove that he had the longest line of noble ancestors would be the one to win, and a special day was appointed to hear the genealogy of each claimant.

(*Opp. p.* 129.)

THE WITCHES' DANCE (VALPURGISNACHT).— Von Kreling.

Ottar, unable to remember the names of more than a few of his progenitors, offered up sacrifices to Freya, entreating her aid. The goddess graciously heard his prayer, appeared before him, changed him into a boar, and rode off upon his back to the dwelling of the sorceress Hyndla, the most renowned witch of the day. By threats and entreaties, Freya compelled this old woman to trace Ottar's genealogy back to Odin, naming every individual in turn, and giving a synopsis of his achievements. Then, fearing lest her votary's memory should prove treacherous, Freya further compelled Hyndla to brew a potion of remembrance, which she gave him to drink.

> "He shall drink
> Delicious draughts.
> All the gods I pray
> To favor Ottar."
> SÆMUND'S EDDA (Thorpe's tr.).

Thus prepared, Ottar presented himself before the Thing on the appointed day, glibly recited his pedigree, and by naming many more ancestors than Angantyr could recollect, obtained possession of the property he coveted.

> "A duty 'tis to act
> So that the young prince
> His paternal heritage may have
> After his kindred."
> SÆMUND'S EDDA (Thorpe's tr.).

Freya was so beautiful that all the gods, giants, and dwarfs longed for her love and in turn tried to secure her as wife. But Freya scorned the ugly old giants and refused to belong even to Thrym, when urged to accept him by Loki and Thor. She was not so obdurate where the gods themselves were concerned, if the various mythologists are to be believed, for as the personification of the earth she is said to have married Odin, the sky, Frey, the fruitful rain, Odur, the sunshine, etc., until it seems as

9

if she deserved the accusation hurled against her by the arch-
fiend Loki, of having loved and married all the gods in turn.

It was customary on solemn occasions to drink Freya's health
with that of the other gods, and when Christianity was introduced in the North this toast was transferred to
the Virgin or to St. Gertrude; Freya herself, like

*Worship of
Freya.*

all the heathen divinities, was declared a demon or witch, and
banished to the mountain peaks of Norway, Sweden, or Germany, where the Brocken is pointed out as her special abode,
and the general trysting place of her demon train on Valpurgisnacht.

CHORUS OF WITCHES.

"On to the Brocken the witches are flocking —
Merry meet — merry part — how they gallop and drive,
Yellow stubble and stalk are rocking,
And young green corn is merry alive,
With the shapes and shadows swimming by.
To the highest heights they fly,
Where Sir Urian sits on high —
Throughout and about,
With clamor and shout,
Drives the maddening rout,
Over stock, over stone;
Shriek, laughter, and moan,
Before them are blown."

GOETHE'S FAUST (Anster's tr.).

As the swallow, cuckoo, and cat were held sacred to Freya in
heathen times, these creatures were supposed to have demonia-
cal properties, and to this day witches are always depicted with
coal-black cats close beside them.

CHAPTER XI.

ULLER.

ULLER, the winter-god, is the son of Sif, and the stepson of Thor. His father, who is never mentioned in the Northern sagas, must have been one of the dreaded frost giants, for Uller loved the cold and delighted in traveling all over the country on his broad snowshoes or glittering skates. This god also delighted in the chase, and pursued his game through the Northern forests, caring but little for ice and snow, against which he was well protected by the thick furs in which he was always clad.

The god of winter.

As god of hunting and archery, he is represented with a quiver full of arrows and a huge bow, and as the yew furnishes the best wood for the manufacture of these weapons, it is said to have been his favorite tree. To have a supply of suitable wood ever at hand ready for use, Uller took up his abode at Ydalir, the vale of yews, where it was always very damp indeed.

> " Ydalir it is called,
> Where Ullr has
> Himself a dwelling made."
> SÆMUND'S EDDA (Thorpe's tr.).

As winter-god, Uller, or Oller, as he was also called, was considered second only to Odin, whose place he usurped during his absence in the winter months of the year, when he exercised full sway over Asgard and Midgard, and even, according to some authorities, took possession of Frigga, Odin's wife, as in the myth

131

of Vili and Ve. But as Uller was very parsimonious, and never bestowed any gifts upon mankind, they gladly hailed the return of Odin, who drove his supplanter away, forcing him to take refuge either in the frozen North or on the tops of the Alps, where, if we are to believe the poets, he had built a summer house into which he retreated until, knowing Odin had departed once more, he again dared appear in the valleys.

Uller was also considered god of death, and was supposed to ride in the Wild Hunt, and at times even to lead it. He is specially noted for his rapidity of motion, and as the snowshoes used in the Northern regions are sometimes made of bone, and turned up in front like the prow of a ship, it was commonly reported that Uller had spoken magic runes over a piece of bone, changing it into a vessel, which bore him over land or sea at will.

Snowshoes being shield-shaped, and the ice with which he yearly enveloped the earth acting also as a shield to protect it from harm during the winter, won for Uller the surname of the shield-god, and as he was thus designated he was specially invoked by all persons about to engage in a duel or in a desperate fight.

In Christian times, St. Hubert, the hunter, was made to take his place in popular worship, and also made patron of the first month of the year, which was dedicated to him, and began on November 22d, as the sun passed through the constellation of Sagittarius, the bowman.

In Anglo-Saxon, Uller was known as Vulder; but in some parts of Germany he was called Holler and considered the husband of the fair goddess Holda, whose fields he covered with a thick mantle of snow, to make them more fruitful when the spring came.

By the Scandinavians, Uller, god of winter, was said to have married Skadi, Niörd's divorced wife, the female personification of winter and cold, and their tastes were so very congenial that they never quarreled in the least.

Numerous temples were dedicated to this god in the North,

and on his altars, as well as on those of all the other gods, lay a sacred ring upon which oaths were sworn. This ring was said to have the power of shrinking so violently as to sever the finger of any premeditated perjurer. The people visited Uller's shrine, especially during the months of November and December, to entreat him to send a thick covering of snow all over their lands, as earnest of a good harvest; and as he was supposed to send out the glorious flashes of light, the aurora borealis, which illumine the Northern sky during its long night, he was considered very nearly akin to Balder, the personification of light.

According to other authorities, Uller was considered Balder's special friend, principally because he too spent part of the year in the dismal depths of Nifl-heim, with Hel, the goddess of death. Uller was supposed to endure a yearly banishment thither, during the summer months, when he was forced to resign his sway over the earth to Odin, the summer god, and there Balder came to join him at Midsummer, the date of his disappearance from Asgard, for then the days began to grow shorter, and the rule of light (Balder) gradually yielded to the ever encroaching power of darkness (Hodur).

CHAPTER XII.

FORSETI.

Son of Balder, god of light, and of Nanna, goddess of immaculate purity, Forseti was the wisest, most eloquent, and most gentle of all the gods. No sooner had his presence been made known in Asgard than the gods awarded him a seat in the council hall, decreed that he should be patron of justice and righteousness, and gave him as abode the radiant palace Glitnir. This dwelling had a silver roof, supported on pillars of gold, and shone so brightly that it could be seen from a great distance.

God of justice and truth.

> "Glitner is the tenth;
> It is on gold sustained,
> And also with silver decked.
> There Forseti dwells
> Throughout all time,
> And every strife allays."
> SÆMUND'S EDDA (Thorpe's tr.).

Here, upon an exalted throne, Forseti, the lawgiver, sat day after day, settling the differences of gods and men, patiently listening to both sides of every question, and finally pronouncing a sentence which was so very equitable that none ever found fault with his decrees. Such were this god's eloquence and his power of persuasion that he always succeeded in touching his hearers' hearts, and never failed to reconcile even the most bitter foes. All who left his presence were thereafter sure to live in peace, for

134

none dared break a vow once made to him, lest they should incur his just anger and immediately fall down dead.

> "Forsete, Balder's high-born son,
>   Hath heard mine oath;
> Strike dead, Forset', if e'er I'm won
>   To break my troth."
> VIKING TALES OF THE NORTH (R. B. Anderson).

As god of justice and eternal law, Forseti was supposed to preside over every judicial assembly, was invariably appealed to by all who were about to undergo a trial, and it was said that he rarely failed to help the deserving.

On one occasion the Frisians selected twelve of their wisest men, the Asegeir, or elders, and bade them collect all the laws of the various families and tribes composing their nation, to compile from them a code which should *The story of Heligoland.* enable them to have uniform laws throughout all the land, and to render justice more easily. The elders, having painstakingly finished their task of collecting this miscellaneous information, embarked upon a small vessel, to seek some secluded spot where they might hold their deliberations in peace. But no sooner had they pushed away from shore than a tempest arose, driving their vessel far out to sea and whirling it around, until they entirely lost their bearings. In their distress the twelve jurists called upon Forseti, begging him to help them reach land once more, and this prayer was scarcely ended when they perceived, to their utter surprise, that the vessel contained a thirteenth passenger.

Seizing the rudder, the newcomer silently brought the vessel around, steered it towards the place where the waves dashed highest, and in an incredibly short space of time brought them to an island, where he motioned to them to disembark. In awe-struck silence the twelve men obeyed; but their surprise was further excited when they saw the stranger fling his battle ax at a distance, and a limpid spring gush forth from the spot on the greensward where it had struck. Imitating the stranger, all drank of this water without saying a word; then they sat down in a circle, marveling because the newcomer resembled each one of them in some particular, but was still very different from them all.

Suddenly the silence was broken, and the stranger began to speak in low tones, which grew firmer and louder, as he clearly expounded a code of laws which combined all the good points of the various existing regulations. This speech being finished, he vanished as suddenly and mysteriously as he had appeared, and the twelve jurists, recovering the power of speech, simultaneously exclaimed that Forseti himself had been among them, and had drawn up the code of laws by which the Frisians would henceforth be ruled. In commemoration of the god's appearance they declared that the island upon which they stood was holy, and laid a solemn curse upon any who might dare to desecrate it by quarrel or bloodshed. This island, known as Forseti's land or Heligoland (holy land), was greatly respected by all the Northern nations, and even the boldest vikings refrained from raiding its shores, lest they should suffer shipwreck or shameful death in punishment for this crime.

Solemn judicial assemblies were frequently held upon this sacred isle, the jurists always drawing water and drinking it in silence, in memory of Forseti's visit there. The waters of his spring were, moreover, considered so holy that all who drank of them were pronounced sacred, and even the cattle who had tasted of them could not be slain. As Forseti was said to hold his assizes in spring, summer, and autumn, but never in winter, it soon became customary, in all the Northern countries, to dispense justice in those seasons, the people declaring that it was only when the light shone clearly in the heavens that right could become apparent to all, and that it would be utterly impossible to render an equitable verdict during the dark winter season. Forseti is seldom mentioned except in connection with Balder. He apparently has no share whatever in the closing battle in which all the other gods play such prominent parts.

CHAPTER XIII.

HEIMDALL.

ODIN was once walking along the seashore when he beheld nine beautiful giantesses, the wave maidens, Gialp, Greip, Egia, Augeia, Ulfrun, Aurgiafa, Sindur, Atla, and Iarnsaxa, sound asleep on the white sand. To secure possession of these charming girls was not much trouble for the god of the sky, who married all nine of them at once, and was very happy indeed when they simultaneously bore him a son called Heimdall.

> "Born was I of mothers nine,
> Son I am of sisters nine."
> SÆMUND'S EDDA (Thorpe's tr.).

The nine mothers now proceeded to nourish this babe on the strength of the earth, the moisture of the sea, and the heat of the sun, which singular diet proved so strengthening that the new god acquired his full growth in a remarkably short space of time, and hastened to join his father in Asgard. There he found the gods proudly contemplating the rainbow bridge Bifröst, which they had just constructed out of fire, water, and air, which three materials can still plainly be seen in its long arch, where glow the three primary colors: the red representing the fire, the blue the air, and the green the cool depths of the sea.

Fearing lest their enemies, the frost giants, should make their way over this bridge, which, connecting heaven and earth, ended under the shade of the mighty world tree Yggdrasil, close beside the fountain where Mimir kept

Guardian of the rainbow.

guard, the gods bade the white-clad Heimdall watch it night and day.

> "Bifrost i' th' east shone forth in brightest green;
> On its top, in snow-white sheen,
> Heimdal at his post was seen."
>
> OEHLENSCHLÄGER (Pigott's tr.).

To enable their watchman to detect the approach of any enemy from afar, the assembled gods gifted him with very keen senses, for he is said to have been able to hear the grass grow on the hillside, and the wool on the sheep's back, to see plainly one hundred miles off by night as well as by day, and to have required less sleep than a bird.

> "'Mongst shivering giants wider known
> Than him who sits unmoved on high,
> The guard of heaven, with sleepless eye."
>
> LAY OF SKIRNER (Herbert's tr.).

Heimdall was further provided with a flashing sword and a marvelous trumpet, called Giallar-horn, which the gods bade him blow whenever he saw their enemies draw near, declaring that its sound would rouse all creatures in heaven, earth, and Nifl-heim; would announce that the last day had come and that the great battle was about to be fought.

> "To battle the gods are called
> By the ancient
> Gjallar-horn.
> Loud blows Heimdall,
> His sound is in the air."
>
> SÆMUND'S EDDA (Thorpe's tr.).

To keep this instrument, which was a symbol of the moon crescent, ever at hand, Heimdall either hung it on a branch of Yggdrasil above his head or sank it in the waters of Mimir's well, where it lay side by side with Odin's eye, which was an emblem of the moon at its full.

Heimdall's palace, called Himinbiorg, was placed on the highest point of the bridge, and here the gods often visited him to quaff the delicious mead which he set before them.

> " 'Tis Himminbjorg called
> Where Heimdal, they say,
> Hath dwelling and rule.
> There the gods' warder drinks,
> In peaceful old halls,
> Gladsome the good mead."
> NORSE MYTHOLOGY (R. B. Anderson).

Heimdall, always clad in resplendent white armor, was therefore called the bright god, as well as the light, innocent, and graceful god, all which titles he fully deserved, for he was as good as beautiful, and all the gods loved him. Connected on his mothers' side with the sea, he was sometimes counted among the Vanas; and as the ancient Northerners, and especially the Icelanders, to whom the surrounding sea appeared the most important element, fancied that all things had risen out of it, they attributed to him a knowledge of all things and imagined him particularly wise.

> " Then said Heimdall,
> Of Æsir the brightest —
> He well foresaw
> Like other Vanir."
> SÆMUND'S EDDA (Thorpe's tr.).

This god was further distinguished by his golden teeth, which flashed when he smiled, and won for him the surname of Gullintani (golden-toothed). He was also the proud possessor of a swift, golden-maned steed called Gull-top, which bore him to and fro over the quivering rainbow bridge. This he crossed many times a day, but particularly in the early morn, when he was considered a herald of the day and bore the name of Heim-dellinger.

> " Early up Bifröst
> Ran Ulfrun's son,
> The mighty hornblower
> Of Himinbiörg."
> SÆMUND'S EDDA (Thorpe's tr.).

Owing to his extreme acuteness of hearing, Heimdall was greatly disturbed one night by hearing soft, catlike footsteps in the direction of Freya's palace, Folkvang. Gazing fixedly towards that side with his eagle eyes, Heimdall soon perceived, in spite of the darkness, that the sound was produced by Loki, who stealthily entered the palace as a fly, stole to Freya's bedside, and strove to purloin her shining golden necklace Brisinga-men, the emblem of the fruitfulness of the earth.

Loki and Freya.

As it happened, however, the goddess had turned in her sleep in such a way that he could not possibly unclasp the necklace without awaking her. Loki stood hesitatingly by the bedside for a few moments, and then rapidly began to mutter the runes which enabled the gods to change their form at will. As he was doing this, Heimdall saw him shrivel up until he was changed to the size and form of a flea, when he crept under the bedclothes and bit Freya's side, thus making her change her position without really rousing her.

The clasp was now free, and Loki, cautiously unfastening it, secured the coveted ornament, with which he proceeded to steal away. Heimdall immediately started out in pursuit of the midnight thief, and drawing his sword from its scabbard, was about to cut off his head when the god suddenly transformed himself into a flickering blue flame. Quick as thought, Heimdall changed himself into a cloud and sent down a deluge of rain to quench the fire; but Loki as promptly altered his form to that of a huge polar bear, and opened wide his jaws to swallow the water. Heimdall, nothing daunted, then assumed the form of a bear also, and fought fiercely with him; but the combat threatening to end disastrously for Loki, he changed himself into a seal, and, Heimdall imitating him, a last struggle took place, at the end of which Loki, vanquished, was forced to give up the necklace, which was duly restored to Freya.

In this myth, Loki is an emblem of the drought, or of the baleful effects of the too ardent heat of the sun, which comes to rob the earth (Freya) of its most cherished ornament (Brisinga-men). Heimdall is a personification of the gentle rain and dew, which, after struggling for a while with his foe the drought, manages to conquer him and force him to relinquish his prize.

Heimdall has several other names, among which we find those of Hallinskide and Irmin, for at times he takes Odin's place and is identified with that god, as well as with the other sword-gods, Er, Heru, Cheru, and Tyr, who are all noted for their shining weapons. He, however, is most generally known as warder of the rainbow, god of heaven, and of the fruitful rains and dews which bring refreshment to the earth. *Heimdall's names.*

This god also shared with Bragi the honor of welcoming heroes to Valhalla, and, under the name of Riger, was considered the ancestor of the various classes which compose the human race, as is set forth in the following myth :

> " Sacred children,
> Great and small,
> Sons of Heimdall ! "
> Sæmund's Edda (Thorpe's tr.).

One day Heimdall left his place in Asgard to wander down upon the earth as the gods were wont to do. He had not gone very far ere he came to a poor hut on the seashore, where he found Ai (great grandfather) and Edda (great grandmother), a poor but worthy couple, who hospitably invited him to share their meager meal of porridge. Heimdall, who gave his name as Riger, gladly accepted this invitation, and remained with them three whole days, teaching them many things. At the end of that time he left them to resume his journey. Some time after his visit, Edda bore a dark-skinned, thick-set male child, whom she called Thrall. *The story of Riger.*

Thrall soon showed uncommon physical strength and a great aptitude for all heavy work ; and having attained marriageable age, he took to wife Thyr, a heavily built girl with sunburnt hands and flat feet, who labored early and late, and bore him many children, from whom all the Northern serfs or thralls are descended.

> "They had children,
> Lived and were happy;
>
> . . . .
>
> They laid fences,
> Enriched the plow-land,
> Tended swine,
> Herded goats,
> Dug peat."
> RIGSMÁL (Du Chaillu's version).

Riger, in the mean while, had pursued his journey, and leaving the barren seacoast had pushed inland, where ere long he came to cultivated fields and a thrifty farmhouse. He entered, and found Afi (grandfather) and Amma (grandmother), who hospitably invited him to sit down and share their plain but bountiful fare.

Riger accepted this invitation also, remained three days with them, and imparted all manner of useful knowledge to his hosts. After his departure from their house, Amma gave birth to a blue-eyed sturdy boy, whom she called Karl. He soon revealed great skill in all agricultural pursuits, and married a buxom and thrifty wife named Snor, who bore him many children, from whom all husbandmen are descended.

> "He did grow
> And thrive well;
> He broke oxen,
> Made plows;
> Timbered houses,
> Made barns,
> Made carts,
> And drove the plow."
> RIGSMÁL (Du Chaillu's version).

After leaving the house of this second couple, Riger went on until he came to a hill, upon which a stately castle was perched, and here he was received by Fadir (father) and Modir (mother), who, delicately nurtured and luxuriously clad, received him cordially, and set before him dainty meats and rich wines.

Riger tarried three days with them ere he returned to Himinbiorg to resume his post as guardian of the Asa-bridge; and the lady of the castle bore a handsome, slenderly built little son, whom she called Jarl. This child early showed a great taste for the hunt and all manner of martial exercises, learned to understand runes, and lived to do great deeds of valor which brought added glory to his name and race. Having attained manhood, Jarl married Erna, an aristocratic, slender-waisted maiden, who ruled his household wisely and bore him many children, all born to rule, the youngest of which, Konur, became the first king of Denmark according to this myth, which is illustrative of the marked sense of classes among the Northern races.

> "Up grew
> The sons of Jarl;
> They brake horses,
> Bent shields,
> Smoothed shafts,
> Shook ash spears.
> But Kon, the young,
> Knew runes,
> Everlasting runes
> And life runes."
>
> RIGSMÁL (Du Chaillu's version).

CHAPTER XIV.

HERMOD.

ANOTHER of Odin's sons, and his special attendant, was Hermod, a bright and beautiful young god, who was gifted with such great rapidity of motion that he was always designated as the swift or nimble god.

> "But there was one, the first of all the gods
> For speed, and Hermod was his name in Heaven ;
> Most fleet he was."
> BALDER DEAD (Matthew Arnold).

As Hermod was so remarkably quick the gods usually employed him as their messenger, and at a mere sign from Odin he was always ready to speed to any part of the world. As a special mark of favor, the king of gods gave him a magnificent corselet and helmet, which he often donned when he took part in war, and sometimes Odin intrusted to his care the precious spear Gungnir, bidding him cast it over the heads of combatants about to engage in battle, and thus kindle their ardor into murderous fury.

> "Let us Odin pray
> Into our minds to enter ;
> He gives and grants
> Gold to the deserving.
> He gave to Hermod
> A helm and corselet."
> SÆMUND'S EDDA (Thorpe's tr.).

As Hermod delighted in battle, he was often called " the valiant in combat," and confounded with the god of the universe, Irmin ;

144

he sometimes accompanied the Valkyrs on their ride to earth, and frequently escorted the warriors to Valhalla, whence he was considered the leader of the heroic dead.

> " To him spake Hermoder and Brage :
>   ' We meet thee and greet thee from all,
> To the gods thou art known by thy valor,
>   And they bid thee a guest to their hall.' "
> Owen Meredith.

Hermod's distinctive attribute, besides his corselet and helmet, was a wand or staff called Gambantein, the emblem of his office, which he carried with him wherever he went.

Once, oppressed by nameless fears for the future, Odin, seeing that the Norns would not answer his questions, bade Hermod don his armor, saddle Sleipnir, which he alone was allowed to ride, and hasten off to the land of the Finns. This people, living in the frozen regions of the pole, were supposed to have great occult powers, and to be able to call up the cold storms which swept down from the North, bringing plenty of ice and snow in their train. *Hermod and the soothsayer.*

The most noted among all these conjuring Finns was Rossthief (the horse thief), who was wont to entice travelers into his realm by magic arts, only to rob and slay them ; but although he could predict the future, he was always very reluctant indeed to do so.

Hermod, " the swift," had no sooner received Allfather's directions than he started out, riding rapidly northward, and brandishing, instead of his own wand, Odin's runic staff, which had the power of dispelling all the obstacles that Rossthief conjured up to hinder his advance. In spite, therefore, of phantom-like monsters and of invisible snares and pitfalls, Hermod safely reached the conjurer's abode, and when the giant began to attack him, soon mastered him, bound him hand and foot, and declared he would set him free only if he promised to reveal all that he wished to know.

Rossthief, seeing there was no hope of escape, pledged him-

10

self to do all the god wished, and as soon as he was free began to mutter terrible incantations, at the mere sound of which the sun hid behind the clouds, the earth trembled and quivered, and the storm winds howled like a pack of hungry wolves.

Pointing to the horizon, the conjurer now bade Hermod look, and the swift god saw a great stream of blood redden all the ground. While he was gazing wonderingly at this stream, a beautiful woman suddenly appeared, and a moment later a little boy stood beside her. To the god's amazement, this child grew with such marvelous rapidity that he soon attained his full growth, and then only did Hermod notice that he fiercely brandished a bow and arrows.

As Hermod was gazing fixedly upon this vision, Rossthiof began to speak, and declared that the stream of blood portended the murder of one of Odin's sons, but that if the father of the gods wooed and won Rinda, in the land of the Ruthenes (Russia), she would bear him a son who would attain his full growth in a few hours and would soon avenge his brother's death.

> "Rind a son shall bear,
> In the western halls:
> He shall slay Odin's son,
> When one night old."
> SÆMUND'S EDDA (Thorpe's tr.).

Satisfied with this prophecy, Hermod returned to Asgard, where he reported all he had seen and heard to Odin. The father of the gods thus definitely ascertained that he was doomed to lose a son by a violent death. He soon consoled himself, however, by the thought that another of his descendants would avenge the murder and thereby obtain all the satisfaction which a true Northerner ever required.

CHAPTER XV.

VIDAR.

ODIN once saw and fell in love with the beautiful giantess Grid, who dwelt in a cave in the desert, and, wooing her, prevailed upon her to become his wife. The offspring of this union between Odin (mind) and Grid (matter) was a son as strong as taciturn, named Vidar, whom the ancients considered a personification of the primeval forest or of the imperishable forces of Nature.

As the gods, through Heimdall, were intimately connected with the sea, they were also bound by close ties to the forests and Nature in general by Vidar, surnamed "the silent," who was destined to survive their destruction and rule over the regenerated earth. This god had his habitation in Landvidi (the wide land), a palace decorated with green boughs and fresh flowers, situated in the midst of an impenetrable primeval forest where reigned the deep silence and solitude which he loved.

> "Grown over with shrubs
> And with high grass
> Is Vidar's wide land."
> NORSE MYTHOLOGY (R. B. Anderson).

This old Scandinavian conception of the silent Vidar is very grand and poetical indeed, and was inspired by the rugged Northern scenery. "Who has ever wandered through such forests, in a length of many miles, in a boundless expanse, without a path, without a goal, amid their monstrous shadows, their sacred gloom, without being filled with deep reverence for the sublime great-

147

ness of Nature above all human agency, without feeling the grandeur of the idea which forms the basis of Vidar's essence ?"

Vidar was tall, well made, and handsome, had a broad-bladed sword, and besides his armor wore a great iron or leather shoe.

Vidar's shoe. According to some mythologists, he owed this peculiar footgear to his mother Grid, who, knowing that he would be called upon to fight against fire on the last day, thought it would protect him from all injury, as her iron gauntlet had shielded Thor in his encounter with Geirrod. But other authorities state that this shoe was made of the leather scraps which Northern cobblers had either given or thrown away. As it was very important that the shoe should be large and strong enough to resist the Fenris wolf's sharp teeth at the last day, it became a matter of religious observance among Northern shoe-makers to give away as many odds and ends of leather as possible.

One day, when Vidar had joined his peers in Valhalla, they welcomed him gaily, for they all loved him and placed their reliance upon him, for they knew he would use his great strength in their favor in time of need. But after he had quaffed the golden mead, Allfather bade him accompany him to the Urdar fountain, where the Norns were busy weaving their web. When questioned by Odin concerning his future and Vidar's destiny, the three sisters answered oracularly each by the following short sentences:

The Norns' prophecy.

"Early begun."

"Further spun."

"One day done."

To which their mother, Wyrd, the primitive goddess of fate, added: "With joy once more won." These mysterious answers would have remained totally unintelligible to the gods, had she not gone on to explain that time progresses, that all must change, but that even if the father fell in the last battle, his son Vidar would be his avenger, and would live to rule over a regenerated world, after having conquered all his enemies.

" There sits Odin's
Son on the horse's back;
He will avenge his father."
NORSE MYTHOLOGY (R. B. Anderson).

At Wyrd's words the leaves of the world tree began to flutter as if agitated by a breeze, the eagle on its topmost bough flapped its wings, and the serpent Nidhug for a moment suspended its work of destruction at the roots of the tree. Grid, joining the father and son, rejoiced with Odin when she heard that their son was destined to survive the older gods and to rule over the new heaven and earth.

" There dwell Vidar and Vale
In the gods' holy seats,
When the fire of Surt is slaked."
NORSE MYTHOLOGY (R. B. Anderson).

Vidar, however, said not a word, but slowly wended his way back to his palace Landvidi, in the heart of the primeval forest, where, sitting down upon his throne, he pondered long about eternity, futurity, and infinity. If he fathomed their secrets he never revealed them, for the ancients averred that he was "as silent as the grave"—a silence which indicated that no man knows what awaits him in the life to come.

Vidar was not only a personification of the imperishability of Nature, but he was also a symbol of resurrection and renewal, proving that new shoots and blossoms are always ready to spring forth to replace those which have fallen into decay.

The shoe he wore was to be his defense against the wolf Fenris, who, having destroyed Odin, would turn all his wrath upon him, and open wide his terrible jaws to devour him. But the old Northerners declared that Vidar would brace the foot thus protected against the monster's lower jaw, and, seizing the upper, would struggle with him until he had rent him to pieces.

As one shoe only is mentioned in the Vidar myths, some mythologists suppose that he had but one leg, and was the personification of a waterspout, which would suddenly rise on the last day to quench the wild fire personified by the terrible wolf Fenris.

CHAPTER XVI.

VALI.

BILLING, the king of the Ruthenes, was greatly dismayed when he heard that a great force was about to invade his kingdom, for

The wooing of Rinda.

he was too old to fight as of yore, and his only child, a daughter named Rinda, although she was of marriageable age, obstinately refused to choose a husband among her many suitors, and thus give her father the assistant he so sorely needed.

While Billing was musing disconsolately in his hall, a stranger suddenly entered his palace. Looking up, the king beheld a middle-aged man wrapped in a wide cloak, with a broad-brimmed hat drawn down over his forehead to conceal the fact that he had but one eye. The stranger courteously inquired the cause of his evident depression, and as soon as he had learned it volunteered to command the army of the Ruthenes.

His services being joyfully accepted, Odin — for it was he — soon won a signal victory for the aged king, and, returning in triumph, asked permission to woo his daughter Rinda to be his wife. Billing, hoping that his daughter would lend a favorable ear to this suitor, who appeared very distinguished in spite of his years, immediately signified his consent. So Odin, still unknown, presented himself before the princess, who scornfully rejected his proposal, and rudely boxed his ears when he attempted to kiss her.

Forced to withdraw, Odin nevertheless clung to his purpose to make Rinda his wife, for he knew, thanks to Rossthiof's prophecy, that none but she could bear the destined avenger of his murdered son. Assuming the form of a smith, Odin therefore soon came back to Billing's hall, fashioned costly ornaments of silver and gold, and so artfully multiplied these precious metals that the king joyfully acquiesced when he inquired whether he might pay his addresses to the princess. The smith Rosterus was, however, as summarily dismissed by Rinda as the successful old general had been; but although his ear tingled with the force of her blow, he was more determined than ever to make her his wife.

A third time Odin now presented himself before the capricious fair one, disguised this time as a dashing warrior, thinking a young soldier might perchance touch the maiden's heart; but when he again attempted to kiss her, she pushed him back so suddenly that he stumbled and fell upon one knee.

> "Many a fair maiden,
> When rightly known,
> Towards men is fickle:
> That I experienced,
> When that discreet maiden I
> Strove to win:
> Contumely of every kind
> That wily girl
> Heaped upon me;
> Nor of that damsel gained I aught."
>
> SÆMUND's EDDA (Thorpe's tr.).

This third insult so enraged Odin that he drew his magic rune stick out of his breast, pointed it at Rinda, and uttered such a terrible spell that she fell back into the arms of her attendants rigid and apparently lifeless.

When Rinda came to life again, the suitor had disappeared, but the king discovered with great dismay that she had entirely lost her senses and was melancholy mad. In vain all the physicians were summoned and all their simples tried; the maiden remained as passive and sad as before, and her distracted father was only too glad when an old woman called Vecha, or Vak, appeared, offering to undertake the cure of the princess. The old woman, who was Odin in disguise, first prescribed a footbath for the patient; but as this did not appear to have any very marked effect, she declared she would be forced to try a severe treatment. This could only be administered if the patient were intrusted to her exclusive care, securely bound so that she could not offer the least resistance. Billing, anxious to save his child, consented to all the strange attendant proposed; and when Odin had thus gained full power over Rinda, he compelled her to marry him, releasing her from bonds and spell only when she had faithfully promised to be his wife.

The prophecy made by Rossthiof was duly fulfilled, for Rinda bore a son named Vali (Ali, Bous, or Beav), a personification of the lengthening days, who grew with such marvelous rapidity, that in the course of a single day he attained his full stature. Without even taking time to wash his face or comb his hair, this young god hastened off to Asgard with bow and arrow to avenge the death of Balder, god of light, by slaying his murderer, Hodur, the blind god of darkness.

Birth of Vali.

> "But, see! th' avenger, Vali, come,
> Sprung from the west, in Rindas' womb,
> True son of Odin! one day's birth!
> He shall not stop nor stay on earth
> His locks to comb, his hands to lave,
> His frame to rest, should rest it crave,
> Until his mission be complete,
> And Baldur's death find vengeance meet."
> VALHALLA (J. C. Jones).

In this myth, Rinda, a personification of the hard-frozen rind of the earth, resists the warm wooing of the sun, Odin, who vainly points out that spring is the time for warlike exploits, and offers the adornments of golden summer. She only yields when, after a shower (the footbath), a thaw set in. Conquered then by the sun's irresistible might, the earth yields to his embrace, is freed from the spell (ice) which made her hard and cold, and brings forth Vali the nourisher, or Bous the peasant, who emerges from his dark hut when the pleasant days have come. The slaying of Hodur by Vali is therefore emblematical of "the breaking forth of new light after wintry darkness."

Vali, who ranked as one of the twelve deities occupying seats in the great hall of Glads-heim, shared with his father the dwelling called Valaskialf, and was destined, even before birth, to survive the last battle and twilight of the gods, and to reign with Vidar over the regenerated earth.

Vali is god of eternal light, just as Vidar of imperishable matter; and as beams of light were often called arrows, he is always represented and worshiped as an archer. For that reason his month in Norwegian calendars is designated by the sign of the bow, and is called Lios-beri, the light-bringing. As it falls between the middle of January and of February, the early Christians dedicated this month to St. Valentine, who was also a skillful archer, and was said, like Vali, to be the harbinger of brighter days, the awakener of tender sentiments, and the patron of all lovers.

Worship of Vali.

CHAPTER XVII.

THE NORNS.

THE Northern goddesses of fate, who were called Norns, were in nowise subject to the other gods, who could neither question nor influence their decrees. They were three sisters, probably descendants of the giant Norvi, from whom sprang Nott (night). As soon as the Golden Age was ended, and sin began to steal even into the heavenly homes of Asgard, the Norns made their appearance under the great ash Yggdrasil, and took up their abode near the Urdar fountain. According to some mythologists, their purpose in coming thus was to warn the gods of future evil, to bid them make good use of the present, and to teach them wholesome lessons from the past.

These three sisters, whose names were Urd, Verdandi, and Skuld, were personifications of the past, present, and future. Their principal occupation was to weave the web of fate; daily to sprinkle the sacred tree with water from the Urdar fountain, and to put fresh clay around its roots, that it might remain fresh and ever green.

> " Thence come the maids
> Who much do know ;
> Three from the hall
> Beneath the tree ;
> One they named *Was*,
> And *Being* next,
> The third *Shall be*."
>
> THE VÖLUSPÁ (Henderson's tr.).

Some authorities further state that the Norns kept watch over the golden apples which hung on the branches of the tree of life, experience, and knowledge, allowing none but Idun to pick the fruit, which had the power of renewing the gods' youth.

The Norns also fed and tenderly cared for the two swans swimming over the mirror-like surface of the Urdar fountain, and from this pair of birds all the swans on earth are supposed to be descended. At times, it is said, the Norns themselves adopted the swan plumage to visit the earth, or sported like mermaids along the coast and in various lakes and rivers, appearing to mortals, from time to time, to foretell the future or give them valuable advice.

The Norns sometimes wove such large webs that one of the weavers stood on a high mountain in the extreme east, while another waded far out into the western sea. The threads of their woof resembled cords, and varied *Their weaving.* greatly in hue, according to the nature of the events about to occur, and a black thread, tending from north to south, was invariably considered an omen of death. As these sisters flashed the shuttle to and fro, they chanted a solemn song. They seemed not to weave according to their own wishes, but blindly, as if reluctantly executing the wishes of Orlog, the eternal law of the universe, an older and superior power, who apparently had neither beginning nor end.

Two of the Norns, Urd and Verdandi, seemed very beneficent indeed, while the third relentlessly undid their work, and often, when it was nearly finished, tore it angrily to shreds, scattering the remnants to the winds of heaven. As personifications of time, the Norns were represented as sisters of different ages and characters, Urd (Wurd, weird) appearing very old and decrepit, continually looking backward, as if absorbed in contemplating past events and people; Verdandi, the second sister, young, active, and fearless, looked straight before her, while Skuld, the type of the future, was generally represented as closely veiled, with head turned in the opposite direction from that where Urd was gazing, and holding a book or scroll which had not yet been opened or unrolled.

These Norns were daily visited by the gods, who loved to consult them; and even Odin himself frequently rode down to the Urdar fountain to bespeak their aid, for they generally answered all his questions, maintaining silence only about his own fate and that of his fellow gods.

> "Rode he long and rode he fast.
>   First beneath the great Life Tree,
>   At the sacred Spring sought he
> Urdar, Norna of the Past;
> But her backward seeing eye
> Could no knowledge now supply.
> Across Verdandi's page there fell
> Dark shades that ever woes foretell;
> The shadows which 'round Asgard hung
> Their baleful darkness o'er it flung;
> The secret was not written there
> Might save Valhal, the pure and fair.
> Last youngest of the sisters three,
> Skuld, Norna of Futurity,
> Implored to speak, stood silent by, —
> Averted was her tearful eye."
>
> VALHALLA (J. C. Jones).

Besides these three principal Norns there were many others, far less important, who seem to have been the guardian spirits of

Other guardian spirits.

mankind, to whom they frequently appeared, lavishing all manner of gifts upon their favorites, and seldom failing to be present at births, marriages, and deaths.

> "Oh, manifold is their kindred, and who shall tell them all?
>   There are they that rule o'er men folk, and the stars that rise and
>   fall:
>
>   .   .   .   .   .
>
> They love and withhold their helping, they hate and refrain the blow;
> They curse and they may not sunder, they bless and they shall not
>   blend;
> They have fashioned the good and the evil, they abide the change
>   and the end."
>
> SIGURD THE VOLSUNG (William Morris).

On one occasion the Norns wandered off to Denmark, and entered the dwelling of a nobleman just as his first child came into the world. Entering the apartment where the mother lay, the first Norn promised that the child should be handsome and brave, and the second that he should be prosperous and a great scald—predictions which filled the parents' hearts with joy and greatly surprised the neighbors, who, crowding in to see the strangers, rudely pushed the third Norn off her chair.

Story of Nornagesta.

Angry at this insult, Skuld proudly rose and declared her sisters' gifts would be of no avail, as she decreed that the child should live only as long as the taper then burning near the bedside. These ominous words filled the mother's heart with terror, and she tremblingly clasped her babe closer to her breast, for the taper was nearly burned out and its extinction could not be very far off. The eldest Norn, however, had no intention of seeing her prediction thus set at naught; but as she could not force her sister to retract her words, she quickly seized the taper, put out the light, and giving the smoking stump to the child's mother, bade her carefully treasure it, and never light it again until her son was weary of life.

> "In the mansion it was night:
> The Norns came,
> Who should the prince's
> Life determine."
> SÆMUND'S EDDA (Thorpe's tr.).

This child was called Nornagesta, in honor of the Norns, and grew up to be as beautiful, brave, and talented as any mother could wish. When he was old enough to comprehend the gravity of the trust, his mother told him the story of the Norns' visit, and placed in his hands the candle end, which he treasured for many a year, placing it for safekeeping inside of the frame of his harp. When his parents were dead, Nornagesta wandered from place to place, taking part and distinguishing himself in every battle, singing his heroic lays wherever he went. As he was of an enthusiastic and poetic temperament, he did not soon become weary of life, and while the other heroes grew wrinkled and old, he remained young at heart and vigorous in frame. He therefore witnessed all the deeds of the heroic ages, was the boon companion of all the ancient warriors, and, after living three hundred years, saw the belief in the old heathen gods gradually supplanted by the teachings of Christian missionaries. Finally Nornagesta came to the court of King Olaf Tryggvesson, who, according to his usual custom, converted him almost by force, and made him receive baptism. Then, wishing to convince his people that the time for superstition was past, the king forced the aged scald to produce and light the taper which he had so carefully guarded for more than three centuries.

In spite of his recent conversion, Nornagesta anxiously watched the flame, and as it flickered and went out, he sank lifeless to the ground, proving that, in spite of the baptism just received, he still believed the words of the Norns.

In the middle ages, and even later, the Norns figure in many a story or myth, appearing as fairies or witches, as, for instance, in the tale of "the Sleeping Beauty," and in Shakespeare's tragedy of "Macbeth."

> "*1st Witch.* When shall we three meet again,
> In thunder, lightning, or in rain?
> *2d Witch.* When the hurlyburly's done,
> When the battle's lost and won:
> *3d Witch.* That will be ere the set of sun."
>
> MACBETH (Shakespeare).

Sometimes the Norns bore the name of Vala, or prophetesses, for they had the power of divination—a power which was held in great honor by all the Northern races, who believed it restricted to the female sex. The predictions of the Vala were never questioned, and it is even said that Drusus, the Roman general, was so terrified by the appearance

The Vala.

of Veleda, one of these women, forbidding his crossing the Elbe, that he actually beat a retreat. She foretold his approaching death, which actually happened shortly after and was occasioned by a fall from his steed.

These prophetesses, who were also known as Idises, Dises, or Hagedises, officiated at the forest shrines and in the sacred groves, and always accompanied invading armies. Riding ahead, or in the very midst of the host, they vehemently urged the warriors on to victory, and when the battle was over they often cut the bloody-eagle upon the captives. The blood was then collected into great tubs, wherein the Dises plunged their naked arms up to the shoulders, previous to joining in the wild dance with which the ceremony ended.

These women were greatly feared, sacrifices were offered to propitiate them, and it was only in later times that they were degraded to the rank of witches, and sent to join the demon host on the Brocken, or Blocksberg, on Valpurgisnacht.

Besides the Norns or Dises, who were also regarded as protective deities, the Northerners ascribed to each human being a guardian spirit named Fylgie, which attended him through life, either in a human or animal shape, and was invisible except at the moment of death by all except the initiated few.

The allegorical meaning of the Norns and of their web of fate is too patent to need any explanation; still some mythologists have made them demons of the air, and state that their web was the woof of clouds, and that the bands of mists which they strung from rock to tree, and from mountain to mountain, were ruthlessly torn apart by the suddenly rising wind. Some authorities, moreover, declare that Skuld, the third Norn, was at times a Valkyr, and at others personated the party-colored goddess of death, the terrible Hel.

CHAPTER XVIII.

THE VALKYRS.

ODIN'S special attendants, the Valkyrs, or battle maidens, were either his daughters, like Brunhild, or the offspring of mortal kings, who were privileged to serve this god and remain immortal and invulnerable as long as they implicitly obeyed his orders and remained virgins. They and their steeds were the personification of the clouds, their glittering weapons being the lightning flashes. The ancients imagined that they swept down to earth at Valfather's command, to choose among the slain the heroes worthy to taste the joys of Valhalla, and brave enough to lend their aid to the gods when the great battle was to be fought.

> "There through some battlefield, where men fall fast,
>   Their horses fetlock-deep in blood, they ride,
>   And pick the bravest warriors out for death,
>   Whom they bring back with them at night to Heaven,
>   To glad the gods and feast in Odin's hall."
>   BALDER DEAD (Matthew Arnold).

These maidens, young and beautiful, with dazzling white arms and flowing golden hair, wore helmets of silver or gold, blood-red corselets, carried glittering spears and shields, and boldly charged hither and thither on their mettlesome white steeds. These horses galloped over the quivering Bifröst and through the realms of air, carrying not only their fair riders, but the heroes slain, who were thus immediately transported to Valhalla, after having received the Valkyrs' kiss of death.

(*Ofp. p.* 160)

VALKYRS RIDING TO BATTLE.—P. N. Arbo.

As the Valkyrs' steeds were also personifications of the clouds, the people fancied that all the hoar frost and dew dropped down upon earth from their glitter- **The clouds.** ing manes as they rapidly dashed to and fro through the air.

"He spake and his harp was with him, and he smote the strings full
    sweet,
And sang of the host of the Valkyrs, how they ride the battle to
    meet,
And the dew from the dear manes drippeth as they ride in the first
    of the sun,
And the tree-boughs open to meet it when the wind of the dawning
    is done:
And the deep dales drink its sweetness and spring into blossoming
    grass,
And the earth groweth fruitful of men, and bringeth their glory to
    pass."

SIGURD THE VOLSUNG (William Morris).

The Valkyrs were not only sent to visit the battlefields upon earth, but often rode over the sea, snatching the dying Vikings away from the sinking vessels. Sometimes they stood upon the strand to beckon them thither, thus warning them that the coming struggle would be their last,—a warning which every Northern hero received with joy.

"Slowly they moved to the billow side;
    And the forms, as they grew more clear,
Seem'd each on a tall pale steed to ride,
    And a shadowy crest to rear,
And to beckon with faint hand
From the dark and rocky strand,
    And to point a gleaming spear.

"Then a stillness on his spirit fell,
    Before th' unearthly train;
For he knew Valhalla's daughters well,
    The choosers of the slain!"

VALKYRIUR SONG (Mrs. Hemans)

The number of Valkyrs differs greatly according to the various mythologists, and ranges from three to sixteen, the greater part of them, however, naming only nine. These Valkyrs, also divinities of the air, were sometimes called Norns, or wish maidens, and Freya and Skuld were often supposed to lead them on to the fray.

Their number and duties.

> "She saw Valkyries
> Come from afar,
> Ready to ride
> To the tribes of god;
> Skuld held the shield,
> Skaugul came next,
> Gunnr, Hildr, Gaundul,
> And Geir-skaugul.
> Thus now are told
> The Warrior's Norns."
>   SÆMUND'S EDDA (Henderson's tr.).

The Valkyrs, as we have seen, were also very busy in Valhalla, where, having laid aside their bloody weapons, they poured out the heavenly mead for the Einheriar. These delighted in this beverage and welcomed the fair maidens as warmly as when they had first seen them on the battlefield and knew that their errand was to transport them where they fain would be.

> "In the shade now tall forms are advancing,
> And their wan hands like snowflakes in the moonlight are gleaming;
> They beckon, they whisper, "Oh! strong Armed in Valor,
> The pale guests await thee — mead foams in Valhalla."
>   FINN'S SAGA (Hewitt).

The Valkyrs were also supposed to own swan plumage, in which they frequently flew down to earth, and which they threw aside when they came near a secluded stream, so that they might indulge in a bath. Any mortal surprising them thus, and securing their plumage, could prevent their ever leaving the earth, and could even force these proud maidens to mate with him if such were his pleasure.

Wayland, smith, and the Valkyrs.

Three of the Valkyrs, Olrun, Alvit, and Svanhvit, were once sporting in the waters, when suddenly the three brothers Egil, Slagfinn, and Völund, or Wayland the smith, came upon them, and securing their swan guise forced them to remain upon earth and become their wives. The Valkyrs, thus detained upon earth, remained with these husbands nine years, but at the end of that time, recovering their plumage, or the spell being broken, they effected their escape.

> " There they stayed
> Seven winters through;
> But all the eighth
> Were with longing seized;
> And in the ninth
> Fate parted them.
> The maidens yearned
> For the murky wood,
> The young Alvit,
> Fate to fulfill."
>
> LAY OF VÖLUND (Thorpe's tr.).

Two of the brothers, Egil and Slagfinn, were so lonely without their wives that, putting on their snow shoes, they went in search of them, disappearing in the cold and foggy regions of the North; but the third brother, Völund, remained at home — knowing all search would be of no avail — contemplating a ring which Alvit had given him as a love token, and constantly hoping she would return. As he was a very clever smith, and could manufacture the most dainty ornaments of silver and gold, as well as magic weapons which no blow could break, he now employed his leisure in making seven hundred rings exactly like the one which his wife had given him. These he bound all together; but one night, on coming home from the hunt, he found that some one had carried away one ring, leaving all the others behind; so he fancied his wife had been there and would soon return for good.

That selfsame night, however, he was surprised in his sleep, and bound and made prisoner by Nidud, King of Sweden, who took possession of his choicest sword, which he reserved for his own use, and of the love ring made of pure Rhine gold, which latter he gave to his only daughter, Bodvild. As for the unhappy Völund himself, he was led captive to a neighboring island, where, after having hamstrung him to prevent his escape, the king made him forge weapons and ornaments for his use day after day. He also compelled him to build an intricate labyrinth, and to this day a maze in Iceland is known as "Völund's house." Völund's rage and despair increased with every new insult offered him by Nidud, and he thought night and day how he might effect his revenge. During the pauses of his labor he furthermore fashioned a pair of wings similar to those his wife had used as a Valkyr, which he intended to don as soon as his vengeance had been accomplished, to escape from the labyrinth on the island. One day the king came to visit him, and brought him the stolen sword that he might repair it; but Völund cleverly substituted another weapon so exactly like the magic sword as to deceive the king when he came to claim it once more. A few days after, Völund the smith enticed the king's sons into his smithy, slew them, and cunningly fashioned drinking vessels for Nidud out of their skulls, and jewels out of their eyes and teeth, which he bestowed upon their mother and sister.

> "But their skulls
> Beneath the hair
> He in silver set,
> And to Nidud gave;
> And of their eyes
> Precious stones he formed,
> Which to Nidud's
> Wily wife he sent.
> But of the teeth
> Of the two
> Breast ornaments he made,
> And to Bödvild sent."
>
> LAY OF VÖLUND (Thorpe's tr.).

These gifts were joyfully accepted, as the royal family did not suspect whence they came; for they fancied the youths had drifted out to sea, where they had been drowned. Some time after this, Bodvild, wishing to have her ring repaired, also visited the smith's hut, where, while waiting for it, she unsuspectingly partook of a magic drug, which sent her to sleep and left her in Völund's power. His last act of vengeance accomplished, Völund donned the pair of wings which he had cunningly fashioned to effect his escape, and grasping his sword and ring slowly rose up in the air. He flew to the palace, and, perched there out of reach, he confessed all his crimes to Nidud. The king, beside himself with rage, summoned Egil, Völund's brother, who had also fallen into his power, and bade him use his marvelous skill as an archer to bring down the impudent bird. Obeying a signal from Völund, Egil aimed for a protuberance under his wing where a bladder full of the young princes' blood was concealed, and Völund flew triumphantly away, declaring that Odin would give his sword to Sigmund — a prediction which was duly fulfilled.

Völund then went to Alf-heim, where, if the legend is to be believed, he found his beloved wife once more, and lived happy with her until the twilight of the gods.

But, even in Alf-heim, this clever smith continued to ply his trade, and manufactured several suits of impenetrable armor, which are described in later heroic poems. Besides Balmung and Joyeuse, Sigmund's and Charlemagne's noted swords, he is reported to have fashioned Miming for his son Heime, and many other remarkable blades.

> "It is the mate of Miming
> Of all swerdes it is king,
> And Weland it wrought,
> Bitterfer it is hight."
> ANGLO-SAXON POETRY (Coneybeare's tr.).

There are countless other tales of swan maidens or Valkyrs, who are said to have consorted with mortals; but the most popular of all is that of Brunhild, the wife of Sigurd, a descendant of Sigmund and the most renowned of Northern heroes.

CHAPTER XIX.

HEL.

HEL, goddess of death, was the daughter of Loki, god of evil, and of the giantess Angur-boda, the portender of ill.   She came

Loki's offspring.
into the world in a dark cave in Jötun-heim, and was closely related to the serpent Iörmungandr and the terrible Fenris wolf, the trio being considered the emblems of pain, sin, and death.

> " Now Loki comes, cause of all ill!
> Men and Æsir curse him still.
>   Long shall the gods deplore,
>   Even till Time be o'er,
> His base fraud on Asgard's hill.
> While, deep in Jotunheim, most fell,
> Are Fenrir, Serpent, and Dread Hel,
> Pain, Sin, and Death, his children three,
> Brought up and cherished; thro' them he
> Tormentor of the world shall be."
>
> VALHALLA (J. C. Jones).

Odin, having become aware of the terrible brood which Loki was cherishing, resolved, as we have already seen, to banish them from the face of the earth.   The serpent was therefore cast into the sea, where his writhing was supposed to cause the most terrible tempests; the wolf Fenris was chained fast, thanks to the dauntless Tyr; and Hel or Hela, the party-colored goddess of death, was hurled down into the depths of Nifl-heim, where Odin gave her power over nine worlds.

" Hela into Niflheim thou threw'st,
And gav'st her nine unlighted worlds to rule,
A queen, and empire over all the dead."
BALDER DEAD (Matthew Arnold).

This realm, which was supposed to be situated under the earth, could only be entered after a painful journey over the roughest roads in the cold, dark regions of the extreme North. The gate was so far from all human abode *Hel's kingdom in Nifl-heim.* that even Hermod the swift, mounted upon Sleipnir, had to journey nine long nights ere he reached the river Giöll. This formed the boundary of Nifl-heim, over which was thrown a bridge of crystal arched with gold, hung on a single hair, and constantly guarded by the grim skeleton Mödgud, who made every spirit pay a toll of blood ere she would allow it to pass.

" The bridge of glass hung on a hair
Thrown o'er the river terrible, —
The Giöll, boundary of Hel.
Now here the maiden Mödgud stood,
Waiting to take the toll of blood, —
A maiden horrible to sight,
Fleshless, with shroud and pall bedight."
VALHALLA (J. C. Jones).

The spirits generally rode or drove across this bridge on the horses or in the wagons which had been burned upon the funeral pyre with the dead to serve that purpose, and the Northern races were very careful to bind upon the feet of the departed a specially strong pair of shoes, called Hel shoes, that they might not suffer during the long journey over rough roads. Soon after the Giallar bridge was passed, the spirit reached the Ironwood, where stood none but bare and iron-leafed trees, and, passing through it, reached Hel-gate, beside which the fierce, blood-stained dog Garm kept constant watch, cowering in a dark hole known as the Gnipa cave. This monster's rage could only be appeased by the offering of a Hel-cake, which never failed those who had ever given bread to the needy.

> " Loud bays Garm
> Before the Gnipa cave."
> SÆMUND'S EDDA (Thorpe's tr.).

Within the gate, amid the intense cold and impenetrable darkness, was heard the seething of the great caldron Hvergelmir, the rolling of the glaciers in the Elivagar and other streams of Hel, among which were the Leipter, by which solemn oaths were sworn, and the Slid, in whose turbid waters naked swords continually rolled.

Further on in this grewsome place was Elvidner (misery), the hall of the goddess Hel, whose dish was Hunger. Her knife was Greed. "Idleness was the name of her man, Sloth of her maid, Ruin of her threshold, Sorrow of her bed, and Conflagration of her curtains."

> " Elvidner was Hela's hall.
> Iron-barred, with massive wall;
> Horrible that palace tall!
> Hunger was her table bare;
> Waste, her knife; her bed, sharp Care;
> Burning Anguish spread her feast;
> Bleached bones arrayed each guest;
> Plague and Famine sang their runes,
> Mingled with Despair's harsh tunes.
> Misery and Agony
> E'er in Hel's abode shall be!"
> VALHALLA (J. C. Jones).

This goddess had many different abodes for the guests who daily came to her, for she received not only perjurers and criminals of all kinds, but also all those who were unfortunate enough to die without shedding blood. To her realm also were consigned all those who died of old age or disease—a mode of decease which was contemptuously called "straw death," as the beds of the people were generally of that material.

> " Temper'd hard by frost,
> Tempest and toil their nerves, the sons of those
> Whose only terror was a bloodless death."
> THOMSON.

Although the innocent were treated kindly by Hel, and enjoyed a state of negative bliss, it is no wonder that the inhabitants of the North shrank from the thought of visiting her cheerless abode. And while the men preferred to mark themselves with the spear points, to hurl themselves down from a precipice, or to be burned ere life was quite extinct, the women did not shrink from equally heroic measures. In the extremity of their sorrow, they did not hesitate to fling themselves down a mountain side, or fall upon the swords which were given them at their marriage, so that their bodies might be burned with those whom they loved and their spirits permitted to join them in the bright home of the gods.

Ideas of the future life.

Further horrors, however, awaited those whose lives had been criminal or impure, for they were banished to Nastrond, the strand of corpses, where they waded in ice-cold streams of venom, through a cave made of wattled serpents, whose poisonous fangs were all turned towards them. After suffering untold agonies there, they were washed down into the caldron Hvergelmir, where the serpent Nidhug ceased for a moment gnawing the root of the tree Yggdrasil to feed upon their bones.

> "A hall standing
> Far from the sun
> In Nåströnd;
> Its doors are northward turned,
> Venom-drops fall
> In through its apertures;
> Entwined is that hall
> With serpents' backs.
> She there saw wading
> The sluggish streams
> Bloodthirsty men
> And perjurers,
> And him who the ear beguiles
> Of another's wife.
> There Nidhog sucks
> The corpses of the dead."
>
> SÆMUND'S EDDA (Thorpe's tr.).

Hel herself was supposed occasionally to leave her dismal abode to range the earth upon her three-legged white horse, and

Pestilence and famine. in times of pestilence or famine she was said to use a rake if a part of the inhabitants escaped, and a broom when whole villages and provinces were depopulated, as was the case during the historical epidemic of the Black Death.

The Northern races further fancied that the spirits of the dead were sometimes allowed to revisit the earth and appear to their relatives, whose sorrow or joy affected them even after death, as is proved by the Danish ballad of Aager and Else, where a dead lover bids his sweetheart smile, so that his coffin may be filled with roses instead of the clotted blood drops produced by her tears.

> " ' Listen now, my good Sir Aager !
> Dearest bridegroom, all I crave
> Is to know how it goes with thee
> In that lonely place, the grave ? '
>
> " ' Every time that thou rejoicest,
> And art happy in thy mind,
> Are my lonely grave's recesses
> All with leaves of roses lined.
>
> " ' Every time that, love, thou grievest,
> And dost shed the briny flood,
> Are my lonely grave's recesses
> Filled with black and loathsome blood.' "
>
> BALLAD OF AAGER AND ELIZA (Longfellow's tr.).

CHAPTER XX.

ÆGIR.

BESIDES Niörd and Mimir, who were both ocean divinities, the one representing the sea near the coast and the other the primeval ocean whence all things were supposed to have sprung, the Northern races recognized another sea-ruler, called Ægir or Hler, who dwelt either in the cool depths of his liquid realm or had his abode on the Island of Lessoe, in the Cattegat, or Hlesey.

God of the sea.

> "Beneath the watery dome,
>   With crystalline splendor,
>   In radiant grandeur,
> Upreared the sea-god's home.
> More dazzling than foam of the waves
> E'er glimmered and gleamed thro' deep caves
> The glistening sands of its floor,
> Like some placid lake rippled o'er."
>
> VALHALLA (J. C. Jones).

Ægir (the sea), like his brothers Kari (the air) and Loki (fire), is supposed to have belonged to an older dynasty of the gods, for he ranked neither with the Æsir, the Vanas, the giants, dwarfs, nor elves, but was considered omnipotent within his realm.

He was supposed to occasion and quiet the great tempests which swept over the deep, and was generally represented as a gaunt old man, with long white beard and hair, his clawlike fingers ever clutching convulsively, as though he longed to have all things within his grasp. Whenever he appeared above the waves, it was only to take fiendish delight in pursuing and over-turning vessels, which he greedily dragged down to the bottom of the sea.

Ægir was mated with his sister, the goddess Ran, whose name means "robber," and who was as cruel, greedy, and insatiable as her husband. Her favorite pastime was lurking near dangerous rocks, whither she enticed mariners. There she spread her net, her most prized possession, and, having entangled the men in its meshes and broken their vessels on the jagged cliffs, she calmly drew them down into her cheerless realm.

Ran.

> " In the deep sea caves
> By the sounding shore,
> In the dashing waves
> When the wild storms roar,
> In her cold green bowers
> In the Northern fiords,
> She lurks and she glowers,
> She grasps and she hoards,
> And she spreads her strong net for her prey."
> STORY OF SIEGFRIED (Baldwin).

Ran was therefore also considered the goddess of death for all who perished at sea, and the Northern nations fancied that she entertained the drowned in her coral caves, where her couches were spread to receive them, and where the mead flowed freely as in Valhalla. The goddess was further supposed to have a great affection for gold, which was called the "flame of the sea," and was used to illuminate her halls. This belief originated when the sailors first noticed the well-known phosphorescent gleams in the deep, and to win Ran's good graces, they were careful to hide some gold about them whenever any special danger threatened them on the sea.

> " Gold, on sweetheart ramblings,
> Pow'rful is and pleasant;
> Who goes empty-handed
> Down to sea-blue Ran,

> Cold her kisses strike, and
> Fleeting her embrace is —
> But we ocean's bride be-
> Troth with purest gold."
> VIKING TALES OF THE NORTH (R. B. Anderson).

Ægir and Ran had nine beautiful daughters, the Waves, or billow maidens, whose snowy arms and bosoms, long golden hair, deep-blue eyes, and willowy, sensuous forms were fascinating in the extreme. These maidens **The Waves.** delighted in playing all over the surface of their father's vast domain, lightly clad in transparent blue, white, or green veils. They were very moody and capricious damsels, however, varying from playful to sullen and apathetic moods, and at times exciting one another almost to madness, tearing their hair and veils, flinging themselves recklessly upon their hard beds, the rocks, chasing one another with frantic haste, and shrieking aloud with joy or despair. These maidens, however, seldom came out to play unless their brother, the Wind, were abroad, and according to his mood they were gentle and playful, or rough and boisterous.

The Waves were generally supposed to go about in triplets, and were often said to play around the ships of vikings whom they favored, smoothing away every obstacle from their course, and helping them speedily to reach their goal.

> "And Æger's daughters, in blue veils dight,
> The helm leap round, and urge it on its flight."
> VIKING TALES OF THE NORTH (R. B. Anderson).

In Anglo-Saxon the sea-god Ægir was known by the name of Eagor, and whenever an unusually large wave came thundering towards the shore, the sailors were wont to cry, **Ægir's brewing** as the Trent boatmen still do, "Look out, Eagor is **kettle.** coming!" He was also known by the name of Hler (the shelterer) among the Northern nations, and of Gymir (the concealer), because he was always ready to hide things in the depths of his realm, never revealing the secrets intrusted to his care. And, because the waters of the sea were frequently said to seethe and hiss, the ocean was often called Ægir's brewing kettle or vat.

His two principal servants, noted for their quickness, were Elde and Funfeng, emblems of the phosphorescence of the sea; they invariably waited upon the guests whom he invited to his banquets in the depths of the sea. Ægir sometimes left his realm to visit the Æsir in Asgard, where he was royally entertained, and took special pleasure in Bragi's tales of the various adventures and achievements of the gods. Excited by the sparkling mead and by these tales, the god on one occasion ventured to invite all the Æsir to celebrate the harvest feast with him in Hlesey, where he promised to entertain them in his turn.

Surprised at this invitation, one of them ventured to remind Ægir that the gods were accustomed to dainty fare; but the

Thor and Hymir. god of the sea declared that as far as eating was concerned they need have no care, as he was sure he could cater to the most fastidious appetites; but he confessed that he was not so confident about drink, as his brewing kettle was rather small. Hearing this, Thor immediately volunteered to procure a suitable kettle, and set out with Tyr to obtain it. The two gods journeyed east of the Elivagar in Thor's goat chariot, left this conveyance at the house of the peasant Egil, Thialfi's father, and wended their way on foot to the dwelling of the giant Hymir, who, they knew, owned a kettle one mile deep and proportionately wide.

> "There dwells eastward
> Of Elivagar
> The all-wise Hymir,
> At heaven's end.
> My sire, fierce of mood,
> A kettle owns,
> A capacious cauldron,
> A rast in depth."
> SÆMUND'S EDDA (Thorpe's tr.).

Only the women were at home, however, and Tyr recognized in the eldest — an ugly old hag with nine hundred heads — his own grandmother, while the youngest, a beautiful young giantess, his mother, hospitably received him and his companion and gave them a drink.

After learning their errand, this woman bade Tyr and Thor hide under some huge kettles resting upon a beam at the end of the hall, for her husband Hymir was very hasty and often slew his would-be guests with a single baleful glance. The gods had no sooner followed her advice than the old giant Hymir came in. When his wife told him that visitors had come, he frowned so portentously, and flashed such a wrathful look towards their hiding place, that the rafter split and the kettles fell with a crash, and were all dashed to pieces with the exception of the largest.

> " In shivers flew the pillar
> At the Jotun's glance;
> The beam was first
> Broken in two.
> Eight kettles fell,
> But only one of them,
> A hard-hammered cauldron,
> Whole from the column."
>
> SÆMUND'S EDDA (Thorpe's tr.).

The giant's wife, however, prevailed upon him to welcome Tyr and Thor, and slay three oxen for their refection; but he was greatly dismayed to see the thunder-god eat two of these for his supper. Muttering that he would have to go fishing early the next morning to secure a breakfast for such a voracious guest, the giant fell asleep. When he went down to the shore at dawn the next day, he was joined by Thor, who declared he would help him. As the giant bade him secure his own bait for fishing, Thor coolly slew his host's largest ox, Himinbrioter (heaven breaker), cut off its head, and, embarking with it, proceeded to row far out to sea. In vain Hymir protested that his usual fishing ground had been reached, and that they might encounter the terrible Midgard snake were they to venture any farther — Thor persistently rowed on, until he fancied they were directly above this monster.

" On the dark bottom of the great salt lake,
  Imprisoned lay the giant snake,
  With naught his sullen sleep to break."
                THOR'S FISHING, OEHLENSCHLÄGER (Pigott's tr.).

Baiting his powerful hook with the ox head, Thor angled for Iörmungandr, while the giant drew up two whales, which seemed enough for an early morning's meal.

As Hymir was about to propose a return, Thor suddenly felt a jerk, and began pulling as hard as he could, for he knew by the resistance of his prey, and the terrible storm lashed up by its writhings, that he had hooked the Midgard snake. In his determined efforts to force him to rise to the surface, Thor braced his feet so strongly against the bottom of the boat that he went through it and stood on the bed of the sea.

After an indescribable struggle, the monster's terrible venom-breathing head appeared, and Thor, seizing his hammer, was about to annihilate it when the giant, frightened by the proximity of Iörmungandr, and fearing lest the boat should sink and he become its prey, drew his knife, cut the fishing line, and thus allowed the monster to drop back like a stone to the bottom of the sea.

" The knife prevails: far down beneath the main
  The serpent, spent with toil and pain,
  To the bottom sank again."
                THOR'S FISHING, OEHLENSCHLÄGER (Pigott's tr.).

Angry with Hymir for his inopportune interference, Thor dealt him a blow with his hammer which knocked him overboard; but Hymir, undismayed, waded ashore, and met him as he returned to the beach. Hymir then took both whales, his share of the fishing, upon his back, to carry them to the house; and Thor, wishing to show his strength also, shouldered boat, oars, and fishing tackle, and followed him.

Breakfast being disposed of, Hymir challenged Thor to show his strength by breaking his goblet; but although the thunder-god threw it with irresistible force against stone pillars and walls, it remained whole and was not even bent. In obedience to a whisper from Tyr's mother, however, Thor suddenly hurled it against the giant's forehead, the only substance tougher than itself, where it was shivered to pieces. Hymir, having thus seen what Thor could do, told him he might have the required kettle, which Tyr vainly tried to lift, and which Thor could raise from the floor only after he had drawn his belt of strength up to the very last hole.

> " Tyr twice assayed
> To move the vessel,
> Yet at each time
> Stood the kettle fast.
> Then Môdi's father
> By the brim grasped it,
> And trod through
> The dwelling's floor."
>
> LAY OF HÝMIR (Thorpe's tr.).

The wrench with which he pulled it up, however, greatly shattered the giant's house and broke his floor to pieces. As Tyr and Thor were departing, the latter having clapped the huge pot on his head in the guise of a hat, Hymir summoned the other frost giants, and proposed that they should slay their inveterate foe. Before they could overtake him, Thor, turning around, became aware of their pursuit, and, hurling Miölnir repeatedly at them, slew them all ere he carried the kettle in triumph to Ægir to enable him to brew enough ale for the harvest feast.

The physical explanation of this myth is, of course, a thunder storm (Thor), in conflict with the raging sea (the Midgard snake), and the breaking up of the polar ice (Hymir's goblet and floor) in the heat of summer.

The gods now joyfully accepted Ægir's invitation to be present at his feast, went there in festive array, and were ever after wont to celebrate the harvest home in his coral caves.

> " Then Vans and Æsir, mighty gods,
> Of earth and air, and Asgard, lords, —

Advancing with each goddess fair,
A brilliant retinue most rare, —
Attending mighty Odin, swept
Up wave-worn aisle in radiant march."

VALHALLA (J. C. Jones).

Ægir, as we have seen, ruled over all the sea with the help of
the treacherous Ran. Both of these divinities were considered
cruel by the Northern nations, who had much to suffer from the
sea, which, surrounding them on all sides, ran far into the heart
of their countries by means of the numerous fiords, and often
swallowed the ships of their vikings, with all the men on board.

" We Goth-folk know indeed
That the sea is a foe full deadly, and a friend that fails at need,
And that Ran, who dwells thereunder, will many a man beguile."

SIGURD THE VOLSUNG (William Morris).

Besides these principal divinities of the sea, the Northern nations believed in mermen and mermaids, the latter having swan
plumage or seal garments, which they sometimes
Other divinities laid for a moment upon the beach, and if a mortal
of the sea.
secured them he could compel the fair maidens to remain ashore.

" She came through the waves when the fair moon shone
(Drift o' the wave and foam o' the sea) ;
She came where I walked on the sands alone,
With a heart as light as a heart may be."

L. E. R.

There were also malignant marine monsters who were known as
Nicors, from whose name has been derived the proverbial Old
Nick. Many of the lesser water divinities had fish tails ; the
females bore the name of Undines, and the males of Stromkarls,
Nixies, Necks, or Neckar. These water spirits often left their
native streams, especially during the middle ages, to appear at
village dances, where they were recognized by the wet hem of
their garments. They often sat beside the flowing brook or river,
playing on a harp, or sang alluring songs while combing out their
long golden or green hair.

" The Neck here his harp in the glass castle plays,
  And mermaidens comb out their green hair always,
  And bleach here their shining white clothes."
                        STAGNELIUS (Keightley's tr.).

The Nixies, Undines, and Stromkarls were particularly gentle and lovable beings, and were very anxious indeed to obtain repeated assurances of their ultimate salvation.

Many stories are therefore told of priests or children meeting these spirits playing by a stream, and taunting them with future damnation, which threat turned the joyful music to pitiful wails. But when priest or children, discovering their mistake, hastened back to the stream and assured the green-toothed water sprites of future redemption, they invariably resumed their happy strain.

" Know you the Nixies, gay and fair?
  Their eyes are black, and green their hair —
  They lurk in sedgy shores."
                        MATHISSON.

Besides Elf or Elb, the water sprite who gave its name to the Elbe River in Germany, the Neck, from whom the Neckar derives its name, and old Father Rhine, with his numerous daughters (tributary streams), the most **River nymphs.** famous of all the lesser water divinities is the Lorelei, the siren maiden who sits upon the Lorelei rock near St. Goar, on the Rhine, and whose alluring song has enticed many a mariner to death. The legends concerning this siren are very numerous indeed, one of the most ancient being as follows :

Lorelei was an immortal, a water nymph, daughter of old Father Rhine; during the day she dwelt in the cool depths of the river bed, but late at night she appeared in the moonlight, sitting aloft upon a pinnacle of rock, in full view of all who passed up or down the stream. At times, the evening breeze wafted some of the notes of her song to the boatmen's ears, when, forgetting time and place in listening to these enchanting melodies, they drifted upon the sharp and jagged rocks, where they invariably perished.

" Above the maiden sitteth,
  A wondrous form, and fair;
With jewels bright she plaiteth
  Her shining golden hair:
With comb of gold prepares it,
  The task with song beguiled;
A fitful burden bears it —
  That melody so wild.

" The boatman on the river
  Lists to the song, spell-bound;
Oh! what shall him deliver
  From danger threat'ning round?
The waters deep have caught them,
  Both boat and boatman brave;
'Tis Loreley's song hath brought them
  Beneath the foaming wave."

SONG, HEINE (Selcher's tr.).

One person only is reported to have seen the Lorelei close by, a young fisherman from Oberwesel, who met her every evening by the riverside, and spent a few delightful hours with her, drinking in her beauty and listening to her entrancing song. Tradition further relates that ere they parted the Lorelei invariably pointed out the places where the youth must cast his nets on the morrow — instructions which he always obeyed, and which invariably brought him success.

The Lorelei and the fisherman.

One night the young fisherman was seen going towards the river, but as he never returned search was made for him. No clew to his whereabouts being found, the credulous Germans finally reported that the Lorelei had dragged him down to her coral caves that she might enjoy his companionship forever.

According to another version, the Lorelei, perching on the rocks above, and luring the fishermen by her songs, caused so many deaths that an armed force was once sent out at nightfall to surround and seize her. But the water nymph used her magic to lay such a powerful spell upon the captain and his men that they could move neither hand nor foot. While they stood mo-

(*Opp. p.* 180.)

LORELEI AND THE FISHERMAN.—Paul Thumann.

tionless around her, the Lorelei divested herself of all her ornaments, which she flung into the waves below; then, chanting a
spell, she lured the waters up to the top of the rock, and the sol-
diers saw her spring into a sea-green chariot drawn by white-
maned steeds, and drive rapidly away. A few moments later the
Rhine had subsided to its usual level, the spell was broken, and
the men recovered the power of motion, and retreated to announce how their efforts had been baffled. Since then, however,
the Lorelei has never been seen, and the peasants declare that
she still resents the insult offered her and will no longer leave her
coral caves.

CHAPTER XXI.

BALDER.

ODIN and Frigga, we are told, were parents of twin sons as dissimilar in character and physical appearance as it was possible to be; for while Hodur, god of darkness, was somber, taciturn, and blind, like the obscurity of sin, which he was supposed to symbolize, Balder, the beautiful, was the pure and radiant god of innocence and light. The snowy brow and golden locks of this Asa seemed to send out beams of sunshine to gladden the hearts of gods and men, by whom he was equally beloved.

> " Of all the twelve round Odin's throne,
> Balder, the Beautiful, alone,
> The Sun-god, good, and pure, and bright,
> Was loved by all, as all love light."
>
> VALHALLA (J. C. Jones).

Balder, attaining his full growth with marvelous rapidity, was admitted to the council of the gods, and married Nanna (blossom),

Nanna. the daughter of Nip (bud), a beautiful and charming young goddess, with whom he lived in perfect unity and peace. He took up his abode in the palace of Breidablik, whose silver roof rested upon golden pillars, and whose purity was such that nothing common or unclean was ever allowed within its precincts.

The god of light was well versed in the science of runes which were carved on his tongue; he knew the various virtues of the simples, one of which, the camomile, was always called " Balder's brow," because its flower was just as immaculately pure as his

182

forehead. The only thing hidden from Balder's radiant eyes, at first, was the perception of his own ultimate fate.

> " His own house
> Breidablik, on whose columns Balder graved
> The enchantments that recall the dead to life.
> For wise he was, and many curious arts,
> Postures of runes, and healing herbs he knew;
> Unhappy! but that art he did not know,
> To keep his own life safe, and see the sun."
> BALDER DEAD (Matthew Arnold).

As Balder the beautiful was always smiling and happy, the gods were greatly troubled when they finally saw the light die out of his blue eyes, a careworn look come into his face, and his step grow heavy and slow. Odin and Frigga, seeing their beloved son's evident depression, tenderly implored him to reveal the cause of his silent grief. Balder, yielding at last to their anxious entreaties, confessed that his slumbers, instead of being peaceful and restful as of yore, had been strangely troubled of late by dark and oppressive dreams, which, although he could not clearly remember them when he awoke, constantly haunted him with a vague feeling of fear.

> " To that god his slumber
> Was most afflicting;
> His auspicious dreams
> Seemed departed."
> LAY OF VEGTAM (Thorpe's tr.).

When Odin and Frigga heard this, they were troubled indeed, but declared they were quite sure nothing would harm their son, who was so universally beloved. Yet, when the anxious father and mother had returned home, they talked the matter over, acknowledged that they also were oppressed by strange forebodings, and having learned from the giants that Balder really was in danger, they proceeded to take measures to avert it.

Frigga, therefore, sent out her servants in every direction, bidding them make all living creatures, all plants, metals, stones —

in fact, every animate and inanimate thing—register a solemn vow not to do any harm to Balder. All creation readily took the oath, for all things loved the radiant god, and basked in the light of his smile. So the servants soon returned to Frigga, telling her that all had been duly sworn except the mistletoe, growing upon the oak stem at the gate of Valhalla, which, they added, was such a puny, inoffensive thing that no harm could be feared from it.

> "On a course they resolved:
> That they would send
> To every being,
> Assurance to solicit,
> Balder not to harm.
> All species swore
> Oaths to spare him;
> Frigg received all
> Their vows and compacts."
> SÆMUND'S EDDA (Thorpe's tr.).

Frigga now resumed her spinning with her usual content, for she knew no harm could come to the child she loved best of all. Odin, in the mean while, also sorely troubled, and wishing to ascertain whether there was any cause for his unwonted depression, resolved to consult one of the dead Valas or prophetesses. He therefore mounted his eight-footed steed Sleipnir, rode over the tremulous bridges Bifröst and Giallar, came to the entrance of Nifl-heim, and, passing the Hel-gate and the dog Garm, penetrated into Hel's dark abode.

The Vala's prophecy.

> "Uprose the king of men with speed,
> And saddled straight his coal-black steed;
> Down the yawning steep he rode,
> That leads to Hela's drear abode."
> DESCENT OF ODIN (Gray).

To his surprise, he noticed that a feast was being spread in this dark realm, and that the couches had all been covered with tapestry and rings of gold, as if some highly honored guest were expected before long. Hastening on, Odin finally reached the grave where the Vala had rested undisturbed for many a year, and solemnly began to chant the magic spell and trace the runes which had the power of raising the dead.

> "Thrice pronounc'd, in accents dread,
>   The thrilling verse that wakes the dead:
>   Till from out the hollow ground
>   Slowly breath'd a sullen sound."
>
> DESCENT OF ODIN (Gray).

Suddenly the grave opened, and the prophetess slowly rose, inquiring who he was and why he thus came to trouble her long rest. Odin, not wishing her to know that he was king of the gods, replied that he was Vegtam, Valtam's son, and that he had awakened her to inquire for whom Hel was spreading her couches and preparing a festive meal. In hollow tones, the prophetess now confirmed all his fears by telling him that the expected guest was Balder, who would shortly be slain by Hodur, his brother, the blind god of darkness.

> "Hodur will hither
>   His glorious brother send;
>   He of Balder will
>   The slayer be,
>   And Odin's son
>   Of life bereave.
>   By compulsion I have spoken;
>   Now I will be silent."
>
> SÆMUND'S EDDA (Thorpe's tr.).

But in spite of these sad tidings, and of the Vala's evident reluctance to answer any other questions, Odin was not yet satisfied, and forced her to tell him who would avenge the murdered man by calling his assassin to account — a spirit of revenge and retaliation being considered a sacred duty among the races of the North.

Then the prophetess told him, as Rossthiof had predicted before, that Rinda, the earth-goddess, would bear a son to Odin, and that this divine emissary, Vali, would neither wash his face nor comb his hair until he had avenged Balder and slain Hodur.

> "In the caverns of the west,
> By Odin's fierce embrace comprest,
> A wondrous boy shall Rinda bear,
> Who ne'er shall comb his raven hair,
> Nor wash his visage in the stream,
> Nor see the sun's departing beam,
> Till he on Hoder's corse shall smile
> Flaming on the fun'ral pile."
>
> DESCENT OF ODIN (Gray).

Having discovered this from the reluctant Vala, Odin, who, thanks to his visit to the Urdar fountain, already knew much of the future, now incautiously revealed some of his knowledge by inquiring who would refuse to weep at Balder's death. When the prophetess heard this question, she immediately knew that it was Odin who had called her out of her grave, and, refusing to speak another word, she sank back into the silence of the tomb, declaring that none would ever be able to lure her out again until the end of the world had come.

> " Hie thee hence, and boast at home,
> That never shall inquirer come
> To break my iron sleep again,
> Till Lok has burst his tenfold chain;
> Never, till substantial Night
> Has reassum'd her ancient right :
> Till wrapt in flames, in ruin hurl'd,
> Sinks the fabric of the world."
>
> DESCENT OF ODIN (Gray).

Odin had questioned the greatest prophetess the world had ever known, and had learned Orlog's (fate's) decrees, which he knew could not be set aside. He therefore remounted his steed, and sadly wended his way back to Asgard, thinking of the time, no longer far distant, when his beloved son would no more be seen in the heavenly abodes, and when the light of his presence would have vanished forever.

On entering Glads-heim, however, Odin was somewhat cheered when he heard of the precautions taken by Frigga to insure their darling's safety, and soon, feeling convinced that if nothing would slay Balder he would surely continue to gladden the world with his presence, he cast aside all care and ordered games and a festive meal.

The gods resumed their wonted occupations, and were soon casting their golden disks on the green plain of Ida, which was called Idavold, the playground of the gods. At last, wearying of this pastime, and knowing that *The gods at play.* no harm could come to their beloved Balder, they invented a new game and began to use him as a target, throwing all manner of weapons and missiles at him, certain that no matter how cleverly they tried, and how accurately they aimed, the objects, having sworn not to injure him, would either glance aside or fall short. This new amusement was so fascinating that soon all the gods were assembled around Balder, at whom they threw every available thing, greeting each new failure with prolonged shouts of laughter. These bursts of merriment soon excited the curiosity of Frigga, who sat spinning in Fensalir; and seeing an old woman pass by her dwelling, she bade her pause and tell what the gods were doing to provoke such great hilarity. The old woman, who was Loki in disguise, immediately stopped at this appeal, and told Frigga that all the gods were throwing stones and blunt and sharp instruments at Balder, who stood smiling and unharmed in their midst, daring them to touch him.

The goddess smiled, and resumed her work, saying that it was quite natural that nothing should harm Balder, as all things loved the light, of which he was the emblem, and had solemnly sworn not to injure him. Loki, the personification of fire, was greatly disappointed upon hearing this, for he was jealous of Balder, the sun, who so entirely eclipsed him and was generally beloved, while he was feared and avoided as much as possible; but he cleverly concealed his chagrin, and inquired of Frigga whether she were quite sure that all objects had joined the league.

Frigga proudly answered that she had received the solemn oath of all things, except of a harmless little parasite, the mistletoe, which grew on the oak near Valhalla's gate, and was too small and weak to be feared. Having obtained the desired information, Loki toddled off; but as soon as he was safely out of sight, he resumed his wonted form, hastened to Valhalla, found the oak and mistletoe indicated by Frigga, and by magic arts compelled the parasite to assume a growth and hardness hitherto unknown.

From the wooden stem thus produced he deftly fashioned a shaft ere he hastened back to Idavold, where the gods were still hurling missiles at Balder, Hodur alone leaning mournfully against a tree, and taking no part in the new game. Carelessly Loki approached him, inquired the cause of his melancholy, and twitted him with pride and indifference, since he would not condescend to take part in the new game. In answer to these remarks, Hodur pleaded his blindness; but when Loki put the mistletoe in his hand, led him into the midst of the circle, and indicated in what direction the novel target stood, Hodur threw his shaft boldly. Instead of the loud shout of laughter which he expected to hear, a shuddering cry of terror fell upon his ear, for Balder the beautiful had fallen to the ground, slain by the fatal blow.

Death of Balder.

> " So on the floor lay Balder dead; and round
> Lay thickly strewn swords, axes, darts, and spears,
> Which all the Gods in sport had idly thrown
> At Balder, whom no weapon pierced or clove;
> But in his breast stood fixed the fatal bough
> Of mistletoe, which Lok, the Accuser, gave
> To Hoder, and unwitting Hoder threw —
> 'Gainst that alone had Balder's life no charm."
>
> BALDER DEAD (Matthew Arnold).

Anxiously the gods all crowded around him, but alas! life was quite extinct, and all their efforts to revive the fallen sun-god were vain. Inconsolable at their loss, they turned angrily upon

(*Opp. p.* 188)

BALDER.

Hodur, whom they would have slain had they not been restrained by the feeling that no willful deed of violence should ever desecrate their peace steads. At the loud sound of lamentation the goddesses came in hot haste, and when Frigga saw that her darling was dead, she passionately implored the gods to go to Niflheim and entreat Hel to release her victim, for the earth could not live happy without him.

As the road was rough and painful in the extreme, none of the gods at first volunteered to go; but when Frigga added that she and Odin would reward the messenger by loving him most of all the Æsir, Hermod signified his readiness to execute the commission. To help him on his way, Odin lent him Sleipnir, and bade him good speed, while he motioned to the other gods to carry the corpse to Breidablik, and directed them to go to the forest and cut down huge pines to make a worthy pyre for his son.

Hermod's errand.

> "But when the Gods were to the forest gone,
>   Hermod led Sleipnir from Valhalla forth.
> And saddled him; before that, Sleipnir brook'd
> No meaner hand than Odin's on his mane,
> On his broad back no lesser rider bore;
> Yet docile now he stood at Hermod's side,
> Arching his neck, and glad to be bestrode,
> Knowing the God they went to seek, how dear.
> But Hermod mounted him, and sadly fared
> In silence up the dark untravel'd road
> Which branches from the north of Heaven, and went
> All day; and daylight waned, and night came on.
> And all that night he rode, and journey'd so,
> Nine days, nine nights, toward the northern ice,
> Through valleys deep-engulph'd by roaring streams.
> And on the tenth morn he beheld the bridge
> Which spans with golden arches Giall's stream,
> And on the bridge a damsel watching, arm'd,
> In the straight passage, at the further end,
> Where the road issues between walling rocks."
>
>   BALDER DEAD (Matthew Arnold).

While Hermod was traveling along the cheerless road to Nifl-heim, the gods hewed and carried down to the shore a vast amount of fuel, which they placed upon the deck of Balder's favorite vessel, Ringhorn, constructing an elaborate funeral pyre, which, according to custom, was decorated with tapestry hangings, garlands of flowers, vessels and weapons of all kinds, golden rings, and countless objects of value, ere the immaculate corpse was brought and laid upon it in full attire.

One by one, the gods now drew near to take a last farewell of their beloved companion, and as Nanna bent over him, her loving heart broke, and she fell lifeless by his side. Seeing this, the gods reverently laid her beside her husband, that she might accompany him even in death; and after they had slain his horse and hounds and twined the pyre with thorns, the emblems of sleep, Odin, the last of the gods, drew near.

In token of affection for the dead and of sorrow for his loss, all laid their most precious possessions upon his pyre, and Odin, bending down, now added to the offerings his magic ring Draupnir. The assembled gods then perceived

The funeral pyre.

that he was whispering in his dead son's ear, but none were near enough to hear what word he said.

These preliminaries ended, the gods now prepared to launch the ship, but found it so heavily laden with fuel and treasures that their combined efforts could not make it stir an inch. The mountain giants, witnessing the sad scene from afar, and noticing their quandary, said that they knew of a giantess called Hyrrokin, who dwelt in Jötun-heim, and was strong enough to launch the vessel without any other aid. The gods therefore bade one of the storm giants hasten off to summon Hyrrokin, who soon appeared, riding a gigantic wolf, which she guided by a bridle made of writhing live snakes. Riding down to the shore, the giantess dismounted and haughtily signified her readiness to give them the required aid, if in the mean while they would but hold her steed. Odin immediately dispatched four of his maddest Berserkers to fulfill this task; but, in spite of their phenomenal strength, they could not hold the monstrous wolf until the giantess had thrown and bound it fast.

Hyrrokin, seeing them now able to manage her refractory steed, marched down the beach, set her shoulder against the stern of Balder's ship Ringhorn, and with one mighty shove sent it out into the water. Such was the weight of the burden she moved, however, and the rapidity with which it shot down into the sea, that all the earth shook as if from an earthquake, and the rollers on which it glided caught fire from the friction. The unexpected shock almost made the gods lose their balance, and so angered Thor that he raised his hammer and would have slain the giantess had he not been restrained by his fellow gods. Easily appeased, as usual — for Thor's violence, although quick, was evanescent — he now stepped up on the vessel once more to consecrate the funeral pyre with his sacred hammer. But, as he was performing this ceremony, the dwarf Lit managed to get into his way so provokingly that Thor, still slightly angry, kicked him into the fire, which he had just kindled with a thorn, where the dwarf was burned to ashes with the corpses of the faithful pair.

As the vessel drifted out to sea, the flames rose higher and higher, and when it neared the western horizon it seemed as if sea and sky were all on fire. Sadly the gods watched the glowing ship and its precious freight, until it suddenly plunged into the waves and disappeared; nor did they turn aside and go back to their own homes until the last spark of light had vanished, and all the world was enveloped in darkness, in token of mourning for Balder the good.

> " Soon with a roaring rose the mighty fire,
>   And the pile crackled; and between the logs
>   Sharp quivering tongues of flame shot out, and leapt
>   Curling and darting, higher, until they lick'd
>   The summit of the pile, the dead, the mast,
>   And ate the shriveling sails; but still the ship
>   Drove on, ablaze above her hull with fire.
>   And the gods stood upon the beach, and gazed;

And while they gazed, the sun went lurid down
Into the smoke-wrapt sea, and night came on.
Then the wind fell with night, and there was calm;
But through the dark they watch'd the burning ship
Still carried o'er the distant waters, on
Farther and farther, like an eye of fire.
So show'd in the far darkness, Balder's pile;
But fainter, as the stars rose high, it flared;
The bodies were consumed, ash choked the pile.
And as, in a decaying winter fire,
A charr'd log, falling, makes a shower of sparks—
So, with a shower of sparks, the pile fell in,
Reddening the sea around; and all was dark."

BALDER DEAD (Matthew Arnold).

Sadly the gods entered Asgard, where no sounds of merriment or feasting were heard, but all hearts were filled with despair, for they knew the end was near, and shuddered at the thought of the terrible Fimbul-winter, which was to herald their death.

Frigga alone cherished some hope, and anxiously watched for the return of her messenger, Hermod the swift, who in the mean while had ridden over the tremulous bridge, along the dark Hel-way, and on the tenth night had crossed the rushing tide of the river Giöll. Here he was challenged by Mödgud, who inquired why the Giallar-bridge trembled more beneath his horse's tread than when a whole army passed, and asked why he, a live man, was attempting to penetrate into the dreaded realm of Hel.

"Who art thou on thy black and fiery horse
Under whose hoofs the bridge o'er Giall's stream
Rumbles and shakes? Tell me thy race and home.
But yestermorn five troops of dead pass'd by,
Bound on their way below to Hela's realm,
Nor shook the bridge so much as thou alone.
And thou hast flesh and color on thy cheeks,
Like men who live, and draw the vital air;
Nor look'st thou pale and wan, like man deceased,
Souls bound below, my daily passers here."

BALDER DEAD (Matthew Arnold).

Hermod explained to Mödgud the reason of his coming, and, having ascertained that Balder and Nanna had ridden over the bridge before him, he hastened on, until he came to the gate of hell, which rose forbiddingly before him.

Nothing daunted by this barrier, Hermod dismounted on the smooth ice, tightened the girths of his saddle, remounted, and burying his spurs deep into Sleipnir's sleek sides, he made him take a prodigious leap, which landed him safely on the other side of Hel-gate.

> "Thence on he journey'd o'er the fields of ice
> Still north, until he met a stretching wall
> Barring his way, and in the wall a gate.
> Then he dismounted, and drew tight the girths,
> On the smooth ice, of Sleipnir, Odin's horse,
> And made him leap the gate, and came within."
>
> BALDER DEAD (Matthew Arnold).

Riding onward, Hermod came at last to Hel's banquet hall, where he found Balder, pale and dejected, lying upon a couch, his wife Nanna beside him, gazing fixedly at the mead before him, which he had no heart to drink.

In vain Hermod informed his brother that he had come to redeem him; Balder sadly shook his head, saying that he knew he must remain in this cheerless abode until the last day should come, but imploring him to take Nanna back with him, as the home of the shades was no place for such a bright and beautiful young creature. But when Nanna heard this request she clung more closely still to her husband's side, vowing that nothing would ever induce her to part from him, and that she would stay with him, even in Nifl-heim, forever.

Result of Hermod's quest.

The whole night was spent in close conversation, ere Hermod sought Hel and implored Balder's release. The churlish goddess listened silently to his request, and finally declared that she would let her victim go providing all things animate and inanimate should prove their sorrow for his loss by shedding a tear.

"Come then! if Balder was so dear beloved,
And this is true, and such a loss is Heaven's —
Hear, how to Heaven may Balder be restored.
Show me through all the world the signs of grief!
Fails but one thing to grieve, here Balder stops!
Let all that lives and moves upon the earth
Weep him, and all that is without life weep;
Let Gods, men, brutes, beweep him; plants and stones '
So shall I know the lost was dear indeed,
And bend my heart, and give him back to Heaven."

BALDER DEAD (Matthew Arnold).

Having received this answer, the ring Draupnir, which Balder sent back to Odin, an embroidered carpet from Nanna for Frigga, and a ring for Fulla, Hermod cheerfully made his way out of Hel's dark realm, whence he hoped soon to rescue Balder the good, for well he knew all Nature sincerely mourned his departure and would shed unlimited tears to win him back.

The assembled gods crowded anxiously around him as soon as he returned, and when he had delivered his messages and gifts, the Æsir sent out heralds to every part of the world to bid all things animate and inanimate weep for Balder.

"Go quickly forth through all the world, and pray
All living and unliving things to weep
Balder, if haply he may thus be won!"

BALDER DEAD (Matthew Arnold).

These orders were rapidly carried out, and soon tears hung from every plant and tree, the ground was saturated with moisture, and metals and stones, in spite of their hard hearts, wept too.

On their way home the messengers passed a dark cave, in which they saw the crouching form of a giantess named Thok, whom some mythologists suppose to have been Loki in disguise; when they asked her also to shed a tear, she mocked them and fled into the dark recesses of her cave, declaring that she would never weep and that Hel might retain her prey forever.

"Thok she weepeth
With dry tears
For Balder's death —
Neither in life, nor yet in death,
Gave he me gladness.
Let Hel keep her prey."
ELDER EDDA (Howitt's version).

As soon as the returning messengers arrived in Asgard, all the gods crowded around them to know the result of their mission; but their faces, all alight with the joy of anticipation, soon grew dark with despair when they heard that, as one creature refused the tribute of tears, they should behold Balder on earth no more.

"Balder, the Beautiful, shall ne'er
From Hel return to upper air!
Betrayed by Loki, *twice* betrayed,
The prisoner of Death is made;
Ne'r shall he 'scape the place of doom
Till fatal Ragnarok be come!"
VALHALLA (J. C. Jones).

The sole consolation left Odin was to fulfill the decree of fate. He therefore departed and achieved the difficult courtship of Rinda, which we have already described. She bore Vali, the Avenger, who, coming into Asgard on the very day of his birth, slew Hodur with his sharp arrow. Thus he punished the murderer of Balder according to the true Northern creed.

The physical explanation of this myth is either the daily setting of the sun (Balder), which sinks beneath the western waves, driven away by darkness (Hodur), or the end of the short Northern summer and reign of the long winter season. "Balder represents the bright and clear summer, when twilight and daylight kiss each other and go hand in hand in these Northern latitudes."

"Balder's pyre, of the sun a mark,
Holy hearth red staineth;
Yet, soon dies its last faint spark,
Darkly then Hoder reigneth."
VIKING TALES OF THE NORTH (R. B. Anderson).

"His death by Hodur is the victory of darkness over light, the darkness of winter over the light of summer; and the revenge by Vali is the breaking forth of new light after the wintry darkness."

Loki, the fire, is jealous of the pure light of heaven, Balder, who alone among the Northern gods never fought, but was always ready with words of conciliation and peace.

> "But from thy lips, O Balder, night or day,
>   Heard no one ever an injurious word
>   To God or Hero, but thou keptest back
>   The others, laboring to compose their brawls."
>   BALDER DEAD (Matthew Arnold).

The tears shed by all things for the beloved god are symbolical of the spring thaw, setting in after the hardness and cold of winter, when every tree and twig, and even the stones drip with moisture; Thok (coal) alone shows no sign of tenderness, as she is buried deep within the dark earth and needs not the light of the sun.

> "And as in winter, when the frost breaks up,
>   At winter's end, before the spring begins,
>   And a warm west wind blows, and thaw sets in —
>   After an hour a dripping sound is heard
>   In all the forests, and the soft-strewn snow
>   Under the trees is dibbled thick with holes,
>   And from the boughs the snow loads shuffle down;
>   And, in fields sloping to the south, dark plots
>   Of grass peep out amid surrounding snow,
>   And widen, and the peasant's heart is glad —
>   So through the world was heard a dripping noise
>   Of all things weeping to bring Balder back;
>   And there fell joy upon the Gods to hear."
>   BALDER DEAD (Matthew Arnold).

From the depths of their underground prison, the sun (Balder) and vegetation (Nanna) try to cheer heaven (Odin) and earth (Frigga) by sending them the ring Draupnir, the emblem of fertility, and the flowery tapestry, symbolical of the carpet of verdure which will again deck the earth and enhance her charms with its beauty.

The ethical signification of the myth is no less beautiful, for Balder and Hodur are symbols of the conflicting forces of good and evil, while Loki impersonates the tempter.

" But in each human soul we find
That night's dark Hoder, Balder's brother blind,
Is born and waxeth strong as he ;
For blind is ev'ry evil born, as bear cubs be,
Night is the cloak of evil ; but all good
Hath ever clad in shining garments stood.
The busy Loke, tempter from of old,
Still forward treads incessant, and doth hold
The blind one's murder hand, whose quick-launch'd spear
Pierceth young Balder's breast, that sun of Valhal's sphere ! "
VIKING TALES OF THE NORTH (R. B. Anderson).

One of the most important festivals was held at the summer solstice, or midsummer's eve, in honor of Balder the good, for it was considered the anniversary of his death and of his descent into the lower world. On that day, the longest in the year, all the people congregated out of doors, made great bonfires, and watched the sun, which in extreme Northern latitudes merely touches the horizon ere it rises upon a new day. From midsummer, the days gradually grow shorter, and the sun's rays less warm, until the winter solstice, which was called the " Mother night," as it was the longest in the year. Midsummer's eve, once celebrated in honor of Balder, is now called St. John's day, that saint having entirely supplanted Balder the good.

Worship of Balder.

CHAPTER XXII.

LOKI.

BESIDES the hideous giant Utgard-Loki, the personification of mischief and evil, whom Thor and his companions visited in Jötun-heim, the ancient Northern nations had another type of sin, whom they called Loki also, and whom we have already seen under many different aspects.

In the beginning, Loki, who by some mythologists is considered the brother of Odin himself, was only the personification of the hearth fire and of the spirit of life. But other authorities assert that Odin and Loki were not related, and had merely gone through the Northern form of swearing blood brotherhood.

> "Odin ! dost thou remember
> When we in early days
> Blended our blood together?
> When to taste beer
> Thou dids't constantly refuse
> Unless to both 'twas offered ? "
> SÆMUND'S EDDA (Thorpe's tr.).

At first a god, Loki gradually becomes " god and devil combined," and ends by being an exact counterpart of the mediæval Lucifer, the prince of lies, "the originator of deceit, and the backbiter" of the Æsir.

While Thor is the embodiment of Northern activity, Loki represents recreation, and the close companionship early established between these two gods shows very plainly how soon our ancestors realized that both were necessary to the welfare of mankind. Thor is ever busy and ever in dead earnest, but Loki

198

makes fun of everything, until at last his love of mischief leads him entirely astray, and he loses all love for good and becomes utterly selfish and malevolent.

He represents evil in the seductive and seemingly beautiful form in which it glides about through the world. On account of this deceptive appearance the gods did not at first avoid him, but considered him one of their number, took him with them wherever they went, and admitted him not only to their banquets and merrymakings, but also to their council hall, where they, unfortunately, too often listened to his advice.

Loki's character.

As we have already seen, Loki played a prominent part in the creation of man, endowing him with the power of motion, and causing the blood to circulate freely through his veins and inspire him with passions. As personification of fire as well as of mischief, Loki (lightning) is often seen with Thor (thunder), whom he accompanies to Jötun-heim to recover his hammer, to Utgard-Loki's castle, and to Geirrod's house. It is he who steals Freya's necklace and Sif's hair, and betrays Idun into the power of Thiassi ; and although he sometimes gives the gods good advice and affords them real help, it is only to extricate them from some predicament into which he has rashly inveigled them.

Some authorities declare that, instead of making part of the creative trilogy (Odin, Hoenir, and Lodur or Loki), this god originally belonged to a pre-Odinic race of deities, and was the son of the great giant Fornjotnr (Ymir), his brothers being Kari (air) and Hler (water), and his sister Ran, the terrible goddess of the sea. Other mythologists, however, make him the son of the giant Farbauti, who has been identified with Bergelmir, the sole survivor of the deluge, and of Laufeia (leafy isle) or Nal (vessel), his mother, thus stating that his connection with Odin was only that of the Northern oath of good fellowship.

Loki (fire) first married Glut (glow), who bore him two daughters, Eisa (embers) and Einmyria (ashes) ; it is therefore very evident that Norsemen considered him emblematic of the hearth fire, and when the flaming wood crackles on the hearth the good-wives in the North are still wont to say that Loki is beating his children. Besides this wife, Loki is also said to have married the giantess Angur-boda (the anguish-boding), who dwelt in Jötunheim, and, as we have already seen, bore him the three monsters, Hel, goddess of death, the Midgard snake Iörmungandr, and the grim wolf Fenris.

> "Loki begat the wolf
> With Angur-boda."
> SÆMUND'S EDDA (Thorpe's tr.).

Loki's third marriage was with Sigyn, who proved a most loving and devoted wife, and bore him two sons, Narve and Vali, **Sigyn.** the latter a namesake of the god who avenged Balder. Sigyn was always faithful to her husband, never forsook him, and stood beside him even after he had definitely been cast out of Asgard and bound in punishment for his sins.

As Loki was the embodiment of evil in the minds of the Northern races, they felt nothing but fear of him, built no temples in his honor, offered no sacrifices to him, and designated the most noxious weeds by his name. The quivering, overheated atmosphere of summer was also supposed to betoken his presence, for the people were then wont to remark that Loki was sowing his oats, and when the sun drew water they said Loki was drinking.

The story of Loki is so inextricably woven in with that of the other gods that most of the myths relating to him have already been told, and there remain but two episodes of his life to relate, one showing his good side before he had degenerated into the arch deceiver, and the other illustrating how he finally induced the gods to defile their peace steads by willful murder.

A giant and a peasant were playing a game together one day (probably a game of chess, which was a favorite winter pastime **Skrymsli and** with the Northern vikings). They of course de-**the peasant's** termined to play for certain stakes, and the giant, **child.** coming off victor, won the peasant's only son, whom he said he

(*Opp. p.* 200.)

LOKI AND SIGYN.— Carl Gebhardt.

would come and claim on the morrow unless the parents could hide him so cleverly that he could not find him.

Knowing that such a feat would be impossible for them to perform, the parents fervently prayed Odin to help them, and in answer to these entreaties the god came down to earth, took the boy, and changed him into a tiny grain of wheat, which he hid in an ear of grain in the midst of a large field, declaring that the giant would never find him. The giant Skrymsli, however, was very wise indeed, and, failing to find the child at home, strode off to the field with his scythe, mowed down the grain, and selected the particular ear where the boy was hidden. Counting over the grains of wheat he was about to lay his hand upon the right one when Odin, hearing the child's cry of distress, suddenly snatched the kernel out of the giant's hand, and restored the boy to his parents, telling them that he had done all in his power to help them. But, as the giant vowed he had been cheated, and would claim his prey on the morrow unless the parents could outwit him, the unfortunate peasants now applied to Hoenir. He changed the boy into a bit of down, which he hid in the breast of a swan swimming in a pond close by. Skrymsli, the giant, coming up a few minutes later, and guessing what had occurred, caught the swan, bit off its neck, and would have swallowed the down, had not Hoenir interfered, wafted it away from his lips and out of reach, restoring the boy safe and sound to his parents, but warning them that he could never aid them again.

Skrymsli having told the parents that he would make a third attempt to secure the child, they now applied in despair to Loki, who carried the boy out to sea, and concealed him, as a tiny egg, in the roe of a flounder. Returning from his expedition, Loki encountered the giant near the shore, and seeing he was bent upon a fishing excursion, insisted upon accompanying him to interfere in case of need. Skrymsli baited his hook, angled awhile, caught several fishes, and finally drew up the identical flounder in which Loki had concealed his little charge. Opening the fish upon his knee, the giant proceeded to count over every egg in the roe, until he found the one which he was seeking; but Loki snatched it out of his grasp, set the child ashore, and secretly bade him run home, passing through the boathouse and closing the door behind him. The terrified boy obeyed, and the giant, in close pursuit, dashed into the boathouse, where Loki had cunningly placed a sharp spike, which pierced his head. The giant sank to the ground with a groan, and Loki, seeing him helpless, cut off one of his legs. Imagine the god's dismay, however, when he saw the pieces join and immediately knit together. Recognizing that magic was at work, Loki cut off the other leg, promptly throwing flint and steel between the severed limb and trunk, and thereby hindering any further sorcery. The peasants, perceiving that their enemy was slain by Loki's agency, ever after considered this god the mightiest of all the heavenly council, for he had delivered them from their foe forever, while the others had only lent temporary aid.

In spite of Bifröst, the tremulous way, and of the watchfulness of Heimdall, the gods could not feel entirely secure in Asgard, and

The giant architect. were often afraid lest the frost giants should make their way into their midst. To obviate this possibility, they finally decided to build an impregnable fortress; and while they were planning how this work could be executed, an unknown architect appeared among them, offering to undertake the construction, provided the gods would give him sun, moon, and Freya, goddess of youth and beauty, as reward. The gods were at first inclined to demur; but, urged by Loki, they finally told the architect that the guerdon should be his, provided the fortress were finished in the course of a single winter, and that he accomplished the work with no other assistance than that of his horse Svadilfare.

> "To Asgard came an architect,
> And castle offered to erect, —
> A castle high
> Which should defy
> Deep Jotun guile and giant raid;
> And this most wily compact made:

> Fair Freya, with the Moon and Sun,
> As price the fortress being done."
>
> VALHALLA (J. C. Jones).

The unknown architect submitted to these conditions, and immediately began his work, hauling ponderous blocks of stone by night, building during the day, and advancing so rapidly that the gods' attention was attracted to the work. Ere long they perceived that more than half the labor was accomplished by the wonderful steed Svadilfare, and trembled when they saw, near the end of winter, that the work was all finished except one portal, which they knew the architect could easily erect during the night.

> " Horror and fear the gods beset;
> Finished almost the castle stood!
> In three days more
> The work be o'er;
> Then must they make their contract good,
> And pay the awful debt."
>
> VALHALLA (J. C. Jones).

Terrified lest they should be called upon to part, not only with the sun and moon, but also with Freya, the personification of all the youth and beauty of the world, the gods sought Loki, and threatened to kill him unless he devised some means of hindering the architect from finishing the work within the specified time.

Changing himself into a mare, at nightfall, Loki rushed out of the forest, and neighed invitingly as Svadilfare passed by, painfully dragging one of the great blocks of stone required for the termination of the work. In a trice the horse kicked his harness to pieces and ran after the mare, closely pursued by his angry and gesticulating master. Loki, the mare, artfully lured horse and master deeper and deeper into the forest, until the night was nearly gone, and it was impossible to finish the work. Discovering the fraud, the architect (a redoubtable Hrim-thurs, in disguise) now returned to Asgard in a towering rage, and, assuming his wonted proportions, would have annihilated all the gods had not Thor suddenly confronted him, and slain him by hurling his magic hammer Miölnir full in his face.

The gods having saved themselves on this occasion only through fraud and by perjury, this murder brought great sorrows upon them, and eventually brought about their downfall and hastened the coming of Ragnarok. Loki, however, felt no remorse for what he had done, and in due time it is said he became the parent of an eight-footed steed called Sleipnir, which, as we have seen, was Odin's favorite mount.

> "But Sleipnir he begat
> With Svadilfari."
> LAY OF HYNDLA (Thorpe's tr.).

Loki performed so many evil deeds during his career that he richly deserved the title of "arch deceiver" which was given him. He was generally hated for his subtle malicious ways, and for an inveterate habit of prevarication which won for him also the title of "prince of lies."

The last crime which he committed, and the one which filled his measure of iniquity, was to induce Hodur to throw the fatal mistletoe at Balder, whom he hated merely on account of his immaculate purity. Had it not been for his obduracy as Thok, perhaps even this crime might have been condoned; but the gods, seeing that nothing but evil remained within him, refused to allow him to remain in Asgard, and unanimously pronounced the sentence of perpetual banishment upon him.

Loki's last crime.

To divert the gods' sadness and make them, for a short time, forget the treachery of Loki and the loss of Balder, Ægir, god of the sea, invited them all to partake of a banquet in his coral caves at the bottom of the sea.

> "Now, to assuage the high gods' grief
> And bring their mourning some relief,
> From coral caves
> 'Neath ocean waves,

> Mighty King Ægir
> Invited the Æsir
> To festival
> In Hlesey's hall;
> That, tho' for Baldur every guest
> Was grieving yet,
> He might forget
> Awhile his woe in friendly feast."
> VALHALLA (J. C. Jones).

The gods gladly accepted the invitation, and donning their richest garb, and wreathing their faces with festive smiles, they appeared in the coral caves at the appointed time. All were present except the radiant Balder, for whom they heaved many a regretful sigh, and the evil Loki, whom none could regret. In the course of the feast, however, this last-named god appeared in their midst like a dark shadow, and when told to depart, gave vent to his rage by vilifying all the gods.

> "Of the Æsir and the Alfar
> That are here within
> Not one has a friendly word for thee."
> ÆGIR'S COMPOTATION, OR LOKI'S ALTERCATION (Thorpe's tr.).

Then, jealous of the praises which Funfeng, Ægir's servant, had won for the dexterity with which he waited upon the guests, Loki suddenly turned all his wrath upon him and slew him. The gods, indignant at this wanton crime, drove Loki away once more, sternly bidding him never appear before them again.

Scarcely had the Æsir recovered from this disagreeable interruption to their feast, and resumed their places at the board, when Loki came creeping in once more, and with venomous tongue resumed his slanders, taunting all the gods with their weaknesses or shortcomings, dwelling maliciously upon their physical imperfections, and deriding them for their mistakes. In vain the gods tried to stem his abuse; his voice rose louder and louder, and he was just uttering some base slander about Sif, when Thor suddenly appeared, angrily brandishing his hammer, at the mere sight of which Loki fled.

> "Silence, thou impure being!
> My mighty hammer, Miöllnir,
> Shall stop thy prating.
> I will thy head
> From thy neck strike;
> Then will thy life be ended."
> ÆGIR'S COMPOTATION, OR LOKI'S ALTERCATION (Thorpe's tr.).

Knowing that he had now lost all hope of ever being admitted into Asgard again, and that sooner or later the gods, seeing the ripening of the crop of evil he had sown, would regret having permitted him to roam about the world, and would try either to bind or slay him, Loki withdrew to the mountains, where he built himself a hut with four doors, which he always left wide open to permit his hasty escape. Carefully laying his plans, he decided that if the gods ever came in search of him he would rush down to the neighboring cataract which is said to have been the Fraananger force or stream, and, changing himself into a salmon, would escape all pursuit. He reasoned, however, that, although he could easily avoid any hook, it would be difficult for him to effect an escape were the gods to fashion a net like that of the sea-goddess Ran.

Haunted by this thought, he wondered if such an implement could be manufactured, and began to make one out of twine. He had not quite finished his work when Odin, Kvasir, and Thor suddenly appeared in the distance; and knowing they had discovered his retreat, and were about to come and make him a prisoner, Loki threw his half-finished net into the fire, and, rushing out, jumped into the waterfall, where, in the shape of a salmon, he hid among the stones.

The gods, finding the hut empty, were about to depart, when Kvasir perceived the remains of the burned net on the hearth, and, examining them closely, advised the gods to weave a similar implement and use it in searching for their foe in the neighboring stream. This advice was immediately followed, and, the net finished, the gods proceeded to drag the stream. Loki eluded them the first time by hiding at the bottom of the river between two stones; but when the gods weighted the net and tried a second time, he effected his escape by jumping up stream. A third attempt to secure him proved successful, however, for, as he once more tried to get away by a sudden leap, Thor caught and held him so fast, that he could not escape. The salmon, whose slipperiness has become proverbial in the North, is noted for its remarkably slim tail, which the people attribute to Thor's tight grasp upon his foe.

The gods, having thus secured Loki and forced him to resume his wonted shape, dragged him down into a cavern, where they made him fast, using as bonds the entrails of his son Narve, who had been torn to pieces by his   **Loki's punishment.** brother Vali, whom the gods had changed into a wolf for this express purpose. One of these fetters was passed under Loki's shoulders, and one under his loins; when he was securely bound, hand and foot, the gods, fearing lest these fetters might give way, changed them into adamant or iron.

> "Thee, on a rock's point,
> With the entrails of thy ice-cold son,
> The gods will bind."
> SÆMUND'S EDDA (Thorpe's tr.).

Skadi, the giantess, a personification of the cold mountain stream, who had joyfully watched the fettering of her foe (subterranean fire), then fastened a venomous serpent directly over his head, so that the poison would fall, drop by drop, upon his upturned face. But Sigyn, Loki's faithful wife, hurried with a cup to his side, gathered up the drops as they fell, and never left her post except when her vessel was full and she was obliged to empty it. During her short absence the drops of venom, falling upon Loki's face, caused such intense pain that he writhed with anguish, shaking all the earth in his efforts to get free, and producing the earthquakes which so frighten mortals.

" Ere they. left him in his anguish,
    O'er his treacherous brow, ungrateful,
Skadi hung a serpent hateful,
Venom drops for aye distilling,
Every nerve with torment filling ;
Thus shall he in horror languish.
By him, still unwearied kneeling,
    Sigyn at his tortured side, —
Faithful wife ! with beaker stealing
    Drops of venom as they fall, —
    Agonizing poison all !
Sleepless, changeless, ever dealing
    Comfort, will she still abide ;
Only when the cup's o'erflowing
    Must fresh pain and smarting cause,
Swift, to void the beaker going,
    Shall she in her watching pause.
        Then doth Loki
        Loudly cry ;
        Shrieks of terror,
        Groans of horror,
Breaking forth in thunder peals !
With his writhings scared Earth reels.
Trembling and quaking,
E'en high Heav'n shaking !
So wears he out his awful doom,
Until dread Ragnarok be come."
                    VALHALLA (J. C. Jones).

In this painful position Loki was condemned to remain until
the twilight of the gods, when his bonds would be loosed, and
he would be free to take part in the last conflict, on the battlefield of Vigrid, where he was destined to fall by the hand of
Heimdall, who would be slain at the same time.

As we have seen, the venom-dropping snake in this myth is
the cold mountain stream, whose waters, falling from time to time
upon the subterranean fire, evaporate, and the steam, escaping
through fissures, produces the earthquakes and geysers with which
the inhabitants of Iceland, for instance, were so familiar.

(*Opp. p.* 208.)

NORWEGIAN WATERFALL.

When the gods were all reduced to the rank of demons by the introduction of Christianity, Loki was confounded with Saturn, who had also been shorn of all his divine attributes, and both were considered the prototypes of Satan. The last day of the week, which was held sacred to Loki, was known in the Norse as Laugardag, or wash day, but in English it was changed to Saturday, and was said to owe its name not to Saturn but to Sataere, the thief in ambush, and the Teutonic god of agriculture, who is supposed to be merely another form of the god Loki.

CHAPTER XXIII.

THE GIANTS.

As we have already seen, the Northern races imagined that the giants were the first creatures who came to life among the icebergs filling the vast abyss of Ginnunga-gap. These giants were from the very beginning the opponents and rivals of the gods, and as the latter were the personifications of all that is good and lovely, the former naturally served to denote all that was ugly and evil.

Slain by the gods, Ymir, the first giant, fell lifeless on the ice, drowning all his progeny in his blood. One couple only, Bergelmir and his wife, effected their escape to the confines of the world, Jötun-heim, where they took up their abode and became the parents of all the giant race. In the North the giants were called by various names, each having a particular meaning. Jötun, for instance, meant "the great eater," for the giants were noted for their enormous appetites as well as for their uncommon size. As they were fond of drinking as well as of eating, they were also called Thurses, a word which some writers claim had the same meaning as thirst, while others think they owed this name to the high towers ("turseis") which they were supposed to have built. As the giants were antagonistic to the gods, the latter always strove to keep them at a distance, and drove them away into Jötun-heim, in the cold regions of the pole, where they condemned them to remain. The giants were almost invariably worsted in their encounters with the gods, for they were heavy and slow witted, and had nothing but stone weapons to oppose the Æsir's bronze. In spite of this in-

Jotun-heim.

210

equality, however, they were sometimes greatly envied by the gods, for they were thoroughly conversant with all knowledge relating to the past. Odin himself was envious of this acquirement, and no sooner had he secured it by a draught from Mimir's spring than he hastened off to Jötun-heim to measure himself against Vafthrudnir, the most learned of the giant band. But he would never have succeeded in defeating his antagonist in this strange encounter had he not ceased inquiring about the past and propounded a question relating to the future.

Of all the gods Thor was the most feared by the Jötuns, for he was continually waging war against the frost and mountain giants, who would fain have hindered agriculture and bound the earth forever in their rigid bands. In fighting against them, Thor, as we have already seen, generally had recourse to his crashing hammer Miölnir, with which he reduced them to powder.

The Germans fancied that the uneven surface of the earth was due to the giants, who, treading upon it while it was still soft and newly created, marred its smoothness, while the giantesses, seeing the valleys made by their huge footprints, shed copious tears, which formed the streams. As such was the Teutonic belief, the people imagined that the giants, who were their personifications of the mountains, were huge uncouth creatures, who could only move about in the darkness or fog, and were petrified as soon as the first rays of sunlight pierced through the gloom or scattered the clouds.

Origin of the mountains.

This belief made them call one of their principal mountain chains the Riesengebirge (giant mountains). The Scandinavians also shared this belief, and to this day the Icelanders designate their highest mountain peaks by the name of Jokul, a modification of the word " Jötun." In Switzerland, where the everlasting snows rest upon the lofty mountain tops, the people still relate old stories of the time when the giants roamed abroad; and when an avalanche comes crashing down the mountain side, they say the giants have restlessly shaken off part of the icy burden from their brows and shoulders.

As the giants were also personifications of snow, ice, cold, stone, and subterranean fire, they were all said to be descended from the primitive Fornjotnr, whom some authorities identify with Ymir. According to this version of the myth, Fornjotnr had three sons: Hler, the sea; Kari, the air; and Loki, fire. These three divinities were the first gods, formed the oldest trinity, and their respective descendants were the sea giants Mimir, Gymir, and Grendel, the storm giants Thiassi, Thrym, and Beli, and the giants of fire and death, such as the Fenris wolf and Hel.

As all the royal dynasties claimed descent from some mythical being, the Merovingians asserted that their first progenitor was a sea giant, who rose up out of the waves in the form of an ox, surprised the queen while she was walking alone on the seashore, and induced her to become his wife. She gave birth to a son named Meroveus, the founder of the first dynasty of Frankish kings.

Many stories have already been told about the most important giants. They reappear in many of the later myths and fairy-tales, and manifest, after the introduction of Christianity, a peculiar dislike to the sound of church bells and the singing of the monks and nuns.

The Scandinavians relate, in this connection, that in the days of Olaf the Saint a giant called Senjemand, who dwelt on the

The giant in love. Island of Senjen, was greatly incensed because a nun on the Island of Grypto daily sang her morning hymn. The sound of this singing troubled his daydreams, for he had fallen in love with a beautiful maiden called Juternajesta, and was trying to gain courage to propose to her. When he made his halting request, however, the fair damsel scornfully rejected him, declaring that he was far too old and ugly to suit her taste.

> "Miserable Senjemand — ugly and gray!
> Thou win the maid of Kvedfiord!
> No — a churl thou art and shalt ever remain."
> BALLAD (Brace's tr.).

(*Onw.* p. 213.)

TORGHATTEN, NORWAY.

In his anger at being thus scornfully refused, the giant swore vengeance, and soon after he shot a great stone arrow from his bow at the maiden, who dwelt eighty miles away. Her lover, Torge, also a giant, seeing her peril and wishing to protect her, flung his hat at the speeding arrow. This hat was a thousand feet high and proportionately broad and thick, but a collision with it only spent the force of the arrow, which, piercing the giant's headgear, fell short of its aim. Senjemand, seeing he had failed, and fearing the wrath of Torge, mounted his steed and prepared to ride away as quickly as possible; but the sun, rising above the horizon just then, turned him into stone, as well as the arrow and Torge's hat, which is now known as the Torghatten mountain. The people still point out the stone arrow, — a huge obelisk, — the hole in the mountain, which is 289 feet high and 88 feet wide, and the horseman on Senjen Island, apparently riding a colossal steed and drawing the folds of his wide cavalry cloak closely about him. As for the nun whose singing had so disturbed Senjemand that he could not propose properly, she was petrified too, and never troubled any one with her psalmody again.

Another legend relates that one of the mountain giants, annoyed by the ringing of church bells more than fifty miles away, once caught up a huge rock, which he hurled at the sacred building, but which fortunately fell short and broke in two. Ever since then, on Christmas eve, the peasants report that the trolls have come to raise the largest piece of stone upon golden pillars, and to dance and feast beneath it. A lady, wishing to know whether this tale were true, once sent her groom to the place. The trolls came forward and hospitably offered him a drink in a horn mounted in gold and ornamented with runes. Seizing the horn, the groom flung its contents away and dashed off at a mad gallop, closely pursued by all the trolls, from whom he escaped only by passing through a stubble field and over running water. A deputation of trolls visited the lady on the morrow to claim this horn, and when she refused to part with it they laid a curse upon her, declaring that

The giant and the church bells.

her castle would burn down every time the horn was removed. This prediction has thrice been fulfilled, and now the family guard their horn with superstitious care. A similar drinking vessel, obtained in much the same fashion by the Oldenburg family, is exhibited in the collection of the King of Denmark.

The giants were not supposed to remain stationary, but were said to move about in the darkness, sometimes transporting masses of earth and sand, which they dropped here and there, thus forming the sandhills in northern Germany and Denmark.

A North Frisian tradition relates that the giants also possessed a colossal ship, called Mannigfual, which constantly cruised about in the Atlantic Ocean. Such was the size of this vessel that the captain was said to pace the deck on horseback. The rigging was so extensive and the masts so high that the sailors who went up as youths came down as gray-haired men, having rested and refreshed themselves in rooms fashioned and provisioned for that purpose in the huge blocks and pulleys.

The giants' ship.

By some mischance it happened that the pilot once directed this immense vessel into the North Sea, and wishing to return to the Atlantic as soon as possible, yet not daring to turn around in such a small space, he steered into the English Channel. Imagine the dismay of all on board when they saw the passage grow narrower and narrower the farther they advanced. When they came to the narrowest spot, between Calais and Dover, it seemed barely possible that the vessel, drifting along with the current, could force its way through. The captain, with laudable presence of mind, promptly bade his men soap the sides of the vessel, laying an extra-thick layer on the starboard, where the rugged Dover cliffs threateningly rose. These orders were no sooner carried out than the vessel entered the narrow space, and, thanks to the captain's precaution, it slipped safely through. The rocks of Dover scraped off so much soap, however, that ever since then they have been very white indeed, and the waves dashing against them still have a particularly foamy appearance.

This exciting experience was not the only one which the Mannigfual passed through, for we are told that it once, nobody knows how, penetrated into the Baltic Sea, where, the water not being deep enough to keep the vessel afloat, the captain ordered all the ballast thrown overboard. Such was the amount of material thus cast on either side the vessel into the sea that it formed the two islands of Bornholm and Christiansoë.

In Thuringia and in the Black Forest the stories of the giants are very numerous indeed, and the peasants delight in telling about Ilse, the lovely daughter of the giant of the Ilsenstein. She was so charming that she was **Princess Ilse.** known far and wide as the beautiful Princess Ilse, and was wooed by many knights, among whom she preferred the lord of Westerburg. But her father did not at all approve of her consorting with a mere mortal, and forbade her seeing her lover. Princess Ilse was willful; and in spite of his prohibitions she daily visited her lover. The giant, exasperated by her persistency and disobedience, finally stretched out his huge hands and, seizing the rocks, tore a great gap between the height where he dwelt and the castle of Westerburg. Princess Ilse, perceiving the cleft which parted her from her lover, recklessly flung herself over the precipice into the raging flood beneath, where she was changed into a bewitching undine. She dwelt here in the limpid waters for many a year, appearing from time to time to exercise her fascinations upon mortals, and even, it is said, captivating the affections of the Emperor Henry, who paid frequent visits to her cascade. Her last appearance, according to popular belief, was at Pentecost, a hundred years ago; and the natives have not yet ceased to look for the beautiful princess, who is said still to haunt the stream and wave her white arms to entice travelers into the cool spray of the waterfall.

> "I am the Princess Ilse,
>   And I dwell at the Ilsenstein;
>   Come with me to my castle,
>   And bliss shall be mine and thine.

"With the cool of my glass-clear waters
Thy brow and thy locks I'll lave;
And thou'lt think of thy sorrows no longer,
For all that thou look'st so grave.

"With my white arms twined around thee,
And lapped on my breast so white,
Thou shalt lie, and dream of elf-land —
Its loves and wild delight."

HEINE (Martin's tr.).

The giants inhabited all the earth before it was given to mankind; they very reluctantly made way for the human race, and

The giant's plaything. retreated into the waste and barren parts of the country, where they brought up their families in strict seclusion. Such was the ignorance of their offspring, that a young giantess, straying away from home, once came to an inhabited valley, where for the first time in her life she saw a farmer plowing on the hillside. Deeming him a pretty plaything, she caught him up with his team, thrust them into her apron, and gleefully carried them home to exhibit them to her father. But the giant immediately bade her carry peasant and horses back to the place where she had found them, and when she had done so he sadly explained that the creatures whom she took for mere playthings, would eventually drive all the giant folk away, and become masters of all the earth.

CHAPTER XXIV.

THE DWARFS.

In the first chapter we saw how the black elves, dwarfs, or Svart-alfar, were bred like maggots in the flesh of the slain giant Ymir. The gods, perceiving these tiny, unformed creatures creeping in and out, gave them form and features, calling them dark elves on account of their swarthy complexions. These small beings were so homely, with their dark skin, green eyes, large heads, short legs, and crow's feet, that they were told to hide underground and never show themselves during the daytime under penalty of being turned into stone. Although less powerful than the gods, they were far more intelligent than men, and as their knowledge was boundless and extended even to the future, gods and men were equally anxious to question them.

They were also known as trolls, kobolds, brownies, goblins, pucks, or Huldra folk, according to the country where they dwelt.

> "You are the gray, gray Troll,
>   With the great green eyes,
> But I love you, gray, gray Troll —
>   You are so wise!
>
> "Tell me this sweet morn,
>   Tell me all you know —
> Tell me, was I born?
>   Tell me, did I grow?"
>   THE LEGEND OF THE LITTLE FAY (Buchanan).

These dwarfs could transport themselves with marvelous celerity from one place to another, loved to conceal themselves behind rocks, and mischievously repeated the last words of every conversation they overheard.   Owing to this well-known trick, the echoes were called dwarfs' talk, and people fancied that the reason why they were never seen was because each dwarf was the proud possessor of a tiny red cap which made the wearer invisible.   This cap was called Tarnkappe, and it was owing to it only that the dwarfs dared appear above the surface of the earth after sunrise without fear of being petrified.

The Tarnkappe.

> "Away! let not the sun view me —
>   I dare no longer stay;
> An Elfin-child, thou wouldst me see,
>   To stone turn at his ray."
>
>   LA MOTTE-FOUQUÉ.

The dwarfs as well as the elves were ruled by a king, who, in various countries of northern Europe, was known as Andvari, Alberich, Elbegast, Gondemar, Laurin, or Oberon. He dwelt in a magnificent subterranean palace, all studded with the gems which his subjects had drawn from the bosom of the earth, and, besides untold riches and the Tarnkappe, he owned a magic ring, an invincible sword, and a belt of strength. At his command his subjects, who were very clever smiths, fashioned marvelous jewels or weapons, which he bestowed upon favorite mortals.

The magic of the dwarfs.

We have already seen how the dwarfs fashioned Sif's golden hair, the ship Skidbladnir, the point of Odin's spear Gungnir, the ring Draupnir, the golden-bristled boar Gullin-bursti, the hammer Miölnir, and Freya's golden necklace Brisinga-men.   They are also said to have made the magic girdle which Spenser describes in his poem of the "Faerie Queene," — a girdle which was said to have the power of revealing whether the wearer were virtuous or a hypocrite.

> "That girdle gave the virtue of chaste love
> And wifehood true to all that did it bear;
> But whosoever contrary doth prove

Might not the same about her middle wear
But it would loose, or else asunder tear."
FAERIE QUEENE (Spenser).

The dwarfs also manufactured the mythical sword Tyrfing, which could cut through iron and stone, and which they gave to Angantyr. This sword, like Frey's, fought of its own accord, and could not be sheathed, after it was once drawn, until it had tasted blood. Angantyr was so proud of this weapon that he had it buried with him; but his daughter Hervor visited his tomb at midnight, recited magic spells, and forced him to rise from his grave to give her the precious blade. She wielded it bravely, and it eventually became the property of another of the Northern heroes.

The dwarfs were generally kindly and helpful; sometimes they kneaded bread, ground flour, brewed beer, performed countless household tasks, and harvested and threshed the grain for the farmers. If ill treated, however, or turned into ridicule, these little creatures forsook the house and never came back again. When the old gods ceased to be worshiped in the Northlands, the dwarfs entirely withdrew from the country, and a ferryman once said that he had been hired to ply his boat back and forth across the river one night, and that at every trip his vessel was so laden down with invisible passengers that it nearly sank. When his night's work was over, he received a rich reward, and his employer informed him that he had helped all the dwarfs across the river, for they were leaving the country forever to punish the people for their unbelief.

According to popular superstition, the dwarfs envied man's taller stature and often tried to improve their race by winning human wives or by stealing unbaptized children, and substituting their own offspring for the human mother to nurse. These dwarf babies were known as changelings, and were recognizable by their puny and wizened forms. To recover possession of her own babe, and to rid herself of the changeling, a woman was obliged either to brew beer in egg-

Changelings.

shells or to grease the soles of the child's feet and hold them so near the flames that, attracted by their offspring's distressed cries, the dwarf parents would hasten to claim their own and return the stolen child.

The female trolls were also said to have the power of changing themselves into Maras or nightmares, and of tormenting any one they pleased ; but if the victim succeeded in stopping up the hole through which a Mara made her ingress into his room, she was entirely at his mercy, and he could even force her to marry him if he chose to do so.   A wife thus obtained was sure to remain as long as the opening through which she had entered the house was closed, but if the plug were removed, either by accident or design, she immediately effected her escape and never returned.

Some writers have ventured a conjecture that the dwarfs so often mentioned in the ancient sagas and fairy-tales were real beings, probably the Phœnician miners, who, work-

A conjecture.   ing the coal, iron, copper, gold, and tin mines of England, Norway, Sweden, etc., took advantage of the simplicity and credulity of the early inhabitants to make them believe that they belonged to a supernatural race and always dwelt underground, in a region which was called Svart-alfa-heim, or the home of the black elves.

DANCE OF THE WILL-O'-THE-WISPS.— W. Kray.

(*Opp. p. 221.*)

CHAPTER XXV.

THE ELVES.

BESIDES the dwarfs there was another numerous class of tiny creatures called Lios-alfar, light or white elves, who inhabited the realms of air between heaven and earth, had their palace in Alf-heim, and were gently governed by the genial god Frey. They were lovely, beneficent beings, so pure and innocent that, according to some authorities, their name was derived from the same root as the Latin word "white" (*albus*), which, in a modified form, was given to the Alps, those snow-covered mountains, and to Albion (England), because of her white chalk cliffs which could be seen from afar.

The elves were so small that they could flit about unseen to care for the flowers, birds, and butterflies; and as they were passionately fond of dancing, they often slipped down to earth on a moonbeam, to dance on the green. Holding one another by the hand, they danced round in circles, thereby making the "fairy rings," which could easily be discovered, as the grass grew greener and more luxuriant in the places their little feet had trod.

> "Merry elves, their morrice pacing
> To aërial minstrelsy,
> Emerald rings on brown heath tracing,
> Trip it deft and merrily."
> WALTER SCOTT.

If any mortal stood in the middle of one of these fairy rings he could, according to the popular belief in England, see the fairies and enjoy their favor; but the Germans and Scandinavians vowed that the unhappy man must die. In connection with this superstition, they tell how Sir Olaf, riding off to his wedding, was enticed by the fairies into their ring. On the morrow, instead of a merry marriage, his friends witnessed a triple funeral, for his mother and bride both died of grief when they beheld his lifeless corpse.

> "Master Olof rode forth ere dawn of the day
> And came where the Elf folk were dancing away.
>   The dance is so merry,
> So merry in the greenwood.
>
> "And on the next morn, ere the daylight was red,
> In Master Olof's house lay three corpses dead.
>   The dance is so merry,
> So merry in the greenwood.
>
> "First Master Olof, and next his young bride,
> And third his old mother — for sorrow she died.
>   The dance is so merry,
> So merry in the greenwood."
>   MASTER OLOF AT THE ELFIN DANCE (Howitt's tr.).

These elves, who in England were called fairies or fays, were also enthusiastic musicians, and delighted especially in a certain tune which was known as the elf dance, and which was so irresistible that no one could hear it without dancing. If a mortal, overhearing the air, ventured to play it, he suddenly found himself incapable of stopping and was forced to play on and on until he died of exhaustion, unless he were deft enough to play the tune backwards, or some one charitably slipped behind him and cut the strings of his violin. His hearers, who were forced to dance as long as the tones continued, could only pause when they ceased.

Fairies or fays.

In the North, in the mediæval ages, the will-o'-the-wisps were known as elf lights, for these tiny sprites were supposed to mislead travelers; and popular superstition claimed that the Jack-o'-lanterns were the restless spirits of mur-

The Will-o'-the-wisps.

derers forced against their will to return to the scene of their crimes. As they nightly walked thither, it is said that they doggedly repeated with every step, " It is right ;" but as they returned they sadly reiterated, " It is wrong."

In later times the fairies or elves were said to be ruled by the king of the dwarfs, who, being an underground spirit, was considered a demon, and allowed to retain the magic power which the missionaries had wrested from the god Frey. In England and France the king of the fairies was known by the name of Oberon; he governed fairyland with his queen Titania, and held his highest revels on earth on Midsummer night. It was then that the fairies all congregated around him and danced most merrily.

Oberon and Titania.

> " Every elf and fairy sprite
> Hop as light as bird from brier ;
> And this ditty after me
> Sing, and dance it trippingly."
> MIDSUMMER-NIGHT'S DREAM (Shakespeare).

These elves, like the brownies, Huldra folk, kobolds, etc., were also supposed to visit human dwellings, and it was said that they took mischievous pleasure in tangling and knotting horses' manes and tails. These tangles were known as elf locks, and whenever a farmer descried them he declared that his steeds had been elf-ridden during the night.

In Germany and Scandinavia sacrifices were offered to the elves to make them propitious. These sacrifices, which consisted either of some small animal, or of a bowl of honey and milk, were known as Alf-blot, and were quite common until the missionaries taught the people that the elves were mere demons. The sacrifice once offered to them was then transferred to the angels, who were long entreated to befriend mortals, and propitiated by the same gifts.

Alf-blot.

Many of the elves were supposed to live and die with the trees or plants which they tended, but these moss, wood, or tree maidens, while remarkably beautiful when seen in front, were hollow like a trough when viewed from behind. They appear in many of the popular tales, but almost always as benevolent and helpful spirits, for they were anxious to do good to mortals and to remain on a friendly footing with them.

In Scandinavia the elves, both light and dark, were worshiped as household divinities, and their images were carved on the doorposts. The Norsemen, who were driven away from home by the tyranny of Harald Harfager in 874, entered their ships, taking these carved doorposts with them. Similar carvings, including images of the gods and heroes, decorated the pillars of their high seats which they also carried away. The exiles showed their trust in their gods by throwing these wooden images overboard when they neared the Icelandic shores, and settling where the waves carried the posts, although the spot scarcely seemed the most desirable. " Thus they carried with them the religion, the poetry, and the laws of their race, and on this desolate volcanic island they kept these records unchanged for hundreds of years, while other Teutonic nations gradually became affected by their intercourse with Roman and Byzantine Christianity." These records, carefully collected by Sæmund the learned, form the Elder Edda, the most precious relic of ancient Northern literature, without which we would know comparatively little of the religion of our forefathers.

Images on doorposts.

The sagas relate that the first Norse settlements in Greenland and Vinland were made in the same way,—the Norsemen piously landing wherever their household gods drifted ashore,—many years before the voyage of Columbus and the accredited discovery of America.

OLD HOUSES WITH CARVED DOORPOSTS, NORWAY.

CHAPTER XXVI.

THE SIGURD SAGA.

WHILE the first part of the Elder Edda consists of a collection of alliterative poems describing the creation of the world, the adventures of the gods, their eventual downfall, and gives a complete exposition of the Northern code of ethics, the second part comprises a series of heroic lays describing the life and adventures of the Volsung family, and especially of their chief representative, Sigurd, the great Northern warrior.

These lays form the basis of the great Scandinavian epic, the Volsunga Saga, and have supplied not only the materials for the Nibelungenlied, the German epic, and for count- The Volsunga less folk tales, but also for Wagner's celebrated Saga. operas, "The Rhinegold," "Valkyr," "Siegfried," and "The Dusk of the Gods." They have also been rewritten by William Morris, the English poet, who has given them the form which they will probably retain in our literature, and it is from his work that almost all the quotations in this chapter are taken in preference to extracts from the Edda.

Sigi, Odin's son, was a powerful man, and generally respected until he killed a man out of jealousy because the latter had slain the most game when they were out hunting together. Sigi. In consequence of this crime, Sigi was driven from his own land and declared an outlaw. But, although he was a criminal, he had not entirely forfeited Odin's favor, for the god now gave him a well-equipped vessel, provided him with a number of brave followers, and promised that victory should ever attend him.

225

Thanks to Odin's protection, Sigi soon won the glorious empire of the Huns and became a powerful monarch. But when he had attained extreme old age his fortune changed, Odin suddenly forsook him, his wife's kindred fell upon him, and after a short encounter he was treacherously slain.

His death was soon avenged, however, for his son Rerir, returning from a journey, put all the murderers to death and

Rerir. claimed the throne. But, in spite of all outward prosperity, Rerir's dearest wish, a son to succeed him, remained unfulfilled for many a year. Finally, however, Frigga decided to grant his constant prayer, and to vouchsafe the heir he longed for. Her swift messenger Gna, or Liod, was dispatched to carry him a miraculous apple, which she dropped into his lap as he was sitting alone on the hillside. Glancing upward, Rerir recognized the emissary of the goddess, and joyfully hastened home to partake of the apple with his wife. The child thus born in answer to their prayers was a handsome little lad called Volsung, who, losing both parents in early infancy, became ruler of all the land.

Every year Volsung's wealth and power increased, and, as he was the boldest leader, many brave warriors rallied around him,

Volsung. and drank his mead sitting beneath the Branstock, a mighty oak, which, rising in the middle of his dwelling, pierced the roof and overshadowed the whole house.

" And as in all other matters 'twas all earthly houses' crown,
    And the least of its wall-hung shields was a battle-world's renown,
    So therein withal was a marvel and a glorious thing to see,
    For amidst of its midmost hall-floor sprang up a mighty tree,
    That reared its blessings roofward and wreathed the roof-tree dear
    With the glory of the summer and the garland of the year."

Volsung did not long remain childless, for ten stalwart sons and one lovely daughter, Signy, came to brighten his home. As soon as this maiden reached marriageable years, many suitors asked for her hand, which was finally pledged to Siggeir, King of the Goths, whom, however, she had never seen.

The wedding day came, and when the bride first beheld her destined groom she shrank back in dismay, for his puny form and lowering glances contrasted oddly with her brothers' strong frames and frank faces. But it was too late to withdraw, — the family honor was at stake, — and Signy so successfully concealed her dislike that none except her twin brother Sigmund suspected how reluctantly she became Siggeir's wife. The wedding of Signy.

The wedding feast was held as usual, and when the merrymakings had reached their height the guests were startled by the sudden entrance of a tall, one-eyed man, closely enveloped in a mantle of cloudy blue. Without vouchsafing word or glance to any in the assembly, the stranger strode up to the Branstock and thrust a glittering sword up to the hilt in its great bole. Then, turning slowly around, he faced the awe-struck assembly, and in the midst of the general silence declared that the weapon would belong to the warrior who could pull it out, and that it would assure him victory in every battle. These words ended, he passed out and disappeared, leaving an intimate conviction in the minds of all the guests that Odin, king of the gods, had been in their midst. The sword in the Branstock.

"So sweet his speaking sounded, so wise his words did seem,
    That moveless all men sat there, as in a happy dream
    We stir not lest we waken; but there his speech had end,
    And slowly down the hall-floor and outward did he wend;
    And none would cast him a question or follow on his ways,
    For they knew that the gift was Odin's, a sword for the world to
        praise."

Volsung was the first to recover the power of speech, and, waiving his own right to try to secure the divine weapon, he invited Siggeir to make the first attempt to draw it out of the tree-trunk. The bridegroom anxiously tugged and strained, but the sword remained firmly embedded in the oak. He resumed his seat, with an air of chagrin, and then Volsung also tried and failed. But the weapon was evidently not intended for either of them, and the young Volsung princes were next invited to try their strength.

"Sons I have gotten and cherished, now stand ye forth and try;
Lest Odin tell in God-home how from the way he strayed,
And how to the man he would not he gave away his blade."

The nine eldest sons were equally unsuccessful; but when Sigmund, the tenth and youngest, laid his firm young hand upon the hilt, it easily yielded to his touch, and he triumphantly drew the sword out without making the least exertion.

Sigmund.

"At last by the side of the Branstock Sigmund the Volsung stood,
And with right hand wise in battle the precious sword-hilt caught,
Yet in a careless fashion, as he deemed it all for naught;
When, lo, from floor to rafter went up a shattering shout,
For aloft in the hand of Sigmund the naked blade showed out
As high o'er his head he shook it: for the sword had come away
From the grip of the heart of the Branstock, as though all loose it
    lay."

All present seemed overjoyed at his success; but Siggeir's heart was filled with envy, for he coveted the possession of the weapon, which he now tried to purchase from his young brother-in-law. Sigmund, however, refused to part with it at any price, declaring that the weapon had evidently been intended for him only. This refusal so offended Siggeir that he secretly resolved to bide his time, to exterminate the proud race of the Volsungs, and thus secure the divine sword.

Concealing his chagrin therefore, he turned to Volsung and cordially invited him to visit his court a month later, bringing all his sons and kinsmen with him. The invitation so spontaneously given was immediately accepted, and although Signy, suspecting evil, secretly sought her father while her husband slept, and implored him to retract his promise and stay at home, he would not consent to appear afraid.

A few weeks after the return of the bridal couple Volsung's well-manned vessels came within sight of Siggeir's shores, and Signy perceiving them hastened down to the beach to implore

THE BRANSTOCK.—Hoffmann.

(*Opp. p.* 229.)

her kinsmen not to land, warning them that her husband had treacherously planned an ambush, whence they could never escape alive. But Volsung and his sons, whom no peril could daunt, calmly bade her return to her husband's palace, and donning their arms they boldly set foot ashore. *Siggeir's treachery.*

"Then sweetly Volsung kissed her: 'Woe am I for thy sake,
But Earth the word hath hearkened, that yet unborn I spake;
How I ne'er would turn me backward from the sword or fire of
    bale; —
—I have held that word till to-day, and to-day shall I change the
    tale?
And look on these thy brethren, how goodly and great are they,
Wouldst thou have the maidens mock them, when this pain hath
    passed away
And they sit at the feast hereafter, that they feared the deadly
    stroke?
Let us do our day's work deftly for the praise and the glory of folk;
And if the Norns will have it that the Volsung kin shall fail,
Yet I know of the deed that dies not, and the name that shall ever
    avail.'"

Marching towards the palace, the brave little troop soon fell into Siggeir's ambuscade, and, although they fought with heroic courage, they were so overpowered by the superior number of their foes that Volsung was soon slain and all his sons made captive. Led bound into the presence of Siggeir, who had taken no part in the fight (for he was an arrant coward), Sigmund was forced to relinquish his precious sword, and he and his brothers were all condemned to die.

Signy, hearing this cruel sentence, vainly interceded for them, but all she could obtain by her prayers and entreaties was that her kinsmen should be chained to a fallen oak in the forest, there to perish of hunger and thirst if the wild beasts spared them. Then, fearing lest his wife should visit and succor her brothers, Siggeir confined her in the palace, where she was closely guarded night and day.

Early every morning Siggeir himself sent a messenger into the forest to see whether the Volsungs were still living, and every morning the man returned saying a monster had come during the night and had devoured one of the princes, leaving nothing but his bones. When none but Sigmund remained alive, Signy finally prevailed upon one of her servants to carry some honey into the forest and smear it over her brother's face and mouth.

That very night the wild beast, attracted by the smell of the honey, licked Sigmund's face, and even thrust its tongue into his mouth. Clinching his teeth upon it, Sigmund, weak and wounded as he was, struggled until his bonds broke and he could slay the nightly visitor who had caused the death of all his brothers. Then he vanished into the forest, where he remained concealed until the daily messenger had come and gone, and until Signy, released from captivity, came speeding to the forest to weep over her kinsmen's remains.

Seeing her evident grief, and knowing she had no part in Siggeir's cruelty, Sigmund stole out of his place of concealment, comforted her as best he could, helped her to bury the whitening bones, and registered a solemn oath in her presence to avenge his family's wrongs. This vow was fully approved by Signy, who, however, bade her brother abide a favorable time, promising to send him a helper. Then the brother and sister sadly parted, she to return to her distasteful palace home, and he to seek the most remote part of the forest, where he built a tiny hut and plied the trade of a smith.

> " And men say that Signy wept
> When she left that last of her kindred ; yet wept she never more
> Amid the earls of Siggeir, and as lovely as before
> Was her face to all men's deeming : nor aught it changed for ruth,
> Nor for fear nor any longing ; and no man said for sooth
> That she ever laughed thereafter till the day of her death was
> come."

Years passed by. Siggeir, having taken possession of the Volsung kingdom, proudly watched the growth of his eldest son, whom Signy secretly sent to her brother as soon as he was ten years of age, bidding Sigmund train the child up to help him, if he were worthy of such a task. Sigmund reluctantly accepted the charge; but as soon as he had **Signy's sons.** tested the boy and found him deficient in physical courage, he either sent him back to his mother, or, as some versions relate, slew him.

Some time after this Sigmund tested Signy's second son, who had been sent to him for the same purpose, and found him wanting also. Evidently none but a pure-blooded Volsung could help him in his work of revenge, and Signy, realizing this, resolved to commit a crime.

"And once in the dark she murmured : 'Where then was the ancient song

That the Gods were but twin-born once, and deemed it nothing wrong

To mingle for the world's sake, whence had the Æsir birth,

And the Vanir, and the Dwarf-kind, and all the folk of earth ?'"

This resolution taken, she summoned a beautiful young witch, exchanged forms with her, and, running into the forest, sought shelter in Sigmund's hut. Deeming her nothing but the gypsy she seemed, and won by her coquetry, he soon made her his wife. Three days later she vanished from his hut, returned to the palace, resumed her own form, and when she gave birth to a little son, she rejoiced to see his bold glance and strong frame.

When this child, Sinfiotli, was ten years of age, she herself made a preliminary test of his courage by sewing his garment to his skin. Then she suddenly snatched it off with **Sinfiotli.** shreds of flesh hanging to it, and as the child did not even wince, but laughed aloud, she confidently sent him to Sigmund. He, too, found the boy quite fearless, and upon leaving the hut one day he bade him take meal from a certain sack, and knead and bake the bread. On returning home Sigmund asked Sinfiotli whether his orders had been carried out. The lad replied by showing the bread, and when closely questioned he artlessly confessed that he had been obliged to knead into the loaf a great adder which was hidden in the meal. Pleased to see that the child, for whom he felt a strange affection, had successfully stood the test which had daunted his predecessors, Sigmund bade him refrain from eating of that loaf, as he alone could taste poison unharmed, and patiently began to teach him all a Northern warrior need know.

"For here the tale of the elders doth men a marvel to wit,
    That such was the shaping of Sigmund among all earthly kings,
    That unhurt he handled adders and other deadly things,
    And might drink unscathed of venom : but Sinfiotli was so wrought
    That no sting of creeping creatures would harm his body aught."

Sigmund and Sinfiotli soon became inseparable companions, and while ranging the forest together they once came to a hut, where they found two men sound asleep. Wolf-skins hanging near them immediately made them conclude that the strangers were werewolves (men whom a cruel spell forced to assume the habits and guise of ravenous wolves, and who could only resume their natural form for a short space at a time). Prompted by curiosity, Sigmund donned one of the wolf skins, Sinfiotli the other, and they were soon metamorphosed into wolves and rushed through the forest, slaying and devouring all they saw.

The were-wolves.

Such were their wolfish passions that they soon attacked each other, and after a fierce struggle Sinfiotli, the younger and weaker, fell down dead. This sudden catastrophe brought Sigmund to his senses. While he hung over his murdered companion in sudden despair, he saw two weasels come out of the forest and fight until one lay dead. The live weasel then sprang back into the thicket, and soon returned with a leaf, which it laid upon its companion's breast. At the contact of the magic herb the dead beast came back to life. A moment later a raven flying overhead dropped a similar leaf at Sigmund's feet, and he, understanding that the gods wished to help him, laid it upon Sinfiotli, who was restored to life.

Afraid lest they might work each other further mischief while in this altered guise, Sigmund and Sinfiotli now crept home and patiently waited until the time of release had come. On the ninth night the skins dropped off and they hastily flung them into the fire, where they were entirely consumed, and the spell was broken forever.

It was now that Sigmund confided the story of his wrongs to Sinfiotli, who swore that, although Siggeir was his father (for neither he nor Sigmund knew the secret of his birth), he would help him to take his revenge. At nightfall, therefore, he accompanied Sigmund to the palace; they entered unseen, and concealed themselves in the cellar, behind the huge beer vats. Here they were discovered by Signy's two youngest children, who were playing with golden rings, which rolled into the cellar, and who thus suddenly came upon the men in ambush.

They loudly proclaimed the discovery they had just made to their father and his guests, but, before Siggeir and his men could don their arms, Signy caught both children by the hand, and dragging them into the cellar bade her brother slay the little traitors. This Sigmund utterly refused to do, but Sinfiotli struck off their heads ere he turned to fight against the assailants, who were rapidly closing around him.

In spite of all efforts Sigmund and his brave young companion soon fell into the hands of the Goths, whose king, Siggeir, sentenced them to be buried alive in the same mound, a stone partition being erected between them so they could neither see nor touch each other. The prisoners were already confined in their living graves, and the men were about to place the last stones on the roof, when Signy drew near, bearing a bundle of straw, which they allowed her to throw at Sinfiotli's feet, for they fancied that it contained only a few provisions which would prolong his agony a little without helping him to escape.

When the workmen had departed and all was still, Sinfiotli undid the sheaf and shouted for joy when he found instead of bread the sword which Odin had given to Sigmund. Knowing that nothing could dull or break the keen edge of this fine weapon, Sinfiotli thrust it through the stone partition, and, aided by Sigmund, sawed an opening, and both soon effected an escape through the roof.

" Then in the grave-mound's darkness did Sigmund the king upstand,
And unto that saw of battle he set his naked hand;
And hard the gift of Odin home to their breasts they drew;
Sawed Sigmund, sawed Sinfiotli, till the stone was cleft atwo,
And they met and kissed together: then they hewed and heaved full hard
Till, lo, through the bursten rafters the winter heavens bestarred!
And they leap out merry-hearted; nor is there need to say
A many words between them of whither was the way."

Sigmund and Sinfiotli, free once more, noiselessly sought the palace, piled combustible materials around it, and setting fire to it placed themselves on either side the door, declaring that none but the women should be allowed to pass through. Then they loudly called to Signy to escape ere it was too late, but she had no desire to live, and after kissing them both and revealing the secret of Sinfiotli's birth she sprang back into the flames, where she perished.

Sigmund's vengeance.

" And then King Siggeir's roof-tree upheaved for its utmost fall,
And its huge walls clashed together, and its mean and lowly things
The fire of death confounded with the tokens of the kings."

The long-planned vengeance had finally been carried out, Volsung's death had been avenged, and Sigmund, feeling that nothing now detained him in Gothland, set sail with Sinfiotli and returned to Hunaland, where he was warmly welcomed and again sat under the shade of his ancestral tree, the mighty Branstock. His authority fully established, Sigmund married Borghild, a beautiful princess, who bore him two sons, Hamond and Helgi, the latter of whom was visited by the Norns when he lay in his cradle, and promised sumptuous entertainment in Valhalla when his earthly career should be ended.

Helgi.

" And the woman was fair and lovely, and bore him sons of fame ;
Men called them Hamond and Helgi, and when Helgi first saw light
There came the Norns to his cradle and gave him life full bright,
And called him Sunlit Hill, Sharp Sword, and Land of Rings,
And bade him be lovely and great, and a joy in the tale of kings."

This young Volsung prince was fostered by Hagal, for Northern kings generally entrusted their sons' education to a stranger, thinking they would be treated with less indulgence than at home. Under this tuition Helgi became so fearless that at the age of fifteen he ventured alone into the palace of Hunding, with whose whole race his family was at feud. Passing all through the palace unmolested and unrecognized, he left an insolent message, which so angered Hunding that he immediately set out in pursuit of the bold young prince. Hunding entered Hagal's house, and would have made Helgi a prisoner had the youth not disguised himself as a servant maid, and begun to grind corn as if it were his wonted occupation. The invaders marveled somewhat at the maid's tall stature and brawny arms, but departed without suspecting that they had been so near the hero whom they sought.

Having thus cleverly escaped, Helgi joined Sinfiotli; they collected an army, and marched openly against the Hundings, with whom they fought a great battle, during which the Valkyrs hovered overhead, waiting to convey the slain to Valhalla. Gudrun, one of the battle maidens, was so charmed by the courage which Helgi displayed, that she openly sought him and promised to be his wife. Only one of the Hunding race, Dag, remained alive, and he was allowed to go free after promising never to try to avenge his kinsmen's death. This promise was not kept, however, for Dag, having borrowed Odin's spear Gungnir, treacherously made use of it to slay Helgi. Gudrun, now his wife, wept many tears at his death, and solemnly cursed his murderer; then, hearing from one of her maids that her slain husband kept calling for her in the depths of his tomb, she fearlessly entered the mound at night and tenderly inquired why he called and why his wounds kept on bleeding even after death. Helgi answered

that he could not rest happy because of her grief, and declared
that for every tear she shed a drop of his blood must flow.

> "Thou weepest, gold-adorned!
> Cruel tears,
> Sun-bright daughter of the south!
> Ere to sleep thou goest;
> Each one falls bloody
> On the prince's breast,
> Wet, cold, and piercing,
> With sorrow big."
> SÆMUND'S EDDA (Thorpe's tr.).

To still her beloved husband's sufferings, Gudrun then ceased
to weep, but her spirit soon joined his, which had ridden over
Bifröst and entered Valhalla, where Odin made him leader of
the Einheriar.   Here Gudrun, a Valkyr once more, continued
to wait upon him, darting down to earth at Odin's command to
seek new recruits for the army which her lord was to lead into
battle when Ragnarok, the twilight of the gods, should come.

Sinfiotli, Sigmund's eldest son, also came to an early death;
for, having quarreled with and slain Borghild's brother, she de-
Death of Sinfiotli. termined to poison him.   Twice Sinfiotli detected
the attempt and told his father there was poison
in his cup.   Twice Sigmund, whom no venom could injure,
drained the bowl; but when Borghild made a third and last
attempt, he bade Sinfiotli let the wine flow through his beard.
Mistaking the meaning of his father's words, Sinfiotli immediately
drained the cup and fell to the ground lifeless, for the poison
was of the most deadly kind.

> "He drank as he spake the words, and forthwith the venom ran
> In a chill flood over his heart, and down fell the mighty man
> With never an uttered death-word and never a death-changed look,
> And the floor of the hall of the Volsungs beneath his falling shook.
> Then up rose the elder of days with a great and bitter cry,
> And lifted the head of the fallen; and none durst come anigh
> To hearken the words of his sorrow, if any words he said
> But such as the Father of all men might speak over Balder dead.

And again, as before the death-stroke, waxed the hall of the
Volsungs dim,
And once more he seemed in the forest, where he spake with naught
but him."

Speechless with grief, Sigmund tenderly raised his son's body in
his arms, and strode out of the hall and down to the shore, where
he deposited his precious burden in the skiff of an old one-eyed
boatman who came at his call. But when he would fain have
stepped aboard also, the boatman pushed off and was soon lost
to sight. The bereaved father then slowly wended his way home
again, knowing that Odin himself had come to claim the young
hero and had rowed away with him " out into the west."

Sigmund repudiated Borghild in punishment for this crime, and
when he was very old indeed he sued for the hand of Hiordis, a
fair young princess, daughter of Eglimi, King of
the Islands. Although this young maiden had   **Hiordis.**
many suitors, among others King Lygni of Hunding's race, she
gladly accepted Sigmund and became his wife. Lygni, the dis-
carded suitor, was so angry at this decision, that he immediately
collected an army and marched against his successful rival, who,
overpowered by superior numbers, fought with the courage of
despair.

Hidden in a neighboring thicket, Hiordis and her maid
anxiously watched the battle, saw Sigmund pile the dead around
him and triumph over every foe, until at last a tall, one-eyed warrior suddenly appeared, broke his matchless sword, and vanished,
leaving him defenseless amid the foe, who soon cut him down.

"But, lo! through the hedge of the war-shafts, a mighty man there
came,
One-eyed and seeming ancient, but his visage shone like flame:
Gleaming gray was his kirtle, and his hood was cloudy blue;
And he bore a mighty twi-bill, as he waded the fight-sheaves through,
And stood face to face with Sigmund, and upheaved the bill to smite.
Once more round the head of the Volsung fierce glittered the
Branstock's light,

The sword that came from Odin : and Sigmund's cry once more
Rang out to the very heavens above the din of war.
Then clashed the meeting edges with Sigmund's latest stroke,
And in shivering shards fell earthward that fear of worldly folk.
But changed were the eyes of Sigmund, the war-wrath left his face ;
For that gray-clad, mighty Helper was gone, and in his place
Drave on the unbroken spear-wood 'gainst the Volsung's empty
    hands :
And there they smote down Sigmund, thē wonder of all lands,
On the foemen, on the death-heap his deeds had piled that day."

All the Volsung race and army had already succumbed, so
Lygni immediately left the battlefield to hasten on and take
possession of the kingdom and palace, where he fully expected
to find the fair Hiordis and force her to become his wife. As
soon as he had gone, however, the beautiful young queen crept
out of her hiding place in the thicket, ran to the dying Sigmund,
caught him to her breast in a last passionate embrace, and tear-
fully listened to his dying words. He then bade her gather up
the fragments of his sword, carefully treasure them, and give them
to the son whom he foretold would soon be born, and who was
destined to avenge his death and be far greater than he.

" 'I have wrought for the Volsungs truly, and yet have I known full
    well
That a better one than I am shall bear the tale to tell :
And for him shall these shards be smithied ; and he shall be my son,
To remember what I have forgotten and to do what I left undone.' "

While Hiordis was mourning over Sigmund's lifeless body, her
watching handmaiden warned her of the approach of a party of
Elf, the   vikings. Retreating into the thicket once more,
viking.   Hiordis exchanged garments with her ; then, bidding her walk first and personate the queen, they went to meet
the viking Elf (Helfrat or Helferich), and so excited his admiration for Sigmund that he buried him with all pomp, and promised
them a safe asylum in his house.
As he had doubted their relative positions from the very first

moment, he soon resorted to a seemingly idle question to ascertain their real rank. The pretended queen, when asked how she knew the hour had come for rising when the winter days were short and there was no light to announce the coming of morn, replied that, as she was in the habit of drinking milk ere she fed the cows, she always awoke thirsty. But when the same question was put to the real Hiordis, she answered that she knew it was morning because the golden ring her father had given her grew cold on her hand.

Elf, having thus discovered the true state of affairs, offered marriage to the pretended handmaiden, Hiordis, promising to foster her child by Sigmund — a promise which he nobly kept. The child was sprinkled with water **Sigurd.** by his hand — a ceremony which our pagan ancestors scrupulously performed — received from him the name of Sigurd, and grew up in the palace. There he was treated as the king's own son, receiving his education from Regin, the wisest of men, who knew all things and was even aware of his own fate, which was to fall by a youth's hand.

"Again in the house of the Helper there dwelt a certain man,
Beardless and low of stature, of visage pinched and wan:
So exceeding old was Regin, that no son of man could tell
In what year of the days passed over he came to that land to dwell:
But the youth of king Elf had he fostered, and the Helper's youth
    thereto,
Yea, and his father's father's: the lore of all men he knew,
And was deft in every cunning, save the dealings of the sword:
So sweet was his tongue-speech fashioned, that men trowed his
    every word;
His hand with the harp-strings blended was the mingler of delight
With the latter days of sorrow; all tales he told aright;
The Master of the Masters in the smithying craft was he;
And he dealt with the wind and the weather and the stilling of the
    sea;
Nor might any learn him leech-craft, for before that race was made,
And that man-folk's generation, all their life-days had he weighed."

Under this tutor young Sigurd grew up to great wisdom. He mastered the smith craft, and the art of carving all manner of runes, learned languages, music, and eloquence, and, last but not least, became a doughty warrior whom none could subdue. By Regin's advice, Sigurd, having reached manhood, asked the king for a war horse — a request which was immediately granted, for he was bidden hasten to Gripir, the stud-keeper, and choose from his flock the steed he liked best.

On his way to the meadow where the horses were at pasture, Sigurd encountered a one-eyed stranger, clad in gray and blue, who bade him drive the horses into the river and select the one which could breast the foaming tide most successfully.

Sigurd, acting according to this advice, noticed that one horse, after crossing, raced around the meadow on the opposite side; then, plunging back into the river, he returned to his former pasture without showing any signs of fatigue. The young hero selected this horse, therefore, calling him Grane or Greyfell. This steed was a descendant of Odin's eight-footed horse Sleipnir, and, besides being unusually strong and indefatigable, was as fearless as his master. A short time after this, while Regin and his pupil were sitting over the fire, the former struck his harp, and, after the manner of the Northern scalds, sang or recited the following tale, which was the story of his life:

Hreidmar, king of the dwarf folk, was the father of three sons. Fafnir, the eldest, was gifted with a fearless soul and a powerful

The treasure of the dwarf king. hand; Otter, the second, with snare and net, and the power of changing form at will; and Regin, the third, could, as we have already seen, command all knowledge and skillfully ply the trade of a smith. To please the avaricious old Hreidmar, this youngest son fashioned for him a house which was all lined with glittering gold and flashing gems, and guarded by Fafnir, whose fierce glances and Ægis helmet none dared encounter.

Now it came to pass that Odin, Hoenir, and Loki once came down upon earth in human guise for one of their wonted expeditions to test the hearts of men, and soon reached the land where Hreidmar dwelt.

"And the three were the heart-wise Odin, the Father of the Slain,
And Loki, the World's Begrudger, who maketh all labor vain,
And Hönir, the Utter-Blameless, who wrought the hope of man,
And his heart and inmost yearnings, when first the work began; —
The God that was aforetime, and hereafter yet shall be
When the new light yet undreamed of shall shine o'er earth and
    sea."

These gods had not wandered very far before Loki perceived an otter basking in the sun. Animated by his usual spirit of destruction, he slew the unoffending beast — which, as it happened, was the dwarf king's second son, Otter — and flung its lifeless body over his shoulders, thinking it would furnish a good dish when meal time came.

Following his companions, Loki came at last to Hreidmar's house, entered with them, and flung his burden down upon the floor. The moment the dwarf king's glance fell upon it he flew into a towering rage, and before the gods could help themselves they were bound by his order, and heard him declare that they should never recover their liberty unless they could satisfy his thirst for gold by giving him enough of that precious substance to cover the otterskin inside and out.

"'Now hearken the doom I shall speak! Ye stranger-folk shall be
    free
When ye give me the Flame of the Waters, the gathered Gold of
    the Sea,
That Andvari hideth rejoicing in the wan realm pale as the grave;
And the Master of Sleight shall fetch it, and the hand that never
    gave,
And the heart that begrudgeth forever, shall gather and give and
    rue.
Lo, this is the doom of the wise, and no doom shall be spoken
    anew.'"

As this otterskin had the property of stretching itself out to a fabulous size, no ordinary treasure could suffice to cover it. The gods therefore bade Loki, who was liberated to procure the ransom, hasten off to the waterfall where the dwarf Andvari dwelt, and secure the treasure he had amassed by magical means.

"There is a desert of dread in the uttermost part of the world,
   Where over a wall of mountains is a mighty water hurled,
   Whose hidden head none knoweth, nor where it meeteth the sea;
   And that force is the Force of Andvari, and an Elf of the dark is he.
   In the cloud and the desert he dwelleth amid that land alone;
   And his work is the storing of treasure within his house of stone."

In spite of diligent search, however, Loki could not find the dwarf; but perceiving a salmon sporting in the foaming waters, he shrewdly concluded the dwarf must have assumed this shape, and borrowing Ran's net he soon had the fish in his power. As he had suspected, it was Andvari, who, in exchange for liberty, reluctantly brought forth his mighty treasure and surrendered it all, including the Helmet of Dread and a hauberk of gold, reserving only the ring he wore, which was gifted with miraculous powers, and, like a magnet, helped him to collect the precious ore. But the greedy Loki, catching sight of it, wrenched it away from him and departed laughing, while the dwarf hurled angry curses after him, declaring that the ring would ever prove its possessor's bane and would cause the death of many.

"That gold
   Which the dwarf possessed
   Shall to two brothers
   Be cause of death,
   And to eight princes,
   Of dissension.
   From my wealth no one
   Shall good derive."
             SÆMUND'S EDDA (Thorpe's tr.).

On arriving at Hreidmar's hut, Loki found the mighty treasure none too great, for the skin widened and spread, and he was even forced to give the ring Andvaranaut (Andvari's loom) to purchase his and his companions' release. The gold thus obtained soon became a curse, as Andvari had predicted, for Fafnir and Regin both coveted a share. As for Hreidmar, he gloated over his treasure night and day, and Fafnir the invincible, seeing that he could not obtain it otherwise, slew his own father, donned the Helmet of Dread and the hauberk of gold, grasped the sword Hrotti, and when Regin came to claim a part drove him scornfully out into the world, where he bade him earn his own living.

Thus exiled, Regin took refuge among men, to whom he taught the arts of sowing and reaping. He showed them how to work metals, sail the seas, tame horses, yoke beasts of burden, build houses, spin, weave, and sew — in short, all the industries of civilized life, which had hitherto been unknown. Years elapsed, and Regin patiently bided his time, hoping that some day he would find a hero strong enough to avenge his wrongs upon Fafnir, whom years of gloating over his treasure had changed into a horrible dragon, the terror of Gnîtaheid (Glittering Heath), where he had taken up his abode.

His story finished, Regin suddenly turned to the attentive Sigurd, told him he knew that he could slay the dragon if he wished, and inquired whether he were ready to help his old tutor avenge his wrongs.

"And he spake: 'Hast thou hearkened, Sigurd? Wilt thou help a
    man that is old
  To avenge him for his father? Wilt thou win that treasure of gold
  And be more than the kings of the earth? Wilt thou rid the earth
    of a wrong
  And heal the woe and the sorrow my heart hath endured o'er long?'"

Sigurd immediately assented, declaring, however, that the curse must be assumed by Regin, for he would have none of it; and, in order to be well prepared for the coming fight, he asked his master to forge him a sword which no *Sigurd's sword.* blow could break. Twice Regin fashioned a marvelous weapon, but twice Sigurd broke it to pieces on the anvil. Then, declaring that he must have a sword which would not fail him in time of need, he begged the broken fragments of Sigmund's weapon from his mother Hiordis, and either forged himself or made Regin forge a matchless blade, whose temper was such that it neatly severed some wool floating gently down the stream, and divided the great anvil in two without being even dinted.

After paying a farewell visit to Gripir, who, knowing the future, foretold every event in his coming career, Sigurd took leave of his mother, and accompanied by Regin set sail from his native land, promising to slay the dragon as soon as he had fulfilled his first duty, which was to avenge his father Sigmund's death.

> " ' First wilt thou, prince,
> Avenge thy father,
> And for the wrongs of Eglymi
> Wilt retaliate.
> Thou wilt the cruel,
> The sons of Hunding,
> Boldly lay low :
> Thou wilt have victory.' "
>
> LAY OF SIGURD FAFNICIDE (Thorpe's tr.).

On his way to the Volsung land Sigurd saw a man walking on the waters, and took him on board, little suspecting that this individual, who said his name was Feng or Fiöllnir, was Odin or Hnikar, the wave stiller. He therefore conversed freely with the stranger, who promised him favorable winds, and learned from him how to distinguish auspicious from unauspicious omens.

After slaying Lygni and cutting the bloody eagle on his foes, Sigurd left his reconquered kingdom and went with Regin to slay

The fight with the dragon. Fafnir. A long ride through the mountains, which rose higher and higher before him, brought him at last to his goal, where a one-eyed stranger bade him dig trenches in the middle of the track along which the dragon daily rolled his slimy length to go down to the river and quench his

(*Opp.* p. 245.)

SIGURD AND THE DRAGON.—K. Dielitz.

thirst. He then bade Sigurd cower in one of those holes, and there wait until the monster passed over him, when he could drive his trusty weapon straight into its heart.

Sigurd gratefully followed this advice, and as the monster's loathsome, slimy folds rolled overhead he thrust his sword under its left breast, and, deluged with blood, sprang out of the trench as the dragon rolled aside in the throes of death.

"Then all sank into silence, and the son of Sigmund stood
On the torn and furrowed desert by the pool of Fafnir's blood,
And the serpent lay before him, dead, chilly, dull, and gray;
And over the Glittering Heath fair shone the sun and the day,
And a light wind followed the sun and breathed o'er the fateful place,
As fresh as it furrows the sea plain, or bows the acres' face."

Regin, who had prudently remained at a distance until all danger was over, seeing his foe was slain, now came up to Sigurd; and fearing lest the strong young conqueror should glory in his deed and claim a reward, he began to accuse him of having murdered his kin, and declared that instead of requiring life for life, as was his right according to Northern law, he would consider it sufficient atonement if Sigurd would cut out the monster's heart and roast it for him on a spit.

"Then Regin spake to Sigurd: 'Of this slaying wilt thou be free?
Then gather thou fire together and roast the heart for me,
That I may eat it and live, and be thy master and more;
For therein was might and wisdom, and the grudged and hoarded lore:—
Or else depart on thy ways afraid from the Glittering Heath.'"

Sigurd, knowing that a true warrior never refused satisfaction of some kind to the kindred of the slain, immediately prepared to act as cook, while Regin dozed until the meat was ready. Feeling of the heart to ascertain whether it were tender, Sigurd burned his fingers so severely that he instinctively thrust them into his mouth to allay the smart. No sooner had Fafnir's blood touched his lips than he discovered, to his utter surprise, that he could understand the songs of the birds, which were already gathering around the carrion. Listening to them attentively, he found they were advising him to slay Regin, appropriate the gold, eat the heart and drink the blood of the dragon; and as this advice entirely coincided with his own wishes, he lost no time in executing it. A small portion of Fafnir's heart was reserved for future consumption, ere he wandered off in search of the mighty hoard. Then, after donning the Helmet of Dread, the hauberk of gold, and the ring Andvaranaut, and loading Greyfell with as much ruddy gold as he could carry, Sigurd sprang on his horse, listening eagerly to the birds' songs to know what he had best undertake next.

Soon he heard them sing of a warrior maiden fast asleep on a mountain and all surrounded by a glittering barrier of flames, through which only the bravest of men could pass in order to arouse her.

The sleeping warrior maiden.

> "On the fell I know
> A warrior maid to sleep;
> Over her waves
> The linden's bane:
> Ygg whilom stuck
> A sleep-thorn in the robe
> Of the maid who
> Would heroes choose."
>
>   LAY OF FAFNIR (Thorpe's tr.).

After riding for a long while through trackless regions, Sigurd at last came to the Hindarfiall in Frankland, a tall mountain whose cloud-wreathed summit seemed circled by fiery flames.

> "Long Sigurd rideth the waste, when, lo! on a morning of day,
> From out of the tangled crag walls, amidst the cloudland gray,
> Comes up a mighty mountain, and it is as though there burns
> A torch amidst of its cloud wreath; so thither Sigurd turns,
> For he deems indeed from its topmost to look on the best of the earth;
> And Greyfell neigheth beneath him, and his heart is full of mirth."

Riding straight up this mountain, he saw the light grow more and more vivid, and soon a barrier of lurid flames stood before him; but although the fire crackled and roared, it could not daunt our hero, who plunged bravely into its very midst.

"Now Sigurd turns in his saddle, and the hilt of the Wrath he shifts,
And draws a girth the tighter; then the gathered reins he lifts,
And crieth aloud to Greyfell, and rides at the wildfire's heart;
But the white wall wavers before him and the flame-flood rusheth apart,
And high o'er his head it riseth, and wide and wild its roar
As it beareth the mighty tidings to the very heavenly floor:
But he rideth through its roaring as the warrior rides the rye,
When it bows with the wind of the summer and the hid spears draw anigh;
The white flame licks his raiment and sweeps through Greyfell's mane,
And bathes both hands of Sigurd and the hilt of Fafnir's bane,
And winds about his war-helm and mingles with his hair,
But naught his raiment dusketh or dims his glittering gear:
Then it fails and fades and darkens till all seems left behind,
And dawn and the blaze is swallowed in mid-mirk stark and blind."

No sooner had Sigurd thus fearlessly sprung into the very heart of the flames than the fire flickered and died out, leaving nothing but a broad circle of white ashes, through which he rode until he came to a great castle, with shield-hung walls, in which he penetrated unchallenged, for the gates were wide open and no warders or men at arms were to be seen. Proceeding cautiously, for he feared some snare, Sigurd at last came to the center of the inclosure, where he saw a recumbent form all cased in armor. To remove the helmet was but a moment's work, but Sigurd started back in surprise when he beheld, instead of a warrior, the sleeping face of a most beautiful woman.

All his efforts to awaken her were quite vain, however, until he had cut the armor off her body, and she lay before him in pure-white linen garments, her long golden hair rippling and waving around her. As the last fastening of her armor gave way, she opened wide her beautiful eyes, gazed in rapture upon the rising sun, and after greeting it with enthusiasm she turned to her deliverer, whom she loved at first sight, as he loved her.

"Then she turned and gazed on Sigurd, and her eyes met the Volsung's eyes.
And mighty and measureless now did the tide of his love arise,
For their longing had met and mingled, and he knew of her heart that she loved,
And she spake unto nothing but him, and her lips with the speech-flood moved."

The maiden now proceeded to inform Sigurd that she was Brunhild, according to some authorities the daughter of an earthly king. Odin had raised her to the rank of a Valkyr, in which capacity she had served him faithfully for a long while. But once she had ventured to set her own wishes above his, and, instead of leaving the victory to the old king for whom he had designated it, had favored his younger and therefore more attractive opponent.

In punishment for this act of disobedience, she was deprived of her office and banished to earth, where Allfather decreed she must marry like any other member of her sex. This sentence filled Brunhild's heart with dismay, for she greatly feared lest it might be her fate to mate with a coward, whom she would despise. To quiet these apprehensions, Odin placed her on Hindarfiall or Hindfell, stung her with the Thorn of Sleep, that she might await in unchanged youth and beauty the coming of her destined husband and surrounded her with a barrier of flame which none but the bravest would venture to pass through.

From the top of the Hindarfiall, Brunhild now pointed out to Sigurd her former home, at Lymdale or Hunaland, telling him he would find her there whenever he chose to come and claim her as his wife; and then, while they stood on the lonely mountain top together, Sigurd placed the ring Andvaranaut upon her hand, in sign of betrothal, swearing to love her alone as long as life endured.

(*Opp. p.* 249.)

BRUNHILD'S AWAKENING.— Th. Pixis.

" From his hand then draweth Sigurd Andvari's ancient Gold ;
   There is naught but the sky above them as the ring together they
      hold,
   The shapen-ancient token, that hath no change nor end,
   No change, and no beginning, no flaw for God to mend :
   Then Sigurd cries: ' O Brynhild, now hearken while I swear
   That the sun shall die in the heavens and the day no more be fair,
   If I seek not love in Lymdale and the house that fostered thee,
   And the land where thou awakedst 'twixt the woodland and the sea !
   And she cried : ' O Sigurd, Sigurd, now hearken while I swear
   That the day shall die forever and the sun to blackness wear,
   Ere I forget thee, Sigurd, as I lie 'twixt wood and sea
   In the little land of Lymdale and the house that fostered me ! ' "

According to some authorities, after thus plighting their troth
the lovers parted; according to others, Sigurd soon sought out
and married Brunhild, with whom he lived for a   The fostering
while in perfect happiness, until forced to leave   of Aslaug.
her and his infant daughter Aslaug. This child, left orphaned at
three years of age, was fostered by Brunhild's father, who, driven
away from home, concealed her in a cunningly fashioned harp,
until reaching a distant land he was murdered by a peasant couple
for the sake of the gold they supposed it to contain. Their surprise and disappointment were great indeed when, on breaking the
instrument open, they found a beautiful little girl, whom they
deemed mute, as she would not speak a word. Time passed on,
and the child, whom they had trained to do all their labor, grew
up to be a beautiful maiden who won the affections of a passing
viking, Ragnar Lodbrog, King of the Danes, to whom she told
her tale. After a year's probation, during which he won glory in
many lands, he came back and married her.

      " She heard a voice she deemed well known,
        Long waited through dull hours bygone,
        And round her mighty arms were cast :
        But when her trembling red lips passed
        From out the heaven of that dear kiss,
        And eyes met eyes, she saw in his

Fresh pride, fresh hope, fresh love, and saw
The long sweet days still onward draw,
Themselves still going hand in hand,
As now they went adown the strand."
THE FOSTERING OF ASLAUG (William Morris).

The story of Sigurd and Brunhild did not end on the Hindarfial, however, for the hero soon went to seek adventures in the great world, where he had vowed, in true knightly fashion, to right the wrong and defend the fatherless and oppressed.

In the course of his wanderings, Sigurd finally came to the land of the Niblungs, the land of continual mist, where Giuki and Grimhild were king and queen. The latter was specially powerful, as she was well versed in magic lore and could not only weave spells and mutter incantations, but could also concoct marvelous potions which would steep the drinker in temporary forgetfulness and make him yield to whatever she wished.

The Niblungs.

The Niblung king was father of three sons, Gunnar, Högni, and Guttorm, who were brave young men, and of one daughter, Gudrun, the gentlest as well as the most beautiful of maidens. Sigurd was warmly welcomed by Giuki, and invited to tarry awhile. He accepted the invitation, shared all the pleasures and occupations of the Niblungs, even accompanying them to war, where he distinguished himself by his valor, and so won the admiration of Grimhild that she resolved to secure him as her daughter's husband at any price. She therefore brewed one of her magic potions, which she bade Gudrun give him, and when he had partaken of it, he utterly forgot Brunhild and his plighted troth, and gazed upon Gudrun with an admiration which by the queen's machinations was soon changed to ardent love.

"But the heart was changed in Sigurd; as though it ne'er had been
His love of Brynhild perished as he gazed on the Niblung Queen:
Brynhild's beloved body was e'en as a wasted hearth,
No more for bale or blessing, for plenty or for dearth."

Although haunted by a vague dread that he had forgotten something important, Sigurd asked for and obtained Gudrun's hand, and celebrated his wedding amid the rejoicings of the people, who loved him very dearly. He gave his bride some of Fafnir's heart to eat, and the moment she had tasted it her nature was changed, and she began to grow cold and silent to all except him. Sigurd further cemented his alliance with the eldest two Giukings (as the sons of Giuki were called) by stepping down into the doom ring with them, cutting out a sod which was placed upon a shield, beneath which they stood while they bared and slightly cut their right arms, and allowing their blood to mingle in the fresh earth, over which the sod was again laid after they had sworn eternal friendship.

But although Sigurd loved his wife and felt true brotherly affection for her brothers, he could not get rid of his haunting sense of oppression, and was seldom seen to smile as radiantly as of old. Giuki having died, Grimhild besought Gunnar, his successor, to take a wife, suggesting that none seemed more worthy to become Queen of the Niblungs than Brunhild, who, it was reported, sat in a golden hall surrounded by flames, whence she had declared she would issue only to marry the warrior who would dare pass through the fire to her side.

Gunnar immediately prepared to seek this bride, and strengthened by one of his mother's magic potions, and encouraged by Sigurd, who accompanied him, he felt very confident of success. But when he would daringly *Gunnar's stratagem.* have ridden straight into the fire, his steed drew back affrighted and he could not induce him to advance a step. Seeing that Greyfell did not flinch, he asked him of Sigurd; but although the steed allowed Gunnar to mount, he would not stir unless his master were on his back. Gunnar, disappointed, sprang to earth and accepted Sigurd's proposal to assume his face and form, ride through the flames, and woo the bride by proxy. This deception could easily be carried out, thanks to the Helmet of Dread, and to a magic potion which Grimhild had given Gunnar.

The transformation having been brought about, Greyfell bounded through the flames with his master, and bore him to the palace door, where he dismounted, and entering the large hall came into the presence of Brunhild, whom he failed to recognize, owing to Grimhild's spell. Brunhild started back in dismay when she saw the dark-haired knight, for she had deemed it utterly impossible for any but Sigurd to cross the flames, and she, too, did not know her lover in his altered guise.

Reluctantly she rose from her seat to receive him, and as she had bound herself by a solemn oath to accept as husband the man who braved the flames, she allowed him to take his lawful place by her side. Sigurd silently approached, carefully laid his drawn sword between them, and satisfied Brunhild's curiosity concerning this singular behavior by telling her that the gods had bidden him celebrate his wedding thus.

> "There they went in one bed together; but the foster-brother laid
> 'Twixt him and the body of Brynhild his bright blue battle-blade,
> And she looked and heeded it nothing; but, e'en as the dead folk
>   lie,
> With folded hands she lay there, and let the night go by:
> And as still lay that image of Gunnar as the dead of life forlorn,
> And hand on hand he folded as he waited for the morn.
> So oft in the moonlit minster your fathers may ye see
> By the side of the ancient mothers await the day to be."

Three days passed thus, and when the fourth morning dawned, Sigurd drew the ring Andvaranaut from Brunhild's hand, replaced it by another, and received her solemn promise that in ten days' time she would appear at the Niblung court to take up her duties as queen and be a faithful wife.

> "I thank thee, King, for thy goodwill, and thy pledge of love I take.
> Depart with my troth to thy people: but ere full ten days are o'er
> I shall come to the Sons of the Niblungs, and then shall we part no
>   more
> Till the day of the change of our life-days, when Odin and Freya
>   shall call."

(*Opp. p. 252.*)

GUDRUN GIVING THE MAGIC DRINK TO SIGURD.—Th. Pixis.

Then Sigurd again passed out of the palace through the ashes lying white and cold, and joined Gunnar, with whom he hastened to exchange forms once more, after he had reported the success of his venture. The warriors rode homeward together, and Sigurd revealed only to Gudrun the secret of her brother's wooing, giving her the fatal ring, which he little suspected would be the cause of many woes.

True to her promise, Brunhild appeared ten days later, solemnly blessed the house she was about to enter, greeted Gunnar kindly, and allowed him to conduct her to the great hall, where she saw Sigurd seated beside Gudrun. He looked up at the selfsame moment, and as he encountered Brunhild's reproachful glance Grimhild's spell was broken and he was struck by an anguished recollection of the happy past. It was too late, however: they were both in honor bound, he to Gudrun and she to Gunnar, whom she passively followed to the high seat, where she sat beside him listening to the songs of the bards.

But, although apparently calm, Brunhild's heart was hot with anger, and she silently nursed her wrath, often stealing out of her husband's palace to wander alone in the forest, where she could give vent to her grief.

In the mean while, Gunnar, seeing his wife so coldly indifferent to all his protestations of affection, began to have jealous suspicions and wondered whether Sigurd had honestly told the whole story of the wooing, and whether he had not taken advantage of his position to win Brunhild's love. Sigurd alone continued the even tenor of his way, doing good to all, fighting none but tyrants and oppressors, and cheering all he met by his kindly words and smile.

One day the queens went down to the Rhine to bathe, and as they were entering the water Gudrun claimed precedence by right of her husband's courage. Brunhild refused to yield what she deemed her right, and a quarrel ensued, in the course of which Gudrun accused her sister-in-law of infidelity, producing the ring Andvaranaut in support of her

Quarrel of the queens.

charge. Crushed by this revelation, Brunhild hastened homeward, and lay on her bed in speechless grief day after day, until all thought she would die. In vain did Gunnar and all the members of the royal family seek her in turn and implore her to speak; she would not utter a word until Sigurd came and inquired the cause of her great grief. Like a long-pent-up stream, her love and anger now burst forth, and she overwhelmed the hero with reproaches, until his heart swelled with grief for her sorrow and burst the tight bands of his strong armor.

> "Out went Sigurd
> From that interview
> Into the hall of kings,
> Writhing with anguish;
> So that began to start
> The ardent warrior's
> Iron-woven sark
> Off from his sides."
> SÆMUND'S EDDA (Thorpe's tr.).

But although he even offered to repudiate Gudrun to reinstate her in her former rights, she refused to listen to his words, and dismissed him, saying that she must never prove faithless to Gunnar. Her pride was such, however, that she could not endure the thought that two living men had called her wife, and the next time her husband sought her presence she implored him to put Sigurd to death, thus increasing his jealousy and suspicions. He refused to grant this prayer because he had sworn good fellowship with Sigurd, and she prevailed upon Högni to work her will. As he, too, did not wish to violate his oath, he induced Guttorm, by means of much persuasion and one of Grimhild's potions, to do the dastardly deed.

In the dead of night, Guttorm stole into Sigurd's chamber, sword in hand; but as he bent over the bed he saw Sigurd's bright eyes fixed upon him, and fled precipitately. Later on he returned and the same scene was repeated; but towards morning, when he stole in for the third time, he found

Death of Sigurd.

the hero asleep and traitorously drove his spear through his back.

Mortally wounded, Sigurd raised himself in bed, grasped his wonderful sword hanging beside him, flung it full at the flying murderer, and cut him in two just as he reached the door. His last remaining strength thus exhausted, Sigurd sank back, whispered a last farewell to the terrified Gudrun, and breathed his last.

" ' Mourn not, O Gudrun, this stroke is the last of ill;
Fear leaveth the house of the Niblungs on this breaking of the morn;
Mayest thou live, O woman belovèd, unforsaken, unforlorn!
It is Brynhild's deed,' he murmured, ' and the woman that loves me well;
Naught now is left to repent of, and the tale abides to tell.
I have done many deeds in my life-days; and all these, and my love they lie
In the hollow hand of Odin till the day of the world go by.
I have done and I may not undo, I have given and I take not again:
Art thou other than I, Allfather, wilt thou gather my glory in vain?' "

Sigurd's infant son was also slain, and poor Gudrun mourned over her dead in speechless, tearless grief; while Brunhild laughed aloud, thereby incurring the wrath of Gunnar, who repented now, but too late, of his share in the dastardly crime.

While the assembled people were erecting a mighty funeral pyre — which they decorated with precious hangings, fresh flowers, and glittering arms, as was the custom for the burial of a prince — Gudrun was surrounded by women, who, seeing her tearless anguish, and fearing lest her heart would break if her tears did not flow, began to recount the bitterest sorrows they had known, one even telling of the loss of all she held dear. But their attempts to make her weep were utterly vain, until they laid her husband's head in her lap, bidding her kiss him as if he were still alive; then her tears began to flow in torrents.

The reaction soon set in for Brunhild also; her resentment was all forgotten when she saw Sigurd laid on the pyre in all his martial array, with the burnished armor, the Helmet of Dread, and the trappings of his horse, which was to be burned with him, as well as several of his faithful servants who could not survive his loss. She withdrew to her apartment, distributed all her wealth among her handmaidens, donned her richest array, and stretching herself out upon her bed stabbed herself.

In dying accents she then bade Gunnar lay her beside the hero she loved, with the glittering, unsheathed sword between them, as it had lain when he had wooed her by proxy. When she had breathed her last, these orders were punctually executed, and both bodies were burned amid the lamentations of all the Niblungs.

"They are gone — the lovely, the mighty, the hope of the ancient
        Earth :
    It shall labor and bear the burden as before that day of their birth :
    It shall groan in its blind abiding for the day that Sigurd hath sped,
    And the hour that Brynhild hath hastened, and the dawn that
        waketh the dead :
    It shall yearn, and be oft-times holpen, and forget their deeds no
        more,
    Till the new sun beams on Balder and the happy sealess shore."

According to another version of the story, Sigurd was treacherously slain by the Giukings while hunting in the forest, and his body was borne home by the hunters and laid at his wife's feet.

Gudrun, still inconsolable, and loathing the kindred who had thus treacherously robbed her of all her joy, fled from her father's house and took refuge with Elf, Sigurd's foster father, who, after Hiordis's death, had married Thora, the daughter of King Hakon. The two women became great friends, and here Gudrun tarried several years, working tapestry in which she embroidered the great deeds of Sigurd, and watching over her little daughter Swanhild, whose bright eyes reminded her so vividly of the husband whom she had lost.

(*Opp. p.* 256.)

BRUNHILD.—Th. Pixis.

In the mean while, Atli, Brunhild's brother, who was now King of the Huns, had sent to Gunnar to demand atonement for his sister's death; and to satisfy these claims Gunnar had promised that in due time he would give him Gudrun's hand in marriage. Time passed, and when at last Atli clamored for the fulfillment of his promise, the Niblung brothers, with their mother Grimhild, went to seek the long-absent Gudrun, and by their persuasions and the magic potion administered by Grimhild succeeded in persuading her to leave little Swanhild in Denmark and become Atli's wife.

Atli, King of the Huns.

Gudrun dwelt, year after year, in the land of the Huns, secretly hating her husband, whose avaricious tendencies were extremely repugnant to her; and she was not even consoled for Sigurd's death and Swanhild's loss by the birth of two sons, Erp and Eitel. As she lovingly thought of the past she often spoke of it, little suspecting that her descriptions of the wealth of the Niblungs excited Atli's greed, and that he was secretly planning some pretext for getting it into his power.

Finally he decided to send Knefrud or Wingi, one of his subjects, to invite all the Niblung princes to visit his court, intending to slay them when he should have them at his mercy; but Gudrun, fathoming this design, sent a runic-written warning to her brothers, together with the ring Andvaranaut, around which she had twined a wolf's hair. On the way, however, the messenger partly effaced the runes, thus changing their meaning; and when he appeared before the Niblungs, Gunnar accepted the invitation, in spite of Högni's and Grimhild's warnings and the ominous dream of his new wife Glaumvor.

Before his departure, however, they prevailed upon him to secretly bury the great Niblung hoard in the Rhine, where it was sunk in a deep hole, the position of which was known to the royal brothers only, and which they took a solemn oath never to reveal.

Burial of the Niblung treasure.

"Down then and whirling outward the ruddy Gold fell forth,
As a flame in the dim gray morning flashed out a kingdom's worth;

Then the waters roared above it, the wan water and the foam
Flew up o'er the face of the rock-wall as the tinkling Gold fell home,
Unheard, unseen forever, a wonder and a tale,
Till the last of earthly singers from the sons of men shall fail."

In martial array they then rode out of the city of the Nib
lungs, which they were never again to see, and after many un-
important adventures came into the land of the

The treachery of Atli.

Huns, where, on reaching Atli's hall and finding
themselves surrounded by foes, they slew the traitor Knefrud, and
prepared to sell their lives as dearly as possible.

Gudrun rushed to meet them, embraced them tenderly, and,
seeing that they must fight, grasped a weapon and loyally helped
them in the terrible massacre which ensued. When the first on-
slaught was over, Gunnar kept up the spirits of his followers by
playing on his harp, which he laid aside only to grasp his sword
and make havoc among the foe. Thrice the brave Niblungs
resisted the assault of the Huns ere, wounded, faint, and weary,
Gunnar and Högni, now sole survivors, fell into the hands of
their foes, who bound them securely and led them off to prison
to await death.

Atli, who had prudently abstained from taking any active part
in the fight, had his brothers-in-law brought in turn before him,
promising freedom if they would only reveal the hiding place of
the golden hoard; but they proudly kept silence, and it was only
after much torture that Gunnar acknowledged that he had sworn
a solemn oath never to reveal the secret as long as Högni lived,
and declared he would believe his brother dead only when his
heart was brought to him on a platter.

"With a dreadful voice cried Gunnar: 'O fool, hast thou heard it told
Who won the Treasure aforetime and the ruddy rings of the Gold?
It was Sigurd, child of the Volsungs, the best sprung forth from the
    best :
He rode from the North and the mountains, and became my summer-
    guest,

My friend and my brother sworn: he rode the Wavering Fire,
And won me the Queen of Glory and accomplished my desire;
The praise of the world he was, the hope of the biders in wrong,
The help of the lowly people, the hammer of the strong:
Ah! oft in the world, henceforward, shall the tale be told of the deed,
And I, e'en I, will tell it in the day of the Niblungs' Need:
For I sat night-long in my armor, and when light was wide o'er the
land
I slaughtered Sigurd my brother, and looked on the work of mine
hand.
And now, O mighty Atli, I have seen the Niblung's wreck,
And the feet of the faint-heart dastard have trodden Gunnar's neck;
And if all be little enough, and the Gods begrudge me rest,
Let me see the heart of Högni cut quick from his living breast
And laid on the dish before me: and then shall I tell of the Gold,
And become thy servant, Atli, and my life at thy pleasure hold.'"

Urged by greed, Atli immediately ordered that Högni's heart
should be brought; but his servants, fearing to lay hands on such
a grim warrior, slew the cowardly scullion Hialli. This trembling
heart called forth contemptuous words from Gunnar, who declared such a timorous organ could never have belonged to his
fearless brother. But when, in answer to a second angry command from Atli, the unquivering heart of Högni was really brought,
Gunnar recognized it, and turning to the monarch solemnly swore
that since the secret now rested with him alone it would never be
revealed.

Livid with anger, the king bade him be thrown, with bound
hands, into a den of venomous snakes, where, his harp having
been flung after him in derision, Gunnar calmly sat, *The last of the*
playing it with his toes, and lulling all the reptiles *Niblungs.*
to sleep save one only. This snake was said to be Atli's mother
in disguise, and it finally bit him in the side, silencing his triumphant song forever.

To celebrate the death of his foes, Atli ordered a great feast,
commanding Gudrun to be present to wait upon him. Then he
heartily ate and drank, little suspecting that his wife had slain

both his sons, and was serving up their roasted hearts and their blood mixed with wine in cups made of their skulls. When the king and his men were intoxicated, Gudrun, according to one version of the story, set fire to the palace, and when the drunken sleepers awoke, too late to escape, she revealed all she had done, stabbed her husband, and perished in the flames with the Huns. According to another version, however, she murdered Atli with Sigurd's sword, placed his body on a ship, which she sent adrift, and then cast herself into the sea, where she was drowned.

" She spread out her arms as she spake it, and away from the earth
   she leapt
And cut off her tide of returning ; for the sea-waves over her swept,
And their will is her will henceforward, and who knoweth the deeps
   of the sea,
And the wealth of the bed of Gudrun, and the days that yet shall
   be ? "

A third and very different version reports that Gudrun was not drowned, but was borne along by the waves to the land where Jonakur was king. There she became his wife, and the mother of three sons, Sörli, Hamdir, and Erp. She also recovered possession of her beloved daughter Swanhild, who, in the mean while, had grown into a beautiful maiden of marriageable age.

Swanhild was finally promised to Ermenrich, King of Gothland, who sent his son, Randwer, and one of his subjects, Sibich, to escort the bride to his kingdom. Sibich, who **Swanhild.** was a traitor, and had planned to compass the death of the royal family that he might claim the kingdom, accused Randwer of having tried to win his young stepmother's affections, and thereby so roused the anger of Ermenrich that he ordered his son to be hanged, and Swanhild to be trampled to death under the feet of wild horses. But such was the beauty of this daughter of Sigurd and Gudrun that even the wild steeds could not be urged to touch her until she had been hidden from their view under a great blanket, when they trod her to death under their cruel hoofs.

HÖGNI THROWING THE TREASURE INTO THE RHINE.— Julius Schnorr.
(*Opp. p.* 260.)

Gudrun, hearing of this, called her three sons to her side, and provided them with armor and weapons against which nothing but stone could prevail. Then, after bidding them depart and avenge their murdered sister, she died of grief, and was burned on a great pyre. The three youths, Sörli, Hamdir, and Erp, invaded Ermenrich's kingdom, but the two eldest, deeming Erp too young to assist them, taunted him with his small size, and finally slew him. They then attacked Ermenrich, cut off his hands and feet, and would have slain him had not a one-eyed stranger suddenly appeared and bidden the bystanders throw stones at the young invaders. His orders were immediately carried out, and Sörli and Hamdir both fell under the shower of stones, which alone had power to injure them according to Gudrun's words.

"Ye have heard of Sigurd aforetime, how the foes of God he slew;
How forth from the darksome desert the Gold of the Waters he
    drew;
How he wakened Love on the Mountain, and wakened Brynhild
    the Bright,
And dwelt upon Earth for a season, and shone in all men's sight.
Ye have heard of the Cloudy People, and the dimming of the day,
And the latter world's confusion, and Sigurd gone away;
Now ye know of the Need of the Niblungs and the end of broken
    troth,
All the death of kings and of kindreds and the Sorrow of Odin the
    Goth."

This story of the Volsungs is supposed by some authorities to be a series of sun myths, in which Sigi, Rerir, Volsung, Sigmund, and Sigurd in turn personify the glowing orb of day. They are all armed with invincible swords, *Interpretation of the Saga.* the sunbeams, and all travel through the world fighting against their foes, the demons of cold and darkness. Sigurd, like Balder, is beloved of all; he marries Brunhild, the dawn maiden, whom he finds in the midst of flames, the flush of morn, and parts from her only to find her again when his career is ended. His body is burned on the funeral pyre, which, like Balder's, represents either the setting sun or the last gleam of summer, of which he too is a type. The slaying of Fafnir is the destruction of the demon of cold or darkness, who has stolen the golden hoard of summer or the yellow rays of the sun.

According to other authorities this Saga is based upon history. Atli is the cruel Attila, the "Scourge of God," while Gunnar is Gundicarius, a Burgundian monarch, whose kingdom was destroyed by the Huns, and who was slain with his brothers in 451. Gudrun is the Burgundian princess Ildico, who slew her husband on her wedding night, as has already been related, using the glittering blade which had once belonged to the sun-god to avenge her murdered kinsmen.

CHAPTER XXVII.

THE TWILIGHT OF THE GODS.

ONE of the distinctive features of Northern mythology is that the people always believed that their gods belonged to a finite race. The Æsir had had a beginning; therefore, it was reasoned, they must have an end; and as they were born from a mixture of the divine and gigantic elements, and were imperfect, they bore within them the germ of death, and were, like men, doomed to endure physical death to attain spiritual immortality.

The whole scheme of Northern mythology was therefore a drama, every step leading gradually to the climax or tragic end, when, with true poetic justice, punishment and reward were impartially meted out. In the fore- going chapters, the gradual rise and decline of the gods has been carefully traced. We have recounted how the Æsir tolerated the presence of evil, personated by Loki, in their midst; how they weakly followed his advice, allowed him to involve them in all manner of difficulties from which they could be extricated only at the price of some of their virtue or peace, and finally permitted him to gain such ascendency over them that he dared rob them of their dearest possession, purity, or innocence, as personified by Balder the good.

Too late now, the gods realized what an evil spirit had found a home among them, and banished Loki to earth, where men, following the gods' example, listened to his teachings, and instead of cultivating virtue became addicted to crime.

263

> " Brothers slay brothers;
> Sisters' children
> Shed each other's blood.
> Hard is the world;
> Sensual sin grows huge.
> There are sword-ages, ax-ages;
> Shields are cleft in twain;
> Storm-ages, murder-ages;
> Till the world falls dead,
> And men no longer spare
> Or pity one another."
> NORSE MYTHOLOGY (R. B. Anderson).

Seeing crime rampant, and all good banished from the earth, the gods realized that the prophecies uttered long before were about to be fulfilled, and that their downfall, Rag- *The Fimbul-winter.* narok, the twilight or dusk of the gods, would soon come to pass. Sol and Mani grew pale with horror, and tremblingly drove their chariots along their appointed paths, gazing with fear behind them at the pursuing wolves which would shortly overtake and devour them; and as their smiles disappeared the earth grew sad and cold, and the terrible Fimbulwinter began. Then snow fell from the four points of the compass at once, the biting winds swept down from the north, and all the earth was covered with a thick layer of ice.

> " Grim Fimbul raged, and o'er the world
> Tempestuous winds and snowstorms hurled;
> The roaring ocean icebergs ground,
> And flung its frozen foam around,
> E'en to the top of mountain height;
>   No warming air
>   Nor radiance fair
> Of gentle Summer's soft'ning light,
> Tempered this dreadful glacial night."
> VALHALLA (J. C. Jones).

This severe winter lasted during three whole seasons without a break, and was followed by three others, equally severe, during which all cheer departed from the earth, where the crimes of men increased with fearful rapidity, and where, in the general struggle for life, the last feelings of humanity and compassion disappeared.

In the dim recesses of the Ironwood the giantess Iarnsaxa or Angur-boda diligently fed the wolves Hati, Sköll, and Managarm, the progeny of Fenris, with the marrow of murderers' and adulterers' bones; and such was **The wolves let loose.** the prevalence of these vile crimes, that the almost insatiable monsters were never stinted in food, and daily gained more strength to pursue Sol and Mani, whom they finally overtook and devoured, deluging the earth with the blood from their dripping jaws.

> "In the east she was seated, that aged woman, in Jarnrid,
> And there she nourished the posterity of Fenrir;
> He will be the most formidable of all, he
> Who, under the form of a monster, will swallow up the moon."
> VOLUSPA (Pfeiffer's tr.).

As this terrible calamity occurred the whole earth trembled and shook, the stars, affrighted, fell from their places, and Loki, Fenris, and Garm, renewing their efforts, rent their chains asunder and rushed forth to take their revenge. At the same moment the dragon Nidhug gnawed through the root of the ash Yggdrasil, which quivered to its topmost bough; the red cock Fialar, perched above Valhalla, loudly crowed an alarm, which was immediately echoed by Gullin-kambi, the rooster in Midgard, and by Hel's dark-red bird in Nifl-heim.

> "The gold-combed cock
> The gods in Valhal loudly crow'd to arms;
> The blood-red cock as shrilly summons all
> On earth and down beneath it."
> VIKING TALES OF THE NORTH (R. B. Anderson).

Heimdall, seeing these ominous portents and hearing the cocks' shrill cry, immediately put the Giallar-horn to his lips and blew the long-expected blast, which was heard throughout the whole world. At the first sound of this rallying call Æsir and Ein-

Heimdall gives the alarm. heriar sprang from their golden couches, armed themselves for the coming fray, sallied bravely out of the great hall, and, mounting their impatient steeds, galloped over the quivering rainbow bridge to the spacious field of Vigrid, where, as Vafthrudnir had predicted so long before, the last battle was to take place.

The terrible Midgard snake Iörmungandr, aroused by the general commotion, writhed and twisted in the bottom of the sea,

The terrors of the sea. wriggled out of the deep, lashed the waters with his tail, and, crawling upon land, hastened to join the fray, in which he was to play a prominent part.

> "In giant wrath the Serpent tossed
> In ocean depths, till, free from chain,
> He rose upon the foaming main;
> Beneath the lashings of his tail,
> Seas, mountain high, swelled on the land;
> Then, darting mad the waves acrost,
> Pouring forth bloody froth like hail,
> Spurting with poisoned, venomed breath
> Foul deadly mists o'er all the Earth,
> Thro' thundering surge, he sought the strand."
>
> VALHALLA (J. C. Jones).

One of the great waves, stirred up by Iörmungandr's struggles, set afloat the fatal ship Nagilfar, constructed entirely out of the nails of the dead, many relatives having failed, in the course of time, to do their duty and show the respect due to the deceased, whose nails should have been pared ere they were laid at rest. As soon as this vessel was afloat, Loki boarded it with the fiery host from Muspells-heim, and steered it boldly over the stormy waters to the place of conflict.

This was not the only vessel bound for Vigrid, however, for out of a thick fog bank towards the north came another ship, steered by Hrym, in which were all the frost giants, armed to the teeth, and eager for a conflict with the Æsir, whom they had always hated.

Through a crevice Hel, the party-colored goddess of death, crept out of her underground home, closely followed by the Hel-hound Garm, all the malefactors of her cheerless realm, and the dragon Nidhug, which flew over the battlefield bearing corpses upon his wings.

Seeing these reinforcements to his party as soon as he landed, Loki welcomed them with joy, and placing himself at their head led them on to the fight.

Just then the skies were suddenly rent asunder, and through the fiery breach rode Surtr with his flaming sword, followed by his sons; and as they attempted to storm Asgard by riding over the bridge Bifröst, the glorious arch sank with a crash beneath their horses' tread.

> "Down thro' the fields of air,
>   With glittering armor fair,
>   In battle order bright,
>   They sped while seething flame
>   From rapid hoofstrokes came.
>   Leading his gleaming band, rode Surtur,
>   'Mid the red ranks of raging fire."
>   VALHALLA (J. C. Jones).

The gods now knew full well that their end was near, and that through weakness and lack of foresight they were laboring under great disadvantages; for Odin had but one eye, Tyr but one hand, and Frey nothing but a stag's horn wherewith to defend himself, instead of his invincible sword. Nevertheless, the Æsir did not show any signs of flinching or despair, but, like true Northern warriors, donned their richest attire, and gaily rode to the battlefield, determined to sell their lives as dearly as possible, and harboring no thought of surrender.

While they were mustering their forces, Odin once more rode down to the Urdar fountain, where, under the wilting Yggdrasil, the Norns sat, with veiled faces, their torn web lying at their feet, obstinately refusing to utter a single word. Once more the father of the gods whispered a mysterious communication to Mimir,

The great battle. then he remounted Sleipnir and went to join the waiting host. On Vigrid's broad plain the combatants were now all assembled; on one side the stern, calm faces of the Æsir, Vanas, and Einheriar, on the other the flashing host of Surtr, the grim frost giants, the pale army of Hel — Loki leading Garm, Fenris, and Iörmungandr, the two latter belching forth fire and smoke and exhaling clouds of noxious, deathly vapors, which filled all heaven and earth with their poisonous breath.

> "The years roll on,
> The generations pass, the ages grow,
> And bring us nearer to the final day
> When from the south shall march the fiery band
> And cross the bridge of heaven, with Lok for guide,
> And Fenris at his heel with broken chain;
> While from the east the giant Rymer steers
> His ship, and the great serpent makes to land;
> And all are marshal'd in one flaming square
> Against the Gods, upon the plains of Heaven."
>
> BALDER DEAD (Matthew Arnold).

At a given signal the opposing hosts close in battle, fighting, as did our ancestors of old, hand to hand and face to face. Rushing impetuously onward, Odin and the Fenris wolf came into contact, while Thor attacked the Midgard snake, and Tyr the dog Garm. Frey closed in with Surtr, Heimdall with Loki, whom he had defeated once before, and the remainder of the gods and all the Einheriar selected foes worthy of their courage and performed unheard-of deeds of valor. But, in spite of their constant practice and glittering arms, Valhalla's host was doomed to defeat, and Odin, after struggling fiercely with the Fenris wolf, saw it suddenly assume colossal proportions, and open its jaws so wide that they embraced all the space between heaven and earth. Then the monster rushed furiously upon the father of the gods and swallowed him whole.

" Fenrir shall with impious tooth
Slay the sire of rolling years:
Vithar shall avenge his fall,
And, struggling with the shaggy wolf,
Shall cleave his cold and gory jaws."

VAFTHRUDNI'S-MAL (W. Taylor's tr.).

None of the gods could lend Allfather a helping hand at that
critical moment, for Frey succumbed beneath Surtr's flashing
sword, Heimdall and Loki fell mutually slain, Tyr and Garm dealt
and received from each other a mortal wound, and Thor, after
an indescribable encounter with the Midgard snake, slew him by
a blow from Miölnir, staggered back nine paces, fell, and was
drowned in the flood of venom which poured from the dying
monster's jaws.

"Odin's son goes
With the monster to fight;
Midgard's Veor in his rage
Will slay the worm;
Nine feet will go
Fiörgyn's son,
Bowed by the serpent
Who feared no foe."

SÆMUND'S EDDA (Thorpe's tr.).

Vidar, seeing that his beloved father had succumbed, now
came rushing from the other end of the plain to avenge his death,
and planting his large shoe upon Fenris's lower jaw, he seized
the monster's upper jaw and with one terrible wrench tore him
asunder.

The other gods who took part in the fray and all the Einheriar
having now perished, Surtr suddenly flung his fiery brands all
over heaven, earth, and the nine kingdoms of Hel. The devouring
The raging flames rose higher and higher, curled fire.
round the stalwart stem of the world ash Yggdrasil, consumed the
golden palaces of the gods, destroyed the vegetation upon earth,
and made all the waters seethe and boil.

> " Fire's breath assails
> The all-nourishing tree,
> Towering fire plays
> Against heaven itself."
> SÆMUND'S EDDA (Thorpe's tr.).

This fire raged most fiercely until everything was consumed, when the earth, blackened and scarred, slowly sank down beneath the boiling waves of the sea. Ragnarok had indeed come; the world tragedy was over, the divine actors were slain, and chaos seemed to have returned to resume all its former sway. But as in a play, after the actors are all slain and the curtain has fallen, the audience still expects the principal favorites to appear and make a bow, so the ancient Northern races fancied that, all evil having perished in Surtr's flames, goodness would rise from the general ruin, to resume its sway over the earth, and some of the gods would return to dwell in heaven forever.

> " All evil
> Dies there an endless death, while goodness riseth
> From that great world-fire, purified at last,
> To a life far higher, better, nobler than the past."
> VIKING TALES OF THE NORTH (R. B. Anderson).

As our ancestors believed fully in regeneration, they declared that after a certain space of time the earth, purged by fire and purified by its immersion in the sea, would rise again in all its pristine beauty and be illumined by the sun, whose chariot was driven by a daughter of Sol's, born before the wolf had devoured her mother. The new orb of day was not imperfect, as the first sun had been, for its rays were no longer so ardent that a shield had to be placed between it and the earth, which soon grew green beneath its beneficent rays, and brought forth flowers and fruit in abundance. Two human beings, a woman, Lif, and a man, Lifthrasir, now emerged from the depths of Hodmimir's (Mimir's) forest. They had taken refuge there when Surtr set fire to the world, and had sunk into peace-

Regeneration.

ful slumbers, unmindful of the destruction around them, and remained, feeding upon the morning dew, until it was safe for them to wander out once more and take possession of the regenerated earth, which their descendants were to people and over which they were to have full sway.

> "We shall see emerge
> From the bright Ocean at our feet an earth
> More fresh, more verdant than the last, with fruits
> Self-springing, and a seed of man preserved,
> Who then shall live in peace, as now in war."
> BALDER DEAD (Matthew Arnold).

All the gods who represented the developing forces of Nature were slain on the fatal field of Vigrid, but the imperishable forces of Nature, typified by Vali and Vidar, returned to the field of Ida, where they were met by Modi and Magni, Thor's sons, the personifications of strength and energy, who saved their father's sacred hammer from the general destruction, and carried it thither with them.

> "Vithar's then and Vali's force
> Heirs the empty realm of gods;
> Mothi's thew and Magni's might
> Sways the massy mallet's weight,
> Won from Thor, when Thor must fall."
> VAFTHRUDNI'S-MAL (W. Taylor's tr.).

Here they were joined by Hoenir, no longer an exile among the Vanas, who, as developing forces, had also vanished forever; and out of the dark underworld where he had languished so long rose the radiant Balder, accompanied by his brother Hodur, with whom he was reconciled, and who was now ready to live with him in perfect amity and peace. Gently and pensively these gods talked of the past, recalled the memory of their former companions, and, searching in the long grass on Idavold, found again the golden disks with which the Æsir had been wont to play.

> " We shall tread once more the well-known plain
>   Of Ida, and among the grass shall find
>   The golden dice with which we play'd of yore;
>   And that will bring to mind the former life
>   And pastime of the Gods, the wise discourse
>   Of Odin, the delights of other days."
>
> BALDER DEAD (Matthew Arnold).

Then, looking towards the place where their lordly dwellings once stood, the assembled gods became aware of the fact that Gimli, the highest heavenly abode, had not been consumed, but rose glittering before them, its golden roof outshining the sun; and when they hastened thither they discovered, with unmixed joy, that it had become the place of refuge of all the virtuous.

> " In Gimli the lofty
>   There shall the hosts
>   Of the virtuous dwell,
>   And through all ages
>   Taste of deep gladness."
>
> LITERATURE AND ROMANCE OF NORTHERN EUROPE (Howitt).

As the Norsemen who settled in Iceland, and through whom the most complete exposition of the Odinic faith has come down to us in the Eddas and Sagas, were not definitely converted until the eleventh century, — although they had come in contact with Christians during their viking raids, nearly six centuries before, — it is very probable that the Northern scalds gleaned some idea of the Christian doctrines, and that this knowledge influenced them to a certain extent, and colored their descriptions of the end of the world and the regeneration of the earth. It was perhaps this vague knowledge, also, which induced them to add to the Edda a verse, which is generally supposed to have been an interpolation, proclaiming that another God, too mighty to name, would rule over Gimli, judge all mankind, separate the bad from the good, banish the former to the horrors of Nastrond, and invite the latter to taste of endless bliss in the halls of Gimli the fair.

One too mighty to name.

"Then comes another,
Yet more mighty.
But Him dare I not
Venture to name.
Few farther may look
Than to where Odin
To meet the wolf goes."

LITERATURE AND ROMANCE OF NORTHERN EUROPE (Howitt).

There were two other heavenly mansions, however, one reserved for the dwarfs and the other for the giants; for as these creatures had no free will, and blindly executed the decrees of fate, they were not held responsible for any harm they had done, and were not punished.

The dwarfs, ruled by Sindri, were said to occupy a hall in the Nida mountains, where they drank the sparkling mead, while the giants took their pleasure in the hall Brimer, situated in the region Okolnur (not cool), for the power of cold was entirely annihilated, and there was no more ice.

Various mythologists have, of course, attempted to explain these myths, and some, as we have already stated, see in the story of Ragnarok the influence of Christian teachings and esteem it only a barbaric version of the end of the world and the coming judgment day, when a new heaven and earth shall arise, and all the good shall enjoy eternal bliss.

CHAPTER XXVIII.

DURING the past fifty years the learned men of many nations have investigated philology and comparative mythology so thoroughly that they have ascertained beyond the possibility of doubt "that English, together with all the Teutonic dialects of the Continent, belongs to that large family of speech which comprises, besides the Teutonic, Latin, Greek, Slavonic, and Celtic, the Oriental languages of India and Persia." "It has also been proved that the various tribes who started from the central home to discover Europe in the north, and India in the south, carried away with them, not only a common language, but a common faith and a common mythology. These are facts which may be ignored but cannot be disputed, and the two sciences of comparative grammar and comparative mythology, though but of recent origin, rest on a foundation as sound and safe as that of any of the inductive sciences." "For more than a thousand years the Scandinavian inhabitants of Norway have been separated in language from their Teutonic brethren on the Continent, and yet both have not only preserved the same stock of popular stories, but they tell them, in several instances, in almost the same words."

Comparative mythology.

This resemblance, so strong in the early literature of nations inhabiting countries which present much the same physical aspect and have nearly the same climate, is not so marked when we compare the Northern myths with those of the genial South. Still, notwithstanding the contrast between the boreal and south temperate zones, where these myths gradually ripened and attained their full growth, there is sufficient analogy between the two mythologies to show that the seeds from whence both sprang were originally the same.

In the foregoing chapters the Northern system of mythology has been outlined as clearly as possible, and the physical significance of the myths has been explained. Now we shall endeavor to set forth the resemblance of Northern mythology to that of the other Aryan nations, by comparing it with the Greek, which, however, it does not resemble as closely as it does the Oriental.

It is, of course, impossible in a brief work of this character to do more than mention the main points of resemblance in the stories forming the basis of these religions; but that will serve to demonstrate, even to the most skeptical, that they must have been identical at a period too remote to indicate now with any certainty.

The Northern nations, like the Greeks, imagined that the world rose out of chaos; and while the latter described it as a vapory, formless mass, the former, influenced by their im- The beginning mediate surroundings, depicted it as a chaos of fire of things. and ice — a combination which is only too comprehensible to any one who has visited Iceland and seen the wild, peculiar contrast between its volcanic soil, spouting geysers, and the great icebergs which hedge it all around during the long, dark winter season.

From these opposing elements, fire and ice, were born the first divinities, who, like the first gods of the Greeks, were gigantic in stature and uncouth in appearance. Ymir, the huge ice giant, and his descendants, are comparable to the Titans, who were also elemental forces of Nature, personifications of subterranean fire; and both, having held full sway for a time, were obliged to yield to greater perfection. After a fierce struggle for supremacy, they all found themselves defeated and banished to the respective remote regions of Tartarus and Jötun-heim.

The triad, Odin, Vili, and Ve, of the Northern myth is the exact counterpart of Jupiter, Neptune, and Pluto, who, superior to the Titan forces, rule supreme over the world in their turn.

In the Greek mythology, the gods, who are also all related to one another, betake themselves to Olympus, where they build golden palaces for their use; and in the Northern mythology the divine conquerors repair to Asgard, and there construct similar dwellings.

Northern cosmogony was not unlike the Greek, for the people imagined that the earth, Mana-heim, was entirely surrounded by the sea, at the bottom of which lay the huge Midgard snake, biting its own tail; and it was perfectly natural that, viewing the storm-lashed waves which beat against their shores, they should declare they were the result of his convulsive writhing. The Greeks, who also fancied the earth was round and compassed by a mighty river called Oceanus, described it as flowing with "a steady, equable current," for they generally gazed out upon calm and sunlit seas. Nifl-heim, the Northern region of perpetual cold and mist, had its exact counterpart in the land north of the Hyperboreans, where feathers (snow) continually hovered in the air, and where Hercules drove the Cerynean stag into a snowdrift ere he could seize and bind it fast.

Cosmogony.

Like the Greeks, the Northern races believed that the earth was created first, and that the vaulted heavens were made afterwards to overshadow it entirely. They also imagined that the sun and moon were daily driven across the sky in chariots drawn by fiery steeds. Sol, the sun maiden, therefore corresponded to Helios, Hyperion, Phœbus, or Apollo, while Mani, the moon (owing to a peculiarity of Northern grammar, which makes the sun feminine and the moon masculine), was the exact counterpart of Phœbe, Diana, or Cynthia.

The phenomena of the sky.

The Northern scalds, who thought that they descried the prancing forms of white-maned steeds in the flying clouds, and the glitter of spears in the flashing light of the aurora borealis, said that the Valkyrs, or battle maidens, were galloping across the sky, while the Greeks saw in the same natural phenomena the white flocks of Apollo guarded by Phaethusa and Lampetia.

As the dew fell from the clouds, the Northern poets declared that it dropped from the manes of the Valkyrs' steeds, while the Greeks, who generally observed that it sparkled longest in the thickets, identified it with Daphne and Procris, whose names are derived from the Sanskrit word "to sprinkle," and who are slain by their lovers, Apollo and Cephalus, personifications of the sun.

The earth was considered in the North as well as in the South as a female divinity, the fostering mother of all things; and it was owing to climatic difference only that the mythology of the North, where people were daily obliged to conquer the right to live by a hand-to-hand struggle with Nature, should represent her as hard and frozen like Rinda, while the Greeks embodied her in the genial goddess Ceres. The Greeks also believed that the cold winter winds swept down from the North, and the Northern races added that they were produced by the winnowing of the wings of the great eagle Hræ-svelgr.

The dwarfs, or dark elves, bred in Ymir's flesh, were like Pluto's servants in that they never left their underground realm, where they, too, sought the precious metals, which they molded into delicate ornaments such as Vulcan bestowed upon the gods, and into weapons which no one could either dint or mar. As for the light elves, who lived aboveground and cared for plants, trees, and streams, they were evidently the Northern substitutes for the nymphs, dryads, oreades, and hamadryads, which peopled the woods, valleys, and fountains of ancient Greece.

Jupiter, like Odin, was the father of the gods, the god of victory, and a personification of the universe. Hlidskialf, Allfather's lofty throne, was no less exalted than Olympus or Ida, whence the Thunderer could observe all that Jupiter and Odin. was taking place; and Odin's invincible spear Gungnir was as terror-inspiring as the thunderbolts brandished by his Greek prototype. The Northern deities feasted continually upon mead and boar's flesh, the drink and meat most suitable to the inhabitants of a Northern climate, while the gods of Olympus preferred the nectar and ambrosia which were their only sustenance.

Twelve Æsir sat in Odin's council hall to deliberate over the wisest measures for the government of the world and men, and an equal number of gods assembled on the cloudy peak of Mount Olympus for a similar purpose. The Golden Age in Greece was a period of idyllic happiness, amid ever-flowering groves and under balmy skies, while the Northern age of bliss was also a time when peace and innocence flourished on earth, and when evil was as yet entirely unknown.

Using the materials near at hand, the Greeks modeled their first images out of clay; hence they naturally imagined that Prometheus had made man out of that substance when called upon to fashion a creature inferior to the gods only. As the Northern statues were all hewed out of wood, the Northern races inferred, as a matter of course, that Odin, Vili, and Ve (who here correspond to Prometheus, Epimetheus, and Minerva, the three Greek creators of man) made the first human couple, Ask and Embla, out of blocks of wood.

Creation of man.

The goat Heidrun, which supplied the heavenly mead, is like Amalthea, Jupiter's first nurse, and the busy, telltale Ratatosk is equivalent to the snow-white crow in the story of Coronis, which was turned black in punishment for its tattling. Jupiter's eagle has its counterpart in the ravens Hugin and Munin, or in the wolves Geri and Freki, which are ever crouching at Odin's feet.

The close resemblance between the Northern Orlog and the Greek Destiny, goddesses whose decrees the gods themselves were obliged to respect, and the equally powerful Norns and Mœræ, is too obvious to need pointing out, while the Vanas are counterparts of Neptune and the other ocean divinities. The great quarrel between the Vanas and the Æsir is merely another version of the dispute between Jupiter and Neptune for the supremacy of the world. Just as Jupiter forces his brother to yield to his authority, so the Æsir remain masters of all, but do not refuse to continue to share their power with their conquered foes, who thus become their allies and friends.

Norns and Fates.

Like Jupiter, Odin is always described as majestic and middle-aged, and both gods are regarded as the divine progenitors of royal races, for while the Heraclidæ claimed Jupiter as their father, the Inglings, Skioldings, etc., said Odin was the founder of their families. The most solemn oaths were sworn by Odin's spear as well as by Jupiter's footstool, and both gods rejoice in a multitude of names, all descriptive of the various phases of their nature and worship.

Odin, like Jupiter, frequently visited the earth in disguise, to judge of the hospitable intentions of mankind, as in the story of Geirrod and Agnar, which resembles that of Philemon and Baucis. The aim was to encourage hospitality, therefore, in both stories, those who showed themselves humanely inclined are richly rewarded, and in the Northern myth the lesson is enforced by the punishment inflicted upon Geirrod, as the scalds believed in poetic justice and saw that it was carefully meted out.

The contest of wit between Odin and Vafthrudnir has its parallel in the musical rivalry of Apollo and Marsyas, or in the test of skill between Minerva and Arachne. Odin further resembled Apollo in that he, too, was god of eloquence and poetry, and could win all hearts to him by means of his divine voice; he was like Mercury in that he taught mortals the use of runes, while the Greek god introduced the alphabet.

The disappearance of Odin, the sun or summer, and the consequent desolation of Frigga, the earth, is merely a different version of the myths of Proserpine and Adonis. **Myths of the seasons.** When Proserpine and Adonis have gone, the earth (Ceres or Venus) bitterly mourns their absence, and refuses all consolation. It is only when they return from their exile that she casts off her mourning garments and gloom, and again decks herself in all her jewels. So Frigga and Freya bewail the absence of their husbands Odin and Odur, and remain hard and cold until their return. Odin's wife Saga, the goddess of history, who lingered by Sokvabek, "the stream of time and events," taking note of all she saw, is like Clio, the muse of history, whom Apollo sought by the inspiring fount of Helicon.

Just as, according to Euhemerus, there was an historical Zeus, buried in Crete, where his grave can still be seen, so there was an historical Odin, whose mound rises near Upsala, where the greatest Northern temple once stood, and where there was a mighty oak which rivaled the famous tree of Dodona.

Frigga, like Juno, was a personification of the atmosphere, the patroness of marriage, of connubial and motherly love, and the

Frigga and Juno. goddess of childbirth. She, too, is represented as a beautiful, stately woman, rejoicing in her adornments; and her special attendant, Gna, rivals Iris in the rapidity with which she executes her mistress's behests. Juno has full control over the clouds, which she can brush away with a motion of her hand, and Frigga is supposed to weave them out of the thread she has spun on her jeweled spinning wheel.

In Greek mythology we find many examples of the way in which Juno seeks to outwit Jupiter. Similar tales are not lacking in the Northern myths. Juno obtains possession of Io, in spite of her husband's reluctance to part with her, and Frigga artfully secures the victory for the Winilers in the Langobardian Saga. Odin's wrath at Frigga's theft of the gold from his statue is equivalent to Jupiter's marital displeasure at Juno's jealousy and interference during the war of Troy. In the story of Gefjon, and the clever way in which she procured land from Gylfi to form her kingdom of Seeland, we have a reproduction of the story of Dido, who obtained by stratagem the land upon which she founded her city of Carthage. In both accounts oxen come into play, for while in the Northern myth these sturdy beasts draw the piece of land far out to sea, in the other an ox hide, cut into strips, serves to inclose the queen's grant.

The Pied Piper of Hamelin, who could attract all living creatures by his music, is like Orpheus or Amphion, whose lyres had

Musical myths. the same power; and Odin, as leader of the dead, is the counterpart of Mercury Psychopompus, both being personifications of the wind, on whose wings disembodied souls were thought to be wafted away from this mortal sphere.

The trusty Eckhardt, who would fain save Tannhäuser and prevent his returning to expose himself to the enchantments of the sorceress in the Hörselberg, is like the Greek Mentor, who not only accompanied Telemachus, but who gave him good advice and wise instructions, and would like to have rescued Ulysses from the hands of Calypso.

Thor, the Northern thunder-god, also has many points of resemblance with Jupiter. He bears the hammer Miölnir, the Northern emblem of the deadly thunderbolt, and, like Jupiter, uses it freely when warring against the giants. In his rapid growth Thor resembles Mercury, for while the former playfully tosses several loads of ox hides about a few hours after his birth, the latter steals Apollo's oxen before he is one day old. In physical strength Thor resembles Hercules, who also gave early proofs of uncommon vigor by strangling the serpents sent to slay him in his cradle, and who delighted, later on, in attacking and conquering giants and monsters. Hercules became a woman and took to spinning to please Omphale, the Lydian queen, and Thor assumed a woman's apparel to visit Thrym and recover his hammer, which had been buried nine rasts underground. The hammer, his principal attribute, was used for many sacred purposes. It consecrated the funeral pyre and the marriage rite, and boundary stakes driven in by a hammer were considered as sacred among Northern nations as the Hermæ or statues of Mercury, whose removal was punished by death.

Thor and the Greek gods.

Thor's wife, Sif, with her luxuriant golden hair, is, as we have already stated, an emblem of the earth, and her hair of its rich vegetation. Loki's theft of these tresses is equivalent to Pluto's rape of Proserpine. To recover the golden locks, Loki must visit the dwarfs (Pluto's servants), crouching in the low passages of the underground world; so Mercury must seek Proserpine in Hades.

The gadfly which hinders Jupiter from recovering possession of Io, after Mercury has slain Argus, reappears in the Northern myth to sting Brock and prevent the manufacture of the magic ring Draupnir, which is merely a counterpart of Sif's tresses, as it also represents the fruits of the earth. It continues to torment the dwarf during the manufacture of Frey's golden-bristled boar, a prototype of Apollo's golden sun chariot, and it prevents the perfect formation of the handle of Thor's hammer.

The magic ship Skidbladnir, also made by the dwarfs, is like the swift-sailing Argo, which was a personification of the clouds sailing overhead; and just as the former was said to be large enough to accommodate all the gods, so the latter bore all the Greek heroes off to the distant land of Colchis.

The Germans, wishing to name the days of the week after their gods, as the Romans had done, gave the name of Thor to Jove's day, and thus made it the present Thursday.

Thor's struggle against Hrungnir is like the fight between Hercules and Cacus or Antæus; while Groa is evidently Ceres, for she, too, mourns for her absent child Orvandil (Proserpine), and breaks out into a song of joy when she hears it will return.

Magni, Thor's son, who when only three hours old exhibits his marvelous strength by lifting Hrungnir's leg off his recumbent father, also reminds us of the infant Hercules; and Thor's voracious appetite at Thrym's wedding feast has its parallel in Mercury's first meal, which consisted of two whole oxen.

Thor's crossing the swollen tide of Veimer reminds us of Jason's wading across the torrent when on his way to visit the tyrant Pelias and recover possession of his father's throne.

The marvelous necklace worn by Frigga and Freya to enhance their charms is like the cestus or girdle of Venus, which Juno borrowed to subjugate her lord, and is, like Sif's tresses and the ring Draupnir, an emblem of luxuriant vegetation or a type of the stars which jewel the firmament.

The Northern sword-god Tyr is, of course, the Roman war-god Mars, whom he so closely resembles that his name was given to the day of the week held sacred to Mars, which is even now known as Tuesday or Tiu's day. Like Mars, Tyr was noisy and courageous; he delighted in the din of battle and warfare, and was quite fearless at all times. He alone dared to brave the Fenris wolf; and the Southern proverb concerning Scylla and Charybdis has its counterpart in the Northern adage, "to get loose out of Læding and to dash out of Droma." The Fenris wolf, also a personification of subterranean fire, is bound, like his prototypes the Titans, in Tartarus.

The similarity between the gentle, music-loving Bragi, with his harp in hand, and Apollo or Orpheus is very great; so is the resemblance between the magic draft Od-hroerir and the waters of Helicon, which were also supposed to serve as inspiration to mortal as well as to immortal poets. Odin dons eagle plumes to bear away this precious mead, and Jupiter assumes a similar guise to secure his cupbearer Ganymede.

Idun, like Adonis and Proserpine, or still more like Eurydice, is also a fair personification of spring. She is borne away by the cruel ice giant Thiassi, who represents the boar which slew Adonis, the kidnapper of Proserpine, or the poisonous serpent which bit Eurydice. Idun is detained for a long, long time in Jötun-heim (Hades), where she forgets all her merry, playful ways, and becomes mournful and pale. She cannot return alone to Asgard, and it is only when Loki (now an emblem of the south wind) comes to bear her away in the shape of a nut or a swallow that she can effect her escape. She reminds us of Proserpine and Adonis escorted back to earth by Mercury (god of the wind), or of Eurydice lured out of Hades by the sweet sounds of Orpheus's harp, which were also symbolical of the soughing of the winds.

The myth of Idun's fall from Yggdrasil into the darkest depths of Nifl-heim, while subject to the same explanation and comparison as the above story, is still more closely related to the tale of Orpheus and Eurydice, for the for- *Idun and Eurydice.* mer, like Bragi, cannot exist without the latter, whom he follows even into the dark realm of death; without her his songs are entirely silenced. The wolfskin in which Idun is enveloped is typical of the heavy snows in Northern regions, which are considered a great blessing, as they preserve the tender roots from the blighting influence of the extreme winter cold.

The Van Niörd, who is god of the sunny summer seas, has his counterpart in Neptune and more especially in Nereus, the personification of the calm and pleasant aspect of the mighty deep. Niörd's wife, Skadi, is the Northern huntress; she therefore resembles Diana. Like her, she bears a quiver full of arrows, and a bow which she handles with consummate skill. Her short gown permits the utmost freedom of motion, also, and she, too, is generally accompanied by a hunting hound.

Skadi and Diana.

The myths of the transference of Thiassi's eyes to the firmament, where they glow like brilliant stars, remind us of many Greek star myths, and especially of Argus's eyes ever on the watch, of Orion and his jeweled girdle, and of his dog Sirius, all changed into stars by the gods to appease angry goddesses. Loki's antics to win a smile from the irate Skadi are considered akin to the quivering flashes of sheet lightning which he personified in the North, while Steropes, the Cyclops, typified it for the Greeks.

The Northern god of sunshine and summer showers, the genial Frey, has many traits in common with Apollo, for, like him, he is beautiful and young, rides the golden-bristled boar which was the Northern conception of the sunbeams, or drives across the sky in a golden car, which reminds us of Apollo's glittering chariot.

Frey has some of the gentle Zephyrus's characteristics besides, for he, too, scatters flowers along his way. His horse Blodughofi is not unlike Pegasus, Apollo's favorite steed, for it can pass through fire and water with equal ease and velocity.

Fro, like Odin and Jupiter, is also identified with a human king, and his mound lies beside Odin's near Upsala. His reign was so happy that it was called the Golden Age, and he therefore reminds us of Saturn, who, exiled to earth, ruled over the people of Italy, and granted them similar prosperity.

Gerda, the beautiful maiden, is like Venus, and also like Atalanta; she is hard to woo and hard to win, like the fleet-footed maiden, but, like her, she yields at last and becomes a happy wife. The golden apples with which Skirnir tries to bribe her remind us of the golden fruit which Hippomenes cast in Atalanta's way, and which made her lose the race.

Freya, the goddess of youth, love, and beauty, like Venus, sprang from the sea, for she is a daughter of the sea-god Niörd. Venus shows that she is not entirely devoid of martial tastes by bestowing her best affections upon Mars and Anchises, while Freya often assumes the garb of a Valkyr, and rides rapidly down to earth to take her part in mortal strife and bear away one half of the heroes slain to feast in her halls. Like Venus, she delights in offerings of fruits and flowers, lends a gracious ear to the petitions of lovers, and favors them as much as she can. Freya also resembles Minerva, for, like her, she wears a helmet and breastplate, and, like her, also, she is noted for her beautiful blue eyes.

Odur, Freya's husband, is like Adonis, and when he leaves her, she, too, sheds countless tears, which, in her case, are turned to gold, while Venus's tears are changed into anemones, and those of the Heliades, mourning **Odur and Adonis.** for Phaeton, harden to amber, which resembles gold in color and in consistency. Just as Venus rejoices at Adonis's return, and all Nature blooms in sympathy with her joy, so Freya becomes lighthearted once more when she has found her husband lover beneath the flowering myrtles of the South. Venus's car is drawn by fluttering doves, while Freya's is swiftly carried along by cats, which are emblems of sensual love, just as the doves were considered types of tenderest love. Freya is so sensitive to beauty that she angrily refuses to marry Thrym, and Venus scorns and finally deserts Vulcan, whom she has been forced to marry much against her will.

The Greeks represented Justice as a blindfolded goddess, with scales in one hand and a sword in the other, to indicate the impartiality and the fixity of her decrees. The corresponding deity of the North was Forseti, who patiently listened to both sides of a question ere he, too, promulgated his impartial and irrevocable sentence.

Uller, the winter-god, resembles Apollo and Orion only in his love for the chase, which he pursues with ardor under all circumstances. He is the Northern bowman, and his skill is quite as unerring as theirs.

Heimdall, like Argus, was gifted with marvelous keenness of sight, which enabled him to perceive even the growth of the grass. His Giallar-horn, which could be heard throughout all the world, proclaiming the gods' passage to and fro over the quivering bridge Bifröst, was like the trumpet of the goddess Renown. As he was related to the water deities on his mother's side, he could, like Proteus, assume any form at will, and made good use of this power on one occasion to frustrate Loki's attempt to steal the necklace Brisinga-men.

Hermod, the quick or nimble, resembles Mercury not only in his marvelous celerity of motion, but he, too, was the messenger of the gods, and, like the Greek divinity, he flashed hither and thither, aided not by winged cap and sandals, but by Odin's steed Sleipnir, whom he alone was allowed to bestride. Instead of the Caduceus, he bore the wand Gambantein. He questioned the Norns and the magician Rossthiof, through whom he learned that Vali would come to avenge his brother Balder and to supplant his father Odin. Instances of similar consultations are found in Greek mythology, where Jupiter would fain have married Thetis, yet desisted when the Fates foretold that she would be the mother of a son destined to surpass his father in glory and renown.

The Northern god of silence, Vidar, has some resemblance to Hercules, for while the latter has nothing but a club with which to defend himself against the Nemean lion, whom he tears asunder, the former, protected by one large shoe, rends the Fenris wolf at Ragnarok.

Odin's courtship of Rinda reminds us of Jupiter's wooing of

Danae, who is also a symbol of the earth; and while the shower of gold in the Greek tale is intended to represent the fertilizing sunbeams, the footbath in the Northern story typi- fies the spring thaw which sets in when the sun has overcome the resistance of the frozen earth. Perseus, the child of this union, has many points of resemblance with Vali, for he, too, is an avenger, and slays his mother's enemies just as surely as Vali destroys Hodur, the murderer of Balder.

Rinda and Danae.

The Fates were supposed to preside over birth in Greece, and to foretell a child's future just as well as the Norns; and the story of Meleager has its unmistakable parallel in that of Nornagesta. Althæa preserves the half-consumed brand in a chest, Nornagesta conceals the candle end in his harp; and while the Greek mother brings about her son's death by casting the brand into the fire, Nornagesta, compelled to light his candle end at Olaf's command, dies as it sputters and goes out.

Hebe and the Valkyrs were the cupbearers of Olympus and Asgard. They were all personifications of youth; and while Hebe married the great hero and demigod Hercules when she retired from office, the Valkyrs were relieved from further attendance when united to heroes like Helgi, Hakon, Völund, or Sigurd.

The Cretan labyrinth has its counterpart in the Icelandic Völundarhaus, and Völund and Dædalus both effect their escape from a maze by a cleverly devised pair of wings, which enables them to fly in safety over land and sea and escape from the tyranny of their respective masters, Nidud and Minos. Völund resembles Vulcan, also, in that he is a clever smith and makes use of his talents to work out his revenge. Vulcan, lamed by a fall from Olympus, and neglected by Juno, whom he had tried to befriend, sends her a golden throne, which is provided with cunning springs to seize and hold her fast. Völund, hamstrung by the suggestion of Nidud's queen, secretly murders her sons, and out of their eyes fashions marvelous jewels, which she unsuspectingly wears upon her breast until he reveals their origin.

Just as the Greeks fancied that the tempests were the effect of

Neptune's wrath, so the Northern races attributed them either to the writings of Iörmungandr, the Midgard snake, or to the anger

Myths of the sea. of Ægir, who, crowned with seaweed like Neptune, often sent his children, the wave maidens (the counterpart of the Nereides and Oceanides), out to play in the tossing billows. Neptune had his dwelling in the coral caves near the Island of Eubœa, while Ægir lived in a similar palace near Cattegat. Here he was surrounded by the nixies, undines, and mermaids, the counterpart of the Greek water nymphs, and by the river-gods of the Rhine, Elbe, and Neckar, who remind us of Alpheus and Peneus, the river-gods of the Greeks.

The frequency of shipwrecks on the Northern coasts made the people describe Ran (the equivalent of the Greek sea-goddess Amphitrite) as greedy and avaricious, and armed with a strong net, with which she drew all things down into the deep. The Greek Sirens had their parallel in the Northern Lorelei, who possessed the same gift of song, and also lured mariners to their death; while Princess Ilse, who was turned into a fountain, reminds us of the nymph Arethusa, who underwent a similar transformation.

In the Northern conception of Nifl-heim we have an almost exact counterpart of the Greek Hades. Mödgud, the guardian of the Giallar-bru (the bridge of death), over which all the spirits of the dead must pass, exacts a tribute of blood as rigorously as Charon demands an obolus from every soul he ferries over Acheron, the river of death. The fierce dog Garm, cowering in the Gnipa hole, and keeping guard at Hel's gate, is like the three-headed monster Cerberus; and the nine worlds of Nifl-heim are not unlike the divisions of Hades, Nastrond being an adequate substitute for Tartarus, where the wicked were punished with equal severity.

The custom of burning dead heroes with their arms, and of slaying victims, such as horses and dogs, upon their pyre, was much the same in the North as in the South; and while Mors or Thanatos, the Greek Death, was represented with a sharp scythe,

Hel was depicted with a broom or rake, which she used as ruthlessly, and with which she did as much execution.

Balder, the radiant god of sunshine, reminds us not only of Apollo and Orpheus, but of all the other heroes of sun myths. His wife Nanna is like Flora, and still more like Proserpine, for she, too, goes down into the underworld, where she tarries for a while. Balder's golden hall of Breidablik is like Apollo's palace in the east; he, too, delights in flowers; all things smile at his approach, and willingly take an oath of allegiance to him. Just as Achilles is vulnerable only in the heel, Balder can be slain only by the harmless mistletoe, and his death is occasioned by Loki's jealousy just as truly as Hercules was slain by Dejanira's. Balder's funeral pyre on Ringhorn reminds us of Hercules's death on Mount Œta, the flames and reddish glow of both fires serving to typify the setting sun. The Northern god of sun and summer could only be released from Nifl-heim if all animate and inanimate objects shed tears; so Proserpine could issue from Hades only upon condition that she had partaken of no food. The trifling refusal of Thok to shed a single tear is like the pomegranate seeds which Proserpine ate, and the result is equally disastrous in both cases, as it detains Balder and Proserpine underground, and the earth (Frigga or Ceres) must continue to mourn their absence.

Balder and Apollo.

Through Loki evil entered into the Northern world; Prometheus's gift of fire brought the same curse down upon the Greeks. The punishment inflicted by the gods upon both culprits is not unlike, for while Loki is bound with adamantine chains underground, and tortured by the continuous dropping of venom from the fangs of a snake fastened above his head, Prometheus is bound to Caucasus by adamantine fetters also, and a ravenous vulture continually preys upon his liver. Loki's punishment has another counterpart in that of Tityus, bound in Hades, and in that of Enceladus, chained beneath Mount Ætna, where his writhing produced earthquakes, and his imprecations were the sudden eruptions of the volcano. Loki further resembles Neptune in that he, too, assumed an equine form and was the parent of a wonderful steed, for Sleipnir rivals Arion both in speed and endurance.

The Fimbulwinter has been compared to the long preliminary fight under the walls of Troy, and Ragnarok, the grand closing drama of Northern mythology, to the burning of that famous city. "Thor is Hector; the Fenris wolf, Pyrrhus, son of Achilles, who slew Priam (Odin); and Vidar, who survives in Ragnarok, is Æneas." The destruction of Priam's palace is the type of the ruin of the gods' golden halls; and the devouring wolves Hati, Sköll, and Managarm, the fiends of darkness, are prototypes of Paris and all the other demons of darkness, who bear away or devour the sun maiden Helen.

According to another interpretation, however, Ragnarok and the consequent submersion of the world is only a Northern version of the Deluge. The survivors, Lif and Lifthrasir, are like Deucalion and Pyrrha, who were destined to repeople the world; and just as the shrine of Delphi alone resisted the destructive power of the great cataclysm, so Gimli stood radiant to receive the surviving gods.

Ragnarok and the Deluge.

We have already seen how closely the Northern giants resembled the Titans; now it only remains to mention that while the Greeks imagined that Atlas was changed into a mountain, so the giants in Germany formed the Riesengebirge, and that the avalanches were the burdens of snow which they impatiently shook off in changing their cramped positions. The apparition of one of the water giants, in the shape of a bull, in order to court the queen of the Francs, has its parallel in the story of Jupiter's wooing of Europa, and Meroveus is evidently the exact counterpart of Sarpedon. A faint resemblance can be traced between the giant ship Mannigfual and the Argo, for while the one is supposed to have cruised all round the Ægean and Euxine Seas, and to have made many places memorable by the dangers it encountered there, so the Northern vessel sailed about the North and Baltic Seas, and is mentioned in connection with the Island of Bornholm and the cliffs of Dover.

While the Greeks imagined that the Nightmares were the evil dreams which escaped from the cave of Somnus, the Northern race fancied they were female dwarfs or trolls, who crept out of the dark recesses of the earth to torment them. All magic weapons in the North were the work of the dwarfs, the underground smiths, while those of the Greeks were manufactured by Vulcan and the Cyclops, under Mount Ætna, or on the Island of Lemnos.

In the Sigurd myth we find Odin one-eyed like the Cyclops, who are also personifications of the sun. Sigurd is instructed by Gripir, the horse trainer, who, like Chiron, the centaur, is not only able to teach a young hero all he need know, and to give him good advice concerning his future conduct, but is also possessor of the gift of prophecy.

The marvelous sword which becomes the property of Sigmund and of Sigurd as soon as they prove themselves worthy to wield it reminds us of the weapon which Ægeus concealed beneath the rock, and which Theseus secured as soon as he had become a man. Sigurd, like Theseus, Perseus, and Jason, seeks to avenge his father's wrongs ere he sets out in search of the golden hoard, the exact counterpart of the golden fleece, which is also guarded by a dragon, and is very hard to secure. Like all the Greek sun-gods and heroes, Sigurd has golden hair and bright blue eyes. His struggle with Fafnir reminds us of Apollo's fight with Python, while the ring Andvaranaut can be likened to Venus's cestus, and the curse attached to its possessor is like the doom which accompanied Helen and caused endless bloodshed wherever she went.

Sigurd could never have conquered Fafnir without the magic sword, just as the Greeks could never have taken Troy without the arrows of Philoctetes, which are also emblems of the all-conquering rays of the sun. The recovery of the stolen treasure is like Menelaus's recovery of Helen, and it apparently brings as little happiness to Sigurd as his recreant wife did to the Spartan king.

Brunhild resembles Minerva in martial tastes, in physical appearance, and in knowledge; but when Sigurd deserts her in favor of Gudrun, she becomes angry and resentful like Œnone, when Paris left her to woo Helen. Brunhild's anger continues to accompany Sigurd through life, and she even seeks to compass his death, while Œnone, feeling she can cure her wounded lover, refuses to do so and permits him to die. Œnone and Brunhild are both overcome by the same remorseful feelings when their lovers have breathed their last, and both insist upon sharing their funeral pyres, and end their lives lying by the side of those whom they had loved.

Containing, as it does, a whole series of sun myths, the Volsunga Saga repeats itself in every phase; and just as Ariadne, forsaken by the sun hero Theseus, finally marries Bacchus, so Gudrun, when Sigurd has departed, marries Atli, the King of the Huns. He, too, ends his life amid the flickering flames of his burning palace or ship. Gunnar, like Orpheus or Amphion, plays such marvelous strains upon his harp that even the serpents are lulled to sleep. According to some interpretations, Atli is like Fafnir, and covets the possession of the gold. Both are therefore probably personifications " of the winter cloud which broods over and keeps from mortals the gold of the sun's light and heat, till in the spring the bright orb overcomes the powers of darkness and tempests, and scatters his gold over the face of the earth."

Swanhild, Sigurd's daughter, is another personification of the sun, as is shown by her blue eyes and golden hair; and her death under the hoofs of black steeds represents the blotting out of the sun by the clouds of storm or of darkness.

Just as Castor and Pollux hasten off to rescue their sister Helen when she has been borne away by Theseus, so Swanhild's brothers, Erp, Hamdir, and Sörli, hasten off to avenge her death.

Such are the main points of resemblance between the mythologies of the North and South, and the analogy serves to prove that they were originally formed from the same materials, and that the difference consists principally in the local coloring unconsciously given by each nation.

INDEX TO POETICAL QUOTATIONS.

Aager and Else, Ballad of, 170.

Anderson, Rasmus B. (translations from the Elder Edda in Norse Mythology, S. C. Griggs & Co., Chicago), 13, 24, 27, 43, 53, 78, 80, 81, 88, 110, 111, 118, 124, 139, 147, 149, 264, 266, 270.

Anster (translation from Goethe), 130.

Arnold, Matthew, 12, 14, 15, 21, 23, 28, 29, 46, 47, 64, 68, 84, 107, 126, 144, 160, 167, 183, 188, 189, 192, 193, 194, 196, 267, 271.

Baldwin, James, Story of Siegfried (Charles Scribner's Sons, New York), 172.

Brace (translation of ballad), 212.

Brand, 120.

Browning, Robert, 33, 34.

Coneybeare (translation from the Anglo-Saxon), 165.

Du Chaillu, Paul, Viking Age (Charles Scribner's Sons, New York), 142, 143.

Edda (Sæmund's, or the Elder), 11, 12, 13, 15, 16, 17, 18, 21, 24, 25, 27, 29, 37, 38, 39, 41, 42,.43, 45, 62, 65, 71, 75, 80, 81, 85, 88, 91, 96, 97, 98, 102, 104, 105, 107, 108, 110, 111, 112, 113, 114, 115, 116, 118, 122, 123, 124, 129, 131, 134, 137, 138, 139, 141, 142, 143, 144, 146, 147, 149, 151, 154, 157, 162, 163, 164, 168, 174, 175, 177, 183, 184, 185, 195, 198, 200, 204, 205, 206, 207, 236, 242, 244, 246, 254, 262, 260, 267, 269, 270, 271, 272.

Edda, The Younger, 53, 77, 78, 79.

Forman (translations), 37, 40, 57, 100.

Goethe, 130.

Gray, 184, 185, 186.

Grotta-Savngr, 122, 123.

Heine, 180, 216.

Hemans, 30, 161.

Henderson (translations), 11, 154, 162.

Herbert (translations), 77, 79, 114, 115, 116, 138.

Herrick, 121.

Hewitt (translation), 162.

Homer, 36.

Howitt, 36, 65, 195, 222, 272, 273.

Jones, Julia Clinton, Valhalla (Bosqui & Co., San Francisco), 11, 16, 53, 62, 86, 89, 90, 91, 101, 102, 103, 152, 156, 166, 167, 168, 171, 178, 182, 195, 203, 205, 208, 264, 266, 267.

Keightley (translation), 179.

Kingsley, Charles, 50, 127.

L. E. R., 178.

La Motte-Fouqué, 218.

Longfellow, Saga of King Olaf, in Tales of a Wayside Inn (Houghton, Mifflin & Co., Boston), 45, 63, 82.

Macdowall, Asgard and the Gods, 51.

Martin (translation from Heine), 216.

Mathisson, 179.

Meredith, Owen, 56, 57, 145.

Morris, William, 19, 24, 61, 113, 128, 156, 178, 226, 227, 228, 229, 230, 231, 232, 234, 235, 237, 238, 239, 241, 242, 243, 245, 246, 247, 248, 249, 250, 252, 255, 256, 258, 259, 260, 261.

Naogeorgus, 119.

Oehlenschläger, 36, 66, 67, 68, 138, 176.

Oxford Carol, 119.

Percy (translation from the Edda), 62.
Pfeiffer (translation), 265.
Pigott (translations from Oehlen-schläger), 66, 67, 68, 138, 176.
Scott, 32, 221.
Selcher (translation), 180.
Shakespeare, 85, 158, 223.
Southey, 35.
Spenser, 219.
Stagnelius, 179.
Stephens (translations from Frid-thiof's Saga in Viking Tales of the North, Rasmus B. Anderson, S. C. Griggs & Co., Chicago), 20, 28, 44, 52, 72, 73, 98, 106, 113, 128, 135, 173, 195, 197, 265, 270.
Taylor (translations from the Sagas), 15, 17, 18, 27, 37, 38, 92, 269, 271.

Tegnér, Fridthiof's Saga, 20, 28, 44, 52, 72, 73, 98, 106, 113, 128, 135, 173, 195, 197, 265, 270.
Thomson, 27, 168.
Thorpe (translations from Sæmund's Edda), 12, 16, 21, 25, 29, 31, 39, 41, 42, 45, 71, 75, 85, 91, 96, 97, 98, 102, 104, 105, 107, 108, 112, 113, 116, 129, 131, 134, 137, 138, 139, 141, 144, 146, 151, 157, 163, 164, 168, 169, 174, 175, 177, 183, 184, 185, 198, 200, 204, 205, 206, 207, 236, 242, 244, 246, 254, 269, 270.
Vail, 29.
Wagner, 37, 40, 57, 100.
Wägner, Asgard and the Gods, 51.
Wordsworth, 30.

GLOSSARY AND INDEX.

AAGER (ä′ger) and Else. Ballad of, 170.

ABEL. Cain in Wild Hunt because of the murder of, 32.

ABUNDANTIA (a-bun-dan′shyà). Same as Fulla, 51.

ABUNDIA. Same as Fulla, 51.

ACHERON (ak′e-ron). Giöll, the Northern, 288.

ACHILLES (a-kil′ēz). Balder, the Northern, 289; father of Pyrrhus, 290.

ADONIS (a-dō′nis). Odin, the Northern, 279; Idun lost like, 283; Odur, the Northern, 285.

ÆGEAN (ē-jē′an). Argo's cruise round the, 290.

ÆGEUS (ē-jē′us). Sigmund's sword compared to that of, 291.

ÆGIR (ā′jir). Tempests caused by, 107; god of the sea, 171–181; banquet in halls of, 204; Neptune, the Greek, 288.

ÆGIS (ē′jis). Fafnir's Helmet of Dread so called, 240.

ÆNEAS (ē-nē′as). Vidar, the Northern, 290.

ÆSIR (ā′sir). Northern gods called, 13; twelve in number, 18; Asgard, home of, 21; dispute between Vanas and, 21; to be supplanted, 38; inhabitants of Asia Minor, 43, 93, 107; Gylfi visits the, 44; Hrungnir feasts with the, 73; Freya visited by the, 77; recovery of hammer pleases the, 79; Fenris bound by the, 91; Suttung slain by the, 97; Idun welcomed by the, 104; Niörd among the, 108; Ægir not ranked with the, 171; Ægir visits the, 174; reward promised to the, 189; heralds sent out by the, 194; Loki slanders the, 198, 205; battle between the giants and the, 210; beginning and end of the, 263; Giallarhorn summons the, 265; giants come to fight the, 266; courage and death of the, 267; golden disks of the, 271; Greek gods compared to the, 277; Greek equivalent of dispute between the Vanas and the, 278.

ÆTNA (et′nà), MOUNT. Northern equivalent for earthquakes in, 289; dwarfs' forge equivalent to Vulcan's in, 291.

AFI (ä′fē). Riger visits, 142.

AFTERNOON. Division of day, 17.

AGNAR. Son of Hrauding, fostered by Frigga, 39, 40; gives Odin a drink, 41; becomes king, 42; Greek equivalent, 279.

AI (ä′ē). Riger visits, 141.

AKU-THOR (ak′u-thor). The charioteer, 64.

ALBERICH (al′bĕr-ikh). King of the dwarfs, 218.

ALBION (al′bi-on). Conjectured origin of name, 221.

ALF-BLOT. Sacrifices offered to elves, 223.

ALF-HEIM (alf′hīm). Home of elves in, 18, 221; Frey, ruler of, 112; Frey's return to, 114; Skirnir's return to, 116; Völund goes to dwell in, 165.

ALI. Same as Vali, 152.

ALLFATHER. The uncreated is, 10; Yggdrasil created by, 19; Odin called, 23; questions Vafthrudnir, 38; wrath of, 48; Longbeards named by, 50; disposes of Hel, Midgard snake, and Fenris, 89; sends Hermod to Finland, 145; goes with Vidar, to consult Norns, 148; dooms Brunhild to marry, 248; is slain, 269.

ALPHEUS (al-fē'us). Greek equivalent of Northern river-god, 288.

ALPINE ROSE. Attendants of Holda crowned with the, 55.

ALPS. Uller's home on the, 132; supposed meaning of the name, 221.

ALSVIDER (äl'svid-er). Steed of moon chariot, 14.

ALSVIN (äl'svin). Steed of sun chariot, 14.

ALTHEA (al-thē'á). Like mother of Nornagesta, 287.

ALVA. Cheru's sword borne by Duke of, 88.

ALVIS. A dwarf, changed to stone, 64, 65.

ALVIT. A Valkyr, marries mortal, 163.

AMALTHEA (am-al-thē'á). Compared to Heidrun, 278.

AMBROSIA. Northern gods eat boar's flesh instead of, 277.

AMERICA. Norsemen real discoverers of, 224.

AMMA. Riger visits, 142.

AMPHION (am-fī'on). Pied Piper like, 280; Gunnar like, 292.

AMPHITRITE (am-fi-trī'tē). Greek equivalent for Ran, 288.

AMSVARTNIR (am-svärt'nir). Lake where Fenris is bound, 91.

ANCHISES (an-kī'sēz). Northern equivalent of, 285.

ANDHRIMNIR (än-dhrim'nir). Cook in Valhalla, 27.

ANDVARANAUT (änd-vä'ra-nout). Ring of Andvari, 243; Sigurd appropriates, 246; Brunhild betrothed with, 248; Sigurd deprives Brunhild of, 252; Gudrun shows, 253; Gudrun sends Gunnar, 257; Greek equivalent, 291.

ANDVARI (änd'vä-rē). King of dwarfs, 218; Loki visits, 242; ring of, 243, 246, 248, 252, 257, 291.

ANGANTYR (än-gän'tēr). Ottar and, 128, 129; Tyrfing, sword of, 219.

ANGLO-SAXON. Heptarchy, 44; Uller called Vulder in, 132; Ægir called Eagor in, 173.

ANGUR-BODA (än-gur-bō'dá). Mother of Hel, Fenris, and Iörmungandr, 89, 166; mother of Gerda, 114; wife of Loki, 200; feeds wolves in Ironwood, 265.

ANNAR. Husband of Nott, 15.

ANTÆUS (an-tē'us). Greek equivalent for Hrungnir, 282.

APOLLO (a-pol'ō). Greek equivalent for Sol, 276; personification of the sun, 277; his contest with Marsyas compared to Odin's with Vafthrudnir, 279; marriage with Clio compared to Odin's with Saga, 279; flocks stolen by Mercury, 281; chariot compared to Frey's boar, 282; god of music, like Bragi, 283; Frey compared to, 284; Uller, a hunter like, 286; sun-god, like Balder, 289; sun myth, like that of Sigurd, 291.

APPLES. Gna's, 51, 226; Idun's, 100, 102, 104; Skirnir gives Gerda golden, 115; emblem of fruitfulness, 117; Norns watch over the magic, 154; Idun only can pick magic, 155; Rerir receives a magic, 226; comparison between Atalanta's and Gerda's, 285.

ARACHNE (a-rak'nē). Vafthrudnir, Northern equivalent, 279.

ARCHANGEL ST. MICHAEL. Wields Cheru's sword, 88.

ARCTIC CIRCLE. Scenery in the, 9.

ARETHUSA (ar-ē-thū'sá). Princess Ilse equivalent to, 288.

ARGO. Like Skidbladnir, 282; like Mannigfual, 290.

ARGUS. Story compared to that of Brock, 281; eyes compared to Thiassi's, 284; eyes compared to Heimdall's, 286.

ARIADNE (ar-i-ad'nē). Compared to Gudrun, 292.

ARION (a-rī'on). Compared to Sleipnir, 290.

ARTHUR. In Wild Hunt, 31, 32.

ARWAKR (ar'wak-r). Steed of sun chariot, 14.

ARYANS (är'yanz). Origin of, 9; myths of, 275.

ASA (ä'sä). Hoenir an, 22; Odin, the almighty, 118; Balder an, 182.

ASA-BRIDGE. Heimdall, guardian of the, 143.

ASABRU (ä'sä-brū). Bridge of gods, 20.

ASEGEIR (ä'se-gīr). Frisian elders, 135.

ASGARD (as'gärd). Home of gods, 18; one root of Yggdrasil in, 19; gods' palaces in, 21; Niörd welcomed in, 22; Odin's seat in, 23; heroes brought to, 26; Ifing separates Jötun-heim from, 38; Odin leaves, 42, 48; Odin returns to, 44; Gylfi visits, 44; Thor admitted into, 61; Bilskirnir in, 61; Brock visits, 68; Hrungnir boasts in, 73; unprotected state of, 76; Thor's return to, 79; Loki's return to, 80; Tyr, a god of, 84; Fenris brought to, 89; Odin brings inspiration to, 96; Idun and Bragi arrive in, 99; Idun to be lured out of, 101; Idun mourns for, 102,103,283; gods return without Idun to, 106; Frey, Freya, and Niörd in, 107; Niörd summoned to 108; Thiassi slain in,104,108; Skadi's honeymoon in, 109; Frey welcomed to, 112; Freya welcomed to, 124, 131; Uller rules in, 131; Balder leaves, 133; Forseti arrives in, 134; Heimdall arrives in, 137; Heimdall leaves, 141; Hermod returns to, 146; Vali comes to, 152; sin enters, 154; Ægir's visit to, 174; Odin's return to, 186; gods' sad return to, 192; messengers' return to, 195; Loki banished from, 200, 204; gods wish to fortify, 202; a Hrim-thurs threatens, 203; Loki forfeits, 206; fire giants storm, 267; Olympus, the

Greek, 276; Valkyrs, cupbearers in, 287.

ASGARDREIA (as-gard-rī'a). Wild Hunt called, 30.

ASIA. Plateau of Iran in, 9; Æsir come from, 43.

ASK (äsk). Ash tree from which gods made man, 19; compared to creation of Prometheus, 278.

ASLAUG (a-sloug'). The fostering of, 249.

ASYNJUR (a-sin'jŏor). Northern goddesses called, 18.

ATALANTA (at-ä-lan'tà). Her apples compared to Gerda's, 285.

ATLA (at'là). One of the wave maidens, 137.

ATLANTIC. Cruise of the Mannigfual in the, 214.

ATLAS. Greek equivalent for Riesengebirge, 290.

ATLI (at'lē). Gudrun wooed by, 257; treachery of, 258; Högni and Gunnar slain by, 259; Gudrun slays, 260; same as Attila, 262; Gudrun's union with, 292.

ATTILA (at'i-là). King of the Huns, has Cheru's sword, 87; same as Atli, 262.

AUD (oud). Son of Nott, 15.

AUDHUMLA (ou-dhŏom'là). Cow nourishes Ymir, 11.

AUGEIA (ou-gī'yà). Wave maiden, 137.

AUGSBURG (awgz'berg). Tyr's city, 84.

AURGIAFA (our-gyä'fà). Wave maiden, 137.

AUSTRI (ou'strē). Dwarf, supporter of heavenly vault at East, 14.

AUSTRIA. Curious custom in, 121.

BACCHUS (bak'kus). Atli compared to, 292.

BALDER (bäl'der). Allfather questions Vafthrudnir about, 38; son of Friggà, 43; Skadi wishes to marry, 109; Uller akin to, 133; Forseti, son of, 134; Forseti's connection with, 136; Vali, the avenger of, 152; god of sun and summer, 182-198; Loki, real murderer of,

204; absent at Ægir's banquet, 205; compared to Sigurd, 261; Loki deprives Æsir of, 263; the return of, 271; his death avenged, 286; Hodur murders, 287; compared to Greek sun-gods, 289.

BALMUNG (bäl'moong). Völund forges, 165; Odin drives into Branstock, 227; Sigmund secures, 228; Siggeir obtains, 229; Sinfiotli makes use of, 233, 234; Odin breaks, 237; Hiordis treasures shards of, 238; forged again, 243; Fafnir slain by, 245; Sigurd cuts off Brunhild's armor with, 247; laid it between Sigurd and Brunhild, 252; Guttorm slain by, 255; it is put on funeral pyre, 256; emblem of sunbeam, 261; compared to sword of Ægeus, 291.

BALTIC SEA. Cruise of Mannigfual in, 215, 290.

BARBAROSSA (bär-bâ-ros'sâ), FREDERICK. Leader of Wild Hunt, 31.

BAUCIS (baw'sis). Story of, compared with Geirrod and Agnar, 279.

BAUGI (bou'gē). Odin serves, 95.

BEAV. Same as Vali, 152.

BELDEGG (bel'deg). King of West Saxony, 44.

BELI (bel'ē). Death of, 117; son of Kari, 212.

BEHMER (bā'mer). Forest in Bohemia, 31.

BERGELMIR (ber-gel'mir). Escapes deluge, 12, 210; same as Farbauti, 199.

BERSERKER (bēr'serk-er). Rage of, 29; wolf held by, 190.

BERTHA (bēr'thâ). Same as Frigga, 58; mother of Charlemagne, 58; patroness of spinning, 59.

BESTLA (best'lâ). Giantess, 12; Æsir's mortal element from, 16.

BETHLEHEM (beth'lē-êm). Peace of Frodi when Christ was born in, 122.

BEYGGVIR (bīg'vir). Servant of Frey, 117.

BEYLA (bī'lâ). Servant of Frey, 117.

BIFRÖST (bē'frēst). Rainbow bridge, 20; Valkyrs ride over, 26, 160; description of, 137; Heimdall, warder of, 138; Odin rides over, 184; insufficieny of, 202; Helgi rides over, 236; downfall of, 267; Giallar-horn proclaims passage of gods over, 285.

BIL. The waning moon, 16.

BILLING. King of Ruthenes, 150; anxious to save Rinda, 152.

BILSKIRNIR (bil'skēr-nir). Thor's palace called, 61; thralls entertained in, 62.

BINGEN (bing'en). Rat Tower near, 35.

BISHOP HATTO. Story of, 35.

BLACK DEATH. Pestilence, 170.

BLACK FOREST. Giants in the, 215.

BLOCKSBERG (bloks'berg). Norns on the, 159.

BLODUG-HOFI (blō'dug-hō'fē). Frey's steed called, 113; Gymir's fire crossed by, 115; compared to Pegasus, 284.

BLOODY EAGLE. Description of, 85; Sigurd cuts the, 244.

BODEN (bō'den). The bowl of offering, 93.

BODVILD (bod'vēld). Betrayed by Völund, 165.

BOHEMIAN FOREST. Same as Behmer, 31.

BOLTHORN (bol'thorn). Giant called, 12.

BOLWERK (bol'wērk). Odin serves, 95.

BÖR (bēr). Marries Bestla, 12; earth created by sons of, 13; divine element of gods in, 16.

BORGHILD (bôrg'hild). Sigmund marries, 234; Sinfiotli poisoned by, 236; Sigmund repudiates, 237.

BORNHOLM (bôrn'holm). The formation of, 215; Mannigfual cruise connected with, 290.

BOUS (bō'us). Same as Vali, 152.

BRAGA-FUL (brä'gâ-ful). Toast in honor of Bragi, 99.

BRAGA-MEN. Northern scalds, 99.

BRAGA-WOMEN. Northern priestesses, 99.

BRAGI (brä'gē). Heroes welcomed to Asgard by, 26; Gunlod, mother of, 43; god of music and eloquence, 93–99; birth of, 97; the absence of, 102; Idun mourns for, 103; Idun sought by, 105; remains with Idun in Nifl-heim, 106; heroes welcomed by Heimdall and, 141; Ægir delights in tales of, 174; compared to Greek divinities, 283.

BRANSTOCK (bran'stok). Oak in Volsungs' hall, 226; sword thrust in the, 227; Sigmund under the, 234.

BRECHTA (brek'tà). Frigga, 58.

BREIDABLIK (bri'dà-blik). Balder's palace, 182; Balder's corpse carried to, 189; compared to Apollo's palace, 289.

BRIMER (bri'mer). Hall of giants, 273.

BRISINGA-MEN (bri-sing'à-men). Necklace of Freya, 127; Loki attempts to steal, 140, 286; emblem of fruitfulness, 141; made by dwarfs, 218.

BROCK. Jealousy of, 66; Loki's wager with, 67; three treasures of, 68; wager won by, 69; story compared with that of Io, 282.

BROCKEN (brŏk'en). Witches' dance on the, 130; Norns on the, 159.

BROWNIES. Same as dwarfs, 217; same as elves, 223.

BRUNHILD (broōn'hild). A Valkyr, 165; Sigurd finds, 247; Sigurd wooes, 248; Sigurd marries, 249; Sigurd forgets, 250; Gunnar loves, 251; Gunnar wooes by proxy, 252; wrath and jealousy of, 253; Högni swears to avenge, 254; rejoices at death of Sigurd, 255; death of, 256; Atli, brother of, 257; compared to Greek divinities, 261, 291, 292.

BRUNNAKER (broōn'na-ker). Idun's grove in, 102.

BURGUNDIAN (bĕr-gun'di-an). Ildico, a princess, 87; Gunnar, a monarch, 262.

BURI (bū'rē). Creation of, 11; giants' war against, 12.

BURI. Grove where Frey and Gerda meet, 116.

BYZANTINE (bi-zan'tin). Teutonic race influenced by that faith, 224.

CACUS (kā'kus). Hrungnir compared to, 282.

CADUCEUS (ka-dū'she-us). Gambantein compared to, 286.

CAIN'S HUNT. The Wild Hunt, 32.

CALAIS (kal'is). Mannigfual passes, 214.

CALYPSO (ka-lip'so). Compared to Holda, 281.

CAMOMILE. Called "Balder's brow," 182.

CAPITOLINE HILL. Vitellius slain on, 87.

CARTHAGE. Compared to Seeland, 280.

CASTOR. Compared to Erp, Sörli, and Hamdir, 292.

CATTEGAT (kat'e-gat). Ægir dwells in, 171, 288.

CAUCASUS (kaw'ka-sus). Loki's punishment compared to Prometheus's on the, 289.

CELTIC (sel'tik). Origin of the language, 274.

CEPHALUS (sef'a-lus). A personification of the sun, 277.

CERBERUS (sĕr'be-rus). Analogy of Garm and, 288.

CERES (sē'rēz). Compared to Rinda, 277; compared to Frigga, 279; compared to Groa, 282; personification of earth, 289.

CERYNEAN STAG (ser-i-nē'an). Story of, 276.

CHANGELINGS. Recipe for riddance of, 31, 219.

CHAOS. World rose from, 10; analogy between Greek and Northern conception of, 275.

CHARIOT. Sun and moon, 14; night and day, 15; Irmin's, 36; Holda's, 57; Nerthus's, 59; Thor's, 64, 69, 78; Frey's, 113; Freya's, 128; comparison between chariots of Greek and Northern gods, 276.

CHARLEMAGNE (shär'le-mān). Leader of Wild Hunt, 31, 32; Bertha, mother of, 58; Freya's temple destroyed by, 128; sword of, 165.

CHARLES V. Alva, general of, 88.

CHARLES'S WAIN. Same as Great Bear, 36.

CHARON (kā'ron). Compared to Mödgud, 288.

CHARYBDIS (ka-rib'dis). Northern parallel to, 283.

CHERU (kēr'ū). Same as Tyr, 86; sword of, 87, 88; Heimdall same as, 141.

CHERUSKI (ke-rŏŏs'kē). The worship of the, 86.

CHIRON (kī'ron). Compared to Gripir, 291.

CHRIST. Peace of Frodi at birth of, 122.

CHRISTIANITY. Attempts to introduce, 58, 88, 130, 212.

CHRISTIANS. Easter feast, 58; Norsemen in contact with, 272.

CHRISTIANSOË. Formation of, 215.

CHRISTMAS. Wild Hunt at, 31; Bertha's visit at, 59; Yule now called, 121; trolls celebrate, 213.

CLIO (klī'ō). Same as Saga, 279.

COLCHIS (kol'kis). Argo sails to, 282.

COLOGNE (ko-lōn'). Odin visits, 86.

COLUMBUS. Norsemen discovered America before, 224.

CORONIS (ko-rō'nis). Ratatosk compared to crow in story of, 278.

CRETAN LABYRINTH. Compared to Völund's house, 287.

CRETE (krēt). Odin's tomb at Upsala compared to Jupiter's in, 280.

CYCLOPS (sī'klops). Compared to Loki, 284; to Northern dwarfs, 291.

CYNTHIA (sin'thi-à). Mani compared to, 276.

DÆDALUS (dē'dà-lus). Compared to Völund, 287.

DAG. Son of Nott, 15; a treacherous Hunding, 235.

DAIN (dā'in). Stag on Yggdrasil, 20.

DANAE (dan'ā-ē). Compared to Rinda, 286.

DANES. Sacrificing place of, 53; Frey, ruler of, 122; Mysinger slays, 123; Ragnar Lodbrog, king of the, 249.

DANISH BALLAD. Aager and Else a, 170.

DANUBE. Cheru's sword buried on banks of, 87.

DAPHNE (daf'ne). Northern equivalent, 277.

DAY. Divisions of, 17; Vafthrudnir's questions about, 37.

DECEMBER. Uller's month, 133.

DEIANEIRA (dē-i-a-nī'rà). Loki's jealousy compared to that of, 289.

DELLINGER (del'ling-er). Third husband of Nott, 15.

DELPHI (del'fī). Compared to Gimli, 290.

DELUGE. Ymir's blood causes, 12; Ragnarok, a version of, 290.

DENMARK. Odin conquers, 43, 44; Frey in, 122; Freya in, 124; Konur, king of, 143; Norns visit, 157; horn in collection of, 214; Gudrun leaves, 257.

DESTINY. Compared to Orlog, 278.

DEUCALION (dū-kā'li-on) and Pyrrha compared to Lif and Lifthrasir, 290.

DIANA (di-a'nà). Mani corresponds to, 276; Skadi compared to, 284.

DIDO (dī'dō). Compared to Gefjon, 280.

DISES (dis'ez). Norns same as, 159.

DODONA (dō-dō'nà). Compared to Upsala, 280.

DOLMENS. Stone altars called, 85.

DONAR (dō'när). Same as Thor, 61.

DOVER. Mannigfual passes, 214, 290.

DRAUPNIR (droup'nir). Odin's ring called, 24; Sindri and Brock make, 67; Odin receives, 68; Skirnir offers Gerda, 115; laid on Balder's pyre, 190; Balder sends Odin, 194; emblem of fertility, 196; dwarfs fashion, 218; Greek equivalent, 282.

DROMA (drō'mà). Chain for Fenris, 90; proverb about, 283.

DRUIDS (drŏŏ'idz). Human sacrifices of, 85.

DRUSUS (drŏŏ'sus). Warned by a Vala, 158.

DRYADS (drī'adz). Northern equivalent for, 277.

DUKE OF ALVA. Cheru's sword found by, 88.

DUNEYR (dū′nīr). Stag on Yggdrasil, 20.

DUNMOW (dun′mou). Flitch of bacon, 121.

DURATHOR (dū′ra-thôr). Stag on Yggdrasil, 20.

"DUSK OF THE GODS." Wagner's opera, 225.

DVALIN (dvä′lin). Stag on Yggdrasil, 20; dwarf visited by Loki, 66.

DWARFS. Black elves called, 18; Ægir does not rank with, 171; one burned with Balder, 191; occupations of, 217–221; home of the, 273; nightmares are, 291.

EAGOR. Same as Ægir, 173.

EAST SAXONY. Conquered by Odin, 44.

EASTER. Same as Ostara, 57; stones, altars to Ostara, 58.

EÁSTRE. Same as Ostara, 57.

ECHO. Dwarf's talk, 218.

ECKHARDT (ek′hart). Tries to stop Tannhäuser, 56; compared to Mentor, 281.

ECLIPSES. Northern belief concerning cause of, 16.

EDDA. Collection of Northern myths, 10, 45, 225, 272; sword-runes in, 85; Frey's wooing related in, 114; Heimdall's visit to earth described in, 141; Sæmund, compiler of Elder, 224; heroic lays in, 225; Younger, 44.

EGIA (ē′gyà). Wave maiden, 137.

EGIL (ē′gil). Marries a Valkyr, 163; arrow of, 165; Thialfi's father, 174.

EGLIMI (eg′li-mē). Father of Hiordis, 237.

EINHERIAR (īn-hä′ri-ar). Odin's guests, 25; meat of, 27; daily battles of, 27; Valkyrs wait on, 162; Helgi, leader of, 236; Giallar-horn calls, 266; muster of, 268; all slain on Vigrid, 269.

EINMYRIA (īn-mē′ri-à). Daughter of Loki, 199.

EIRA (ī′rà). Goddess of medicine, 53.

EISA (ī′sà). Daughter of Loki, 199.

EITEL (ī′tel). Son of Atli and Gudrun, 257.

ELB. Water sprite, 179; god of the Elbe, 288.

ELBE (el′be). Drusus stopped at, 159; river named after Elb, 179.

ELBEGAST (el′be-gast). King of the dwarfs, 218.

ELDE (el′de). Ægir's servant, 174.

ELDHRIMNIR (el-dhrim′nir). Kettle in Valhalla, 27.

ELF. Water sprite, 179; elf lights, 222; elf locks, 223.

ELF. Sigmund buried by, 238; Hiordis marries, 239; second marriage of, 256.

ELIVAGAR (el-i-vag′ar). Streams of ice from Hvergelmir, 10, 12; Thor crosses, 76; rolling ice in, 168; Thor's journey east of, 171.

ELLI (el′lē). Thor wrestles with, 72, 73.

ELSE (el′sa). Ballad of Aager and, 170.

ELVES. Light elves, 18; occupation of the, 221–225; Ægir does not rank with the, 171.

ELVIDNER (el-vid′ner). Hel's hall, 168.

EMBLA (em′blà). The elm or first woman, 19; wooden, 278.

ENCELADUS (en-sel′a-dus). Compared to Loki, 289.

ENGLAND. Wild Hunt in, 32; Mayday in, 42; Yule in, 119; flitch of bacon in, 120, 121; miners in, 220; Albion same as, 221; fairies in, 221, 222; Oberon, fairy king in, 223.

ENGLISH CHANNEL. Mannigfual in, 214.

EPIMETHEUS (ep-i-mē′thŭs). Compared to Northern creators, 278.

ER. Same as Tyr, 86; Heimdall same as, 141.

ERDA. Same as Jörd, 61.

ERMENRICH (ēr′men-rēkh). Swanhild marries, 260; Gudrun's sons attack, 261.

ERNA. Jarl marries, 143.

ERP. Son of Atli and Gudrun, 257; son of Jonakur and Gudrun, 260;

slain by brothers, 261; to avenge Swanhild, 292.

ESKIMO. Skadi's dog, 111.

EUBŒA (ū-bē'à). Ægir's palace resembles Neptune's home in, 288.

EUHEMERUS (ū-hem'er-us). Historical theory of, 280.

EUROPA (ū-rō'på). Northern equivalent for story of, 290.

EUROPE. Æsir migrate into, 43; discovery of, 274.

EURYDICE (ū-rid'i-sē). Compared to Idun, 283.

EUXINE SEA (ūk'sin). Mannigfual's cruise compared to Argo's in, 290.

EVENING. Part of day, 17.

EXORCISM. Of spectral hound, 31; of changelings, 219, 220.

FADIR (fä'dir). Heimdall visits, 143.

"FAERIE QUEENE." Girdle in, 218.

FAFNIR (faf'nir). Son of Hreidmar, 240; gold seized by, 243; Sigurd goes to slay, 244, 245, 246; Gudrun eats heart of, 251; personification of cold and darkness, 262, 292; compared to Python, 291.

FAIRY RINGS. Magic spell of, 221.

FAIRYLAND. Alf-heim is, 112.

FARBAUTI (far-bou'tē). Same as Bergelmir, 199.

FAROE ISLANDS. Thor's name in, 81.

FATES. Yggdrasil sprinkled by Northern, 20; compared to Norns, 286, 287.

FEBRUARY. Vali's month is, 153.

FENG. Same as Odin, 244.

FENIA. Giantess slave of Frodi, 122.

FENRIS (fen'ris). Birth and capture of, 89; story of, 89–92; shoe to defend Vidar against, 148; prediction concerning, 149; Hel related to, 166; birth of, 200; Loki, father of, 212; released from bonds, 265; Loki leads, 268; death of, 269; Tyr alone dare face, 283; compared to Nemean lion, 286; compared to Pyrrhus, 290.

FENSALIR (fen'säl-ir). Frigga's palace, 47; Frigga spinning in, 187.

FIALAR (fyäl'ar). 1. Kvasir slain by, 93. 2. Red cock of Valhalla, 265.

FIMBULWINTER (fim'bul-win-ter). Prediction of coming, 192; terror of people at approach of, 264; Greek equivalent, 290.

FINITE NATURE. Of gods, 16.

FINNS. Hermod visits the, 145.

FIOLNIR (fyol'nir). 1. Birth of, 117. 2. Same as Odin, 244.

FIORGYN (fyôr'gēn). Genealogy of, 43; Frigga, daughter of, 46.

FLAX. Discovery of, 54–56.

FLINT. Origin of, 75, 76.

FLITCH. Of bacon, 120, 121.

FLORA. Nanna compared to, 289.

FOLKVANG (fōk'vang). Freya's home, 77, 124; warriors and wives in, 125; Loki enters, 140.

FORENOON. Part of day, 17.

FORNJOTNR (fôrn-yōt'nr). Same as Ymir, 199; giants descended from, 212.

FORSETI (fôr-set'e). God of justice, 134–137; Greek equivalent for, 286; the land of, 136.

FRAANANGER (frā-nan'ger). Loki takes refuge in, 206.

FRANCE. Golden age in, 58; Oberon, fairy king in, 223.

FRANCONIA. Conquered by Odin, 44.

FRANKISH. Kings' descent, 212: queen marries giant, 290.

FRANKLAND. Hindarfiall in, 246.

FRANKS. Worship of Tyr among the, 85; martial games of the, 88.

FRAU GODE (frou gō'dä). Same as Frigga, 59.

FRAU HOLLE. Same as Frigga, 54.

FRAU VENUS. Same as Holda, 56.

FREDERICK BARBAROSSA. Wild Hunt led by, 31.

FREKI (frek'ē). Odin's wolf, 24, 278.

FRENCH REVOLUTION. Wild Hunt announces, 32.

FREY (frī). Comes to Asgard, 22, 107; present for, 66; Gullin-bursti and Skidbladnir for, 68; toast to, 111; god of summer, 112–124; Freya, sister of, 124; rides with Freya, 128; Freya marries, 129; sword of, 219; elves governed by, 221; deprived of power, 223;

weapon, a stag's horn, 267; fights Surtr, 268; death of, 269; boar of, 282; Greek equivalent, 284.

FREYA (frī'á). Comes to Asgard, 22, 107; Hrungnir wants, 74; Loki borrows falcon plumes of, 77, 103; anger of, 77; Thor borrows garments of, 78; Thor personates, 79; Freya, goddess of beauty, 124–130; Friday sacred to, 128; Loki steals necklace of, 140, 199; the earth is, 141; Valkyrs led by, 162; promised to giant, 202; gods fear to lose, 203; dwarfs make necklace for, 218; Greek equivalents, 279, 282, 285.

FREYGERDA (frī-gēr'dá). Wife of Fridleef, 122.

FRIDAY. Sacred to Freya, 128.

FRIDLEEF (frid'leef). Same as Frey, 122.

FRIGGA (frig'á). Sits on Hlidskialf, 23; Odin disguises himself by advice of, 37; Agnar fostered by, 40; Odin outwitted by, 41, 49; wife of Vili and Ve, 42; Odin's wife, 43; seven sons of, 44; goddess of earth, 44–60; goddess of atmosphere, 46; secrecy of, 46; worshiped with Odin, 54; Thor, son of, 61; Nerthus same as, 108; Freya same as, 124; Uller marries, 131; Balder and Hodur, sons of, 182; Balder's depression noticed by, 183; all things swear to, 184; Loki wrests secret from, 187, 188; Hermod departs at request of, 189; the hope of, 192; emblem of earth, 196; grants Rerir's wish, 226; Greek equivalents, 279, 280, 282, 289.

FRISIANS (friz'ianz). Want new laws, 135; tradition of, 214.

FRO. Same as Frey, 112, 120, 284.

FRODI (frō'dē). Mill of, 122; death of, 123.

FULLA (ful'á). Attendant of Frigga, 48, 50, 57; Nanna sends ring to, 194.

FUNFENG (fun'feng). Ægir's servant, 174; Loki jealous of, 205.

FYLGIE (fēl'gye). Guardian spirit, 159.

GABRIEL'S HOUNDS. Wild Hunt in England, 30.

GALAR (gäl'ar). Kvasir slain by, 93.

GAMBANTEIN (gam'ban-tīn). Wand of Hermod, 145; like Caduceus, 286.

GAMLA UPSALA (gam'lá up-sä'lá). Odin's, Frey's, and Thor's mounds near, 118.

GANGLER (gang'ler). Deludes Gylfi, 44.

GANGRAD (gang'räd). Odin as, 37.

GANYMEDE (gan'i-mēd). Northern equivalent for story of, 283.

GARM. Dog of Hel, 167; Odin passes, 184; Hel followed by, 267; Loki leads, 268; death of, 269; compared to Cerberus, 288.

GEFJON (gef'yon). Gylfi visited by, 52; compared to Dido, 280.

GEFN. Same as Freya, 125.

GEIR ODDS (gīr odz). Carving of, 44, 169.

GEIRROD (gīr'rod). 1. Story of, 39–41. 2. Loki visits, 79; Thor visits, 80, 81, 148; Loki accompanies Thor to, 199; Greek equivalent, 279.

GELGIA (gel'gyà). End of Fenris's fetter, 92.

GERDA (gēr'dà). Wooed by Frey, 114, 115, 116; Greek counterparts of, 285.

GERI (gēr'ē). Odin's wolf, 24, 278.

GERMAN. Cheru's sword belongs to a, 86; Langobart, a long beard in, 50; Eckhardt the mentor, 56; belief in Lorelei, 180; topographical belief, 211; belief in fairies, 222; epic, Nibelungenlied, 225.

GERMANY. Wild Hunt in, 32; Odin conquers, 43; Abundantia worshiped in, 51; worship of Frigga in, 54; Easter-stones in, 58; golden age in, 58; belief in White Lady in, 59; Thor, kettle vender in, 64; storms in, 69; Nerthus in, 108; Frey is Fro in, 112; Yule in, 119; Freya's worship in, 124, 125; temple in Magdeburg in, 128; Freya now a witch in, 130; Uller in, 132; the Elbe in, 179; sandhills in, 214; sacrifices to elves in, 223.

GERSEMI (gēr'se-mē). Freya's daughter, 125.

GERTRUDE (gēr'trōōd). Replaces Freya in Germany, 130.

GIALLAR (gyäl'lar). Bridge in Nifl-heim, 167; Odin rides over, 184; trembling of, 192; Greek equivalent, 288.

GIALLAR-HORN. Heimdall's trumpet, 21, 138; last blast of the, 265; Greek equivalent, 286.

GIALP (gyälp). Incantation of, 80; Thor breaks the back of, 81; wave maiden called, 137.

GIANTS. Birth of ice, 11; gods slay the, 12; Ægir does not belong to the, 171; Hyrrokin summoned by the, 190; general account of the, 210-217; Brimer, hall of, 273.

GILLING (gil'ling). Giant slain by dwarfs, 93; death of wife of, 94.

GIMLI (gim'lē). Not consumed in Ragnarok, 272; compared to Delphi, 290.

GINNUNGA-GAP (ge-nōōn'gà-gap). Primeval abyss, 10; giants come to life in, 210.

GIOLL (gyol). Rock to which Fenris is bound, 92.

GIÖLL (gyēl). River boundary of Nifl-heim, 167; Hermod crosses, 192; like Acheron, 288.

GIUKI (gi-'ōōki). Niblung king, 250; Sigurd, blood brother of sons of, 251.

GIUKINGS. Sons of Giuki, 251; Sigurd slain by, 256.

GLADS-HEIM (glädz-hīm). Twelve seats in, 25; Tyr welcomed in, 84; Vali dwells in, 153; Odin returns to, 187.

GLASIR (glä'sir). The golden grove of, 25.

GLAUMVOR (gloum'vor). Second wife of Gunnar, 257.

GLAUR (glour). Husband of Sol, 14.

GLEIPNIR (glīp'nir). Manufacture of, 90, 91.

GLITNIR (glit'nir). Forseti's hall, 134.

GLITTERING HEATH. Fafnir on the, 243.

GLUT (glōōt). Loki's first wife, 199.

GNA (gnä). Messenger of Frigga, 51; carries apple to Rerir, 226; compared to Iris, 280.

GNIPA (gnē'pà). Cave in Nifl-heim, 167; Garm in, 288.

GNÎTAHEID (gnē'tà-hīd). Fafnir on, 243.

GNOMES (nōmz). Same as dwarfs, 18.

GOBLINS. Same as dwarfs, 217.

GODE (gō'de). Same as Frigga, 59.

GODEY. Thor's temple at, 82.

GODI. Human sacrifices by, 85.

GOLD. Freya's tears are, 126; the flame of the sea, 172.

GOLDEN AGE, 19; Norns arrive after, 154; Greek equivalent for Northern, 278; Frey's reign the, 284.

GONDEMAR (gon'de-mar). King of the dwarfs, 218.

GOTHLAND. Thor's temple in, 82; Sigmund leaves, 234; Ermenrich, king of, 260.

GOTHS. Siggeir, king of the, 226; Sigmund and Sinfiotli, prisoners of the, 233.

GRANE (grä'nē). Sigurd chooses, 240.

GREAT BEAR. Odin's Wain, 36.

GREENLAND. First settlement, 224.

GREIP (grīp). Thor breaks the back of, 81; a wave maiden called, 137.

GRENDEL. Son of Hler, 213.

GREYFELL (grä'fel). Same as Grane, 240; Sigurd loads hoard on, 246; Gunnar borrows, 251; Sigurd rides through flames on, 252; burned with Sigurd, 256.

GRID. Wife of Odin, 43, 80, 147; gives Vidar shoe, 148; with Vidar and Odin, 149.

GRIMHILD (grim'hild). Queen of the Niblungs, 250; wishes Gunnar to marry, 251, 252, 253; gives magic potion to Guttorm, 254; to Gudrun, 257.

GRIMNIR. Odin as, 41.

GRIOTTUNAGARD (gryot-tū'na-gärd). The dual in, 74.

GRIPIR (grē'pir). Stud-keeper of Elf, 240; prophecies of, 244; compared to Chiron, 291.

GROA (grō'ä). Incantations of, 76; compared to Ceres, 282.

GROTTI. Magic mill, 122, 123.

GRYPTO. Nun on, 212.

GUDRUN (goo-droon'). 1. A Valkyr marries Helgi, 235; self-sacrifice of, 236. 2. Gives magic potion to Sigurd, 250; marries Sigurd, 251; Sigurd gives ring to, 253; Sigurd offers to repudiate, 254; mourning of, 255; goes to Denmark, 256; wooed by Atli, 257; Niblungs helped by, 258; slays her children, 259; revenge of, 260; sends sons to avenge Swanhild, 261; same as Ildico, 262; Greek equivalent, 292.

GULL-TOP (gool-top). Heimdall's steed, 139.

GULLFAXI (gool-fax'ē). Hrungnir's steed, 73; Magni receives, 75.

GULLIN-BURSTI (gool'in-bērs-tē). Making of, 67; Frey receives, 68, 113; dwarfs manufacture, 218.

GULLIN-KAMBI (gool'in-käm-bē). Midgard rooster, 265.

GULLIN-TANI (gool'in-tä-nē). Same as Heimdall, 139.

GUNDICARIUS (goon-di-cär'i-us). Same as Gunnar, 262.

GUNGNIR (goong'nir). Odin's spear, 24; made of Yggdrasil wood, 37; runes on, 39; Dvalin makes point of, 66, 218; Odin receives, 68; Hermod throws, 144; Dag borrows, 235; Greek equivalent, 277.

GUNLOD (goon'lod). Mother of Bragi, 43; guardian of inspiration, 94; Odin visits, 95, 96.

GUNNAR (gun'när). Son of Giuki, 250; wooing of Brunhild by, 251; Brunhild marries, 253; repentance of, 255; Brunhild burned by order of, 256; Atli asks compensation for death of the sister of, 257; courage and oath of, 258; death of, 259; same as Gundicarius, 262; Greek equivalents, 292.

GUTTORM (goot'torm). Son of Giuki, 250; Sigurd slain by, 254; death of, 255.

GYLFI (gēl'fē). Odin welcomed by, 43; delusion of, 44; Gefjon visits, 52; Greek equivalent, 280.

GYMIR (gē'mir). Gerda, daughter of, 114; dwelling of, 115; Ægir same as, 173; son of Hler, 212.

HADES (hä'dēz). Compared to Niflheim, 281, 289; Jötun-heim compared to, 283.

HAGAL. Fosters Helgi, 235.

HAGEDISES (hag'e-dis-ez). Norns called, 159.

HAKON (hä'kon). Thora, daughter of, 256; marries a Valkyr, 287.

HALLINSKIDE (häl'lin-skē-de). Heimdall, same as, 141.

HAMADRYADS. Northern equivalents, 277.

HAMDIR (ham'dir). Son of Gudrun, 260; death of, 261; Greek equivalent, 292.

HAMELIN (ham'e-lin). Story of Pied Piper of, 33, 34; Greek equivalent, 280.

HAMMER. To dedicate boundaries, homes, marriages, 64; effect of, 70; the theft of the, 76; sign of the, 99.

HAMOND. Son of Sigmund, 234.

HANS VON HACKELBERG. Leader of Wild Hunt, 31, 32.

HAR. One of the triad seen by Gylfi, 44.

HARALD HARFAGER (här'fag-er). Norseman driven away by, 224.

HATI (hä'tē). Wolf pursuing orbs, 16; fed in Ironwood, 265; demon of darkness, 290.

HATTO. Bishop of Mayence, 35.

HÁVAMÁL (hav'a-mal). Code of laws and ethics, 45.

HEBE (hē'bē). Compared to Valkyrs, 287.

HECTOR. Northern equivalent, 290.

HEIDRUN (hī'droon). Goat supplying mead, 20; compared to Amalthea, 278.

HEIM-DELLINGER. Same as Heimdall, 139.

HEIMCHEN. Unborn children, 58.

HEIMDALL (hīm'däl). Bifröst guarded by, 21; nine mothers of, 43; Thor advised by, 78; Idun sought by, 105; Brisinga-men saved by, 127; watch-warder of Asgard, 137–143; connected with Æsir, 147; watchfulness of, 202; Loki to be slain by, 208; horn blown by, 265; Loki fights, 268; death of, 269; Greek equivalents, 286.

HEIME. Miming, the sword of, 165.

"HEIMSKRINGLA" (hīmz'kring-lå). Northern chronicle, 117.

HEL. Goddess of death, 32; birth and banishment of, 89, 200; realm of, 98; Idun's sojourn with, 105, 106; Uller with, 133; Skuld as, 159; the home of, 166–170; Odin visits, 184; daughter of Loki, 212; Hermod goes to, 184; couches spread by, 185; Hermod visits, 189; challenged, 192; urged to release Balder, 193; Hermod leaves, 194; the bird of, 265; arrives on Vigrid, 267; army of, 268; realm burned, 269; Garm guards gate of, 288; rake of, 289.

HEL-CAKE. Provided for Garm, 167.

HEL-GATE. Hermod passes, 167, 193.

HEL-SHOES. For feet of dead, 167.

HEL-WAY. Hermod journeys along the, 192.

HELA. Same as Hel, 166.

HELEN. Northern equivalents, 290, 291, 292.

HELFERICH (hel'fer-ēkh). Same as Elf, 238.

HELFRAT (hel'frat). Same as Elf, 238.

HELGI. Glorious career of, 234, 235; marriage of, 287.

HELIADES (he-lī'a-dēz). Northern equivalent, 285.

HELICON. Compared to Sokvabek, 279; to Od-hroerir, 283.

HELIGOLAND (hel'i-go-länd). Naming of, 131.

HELIOS (hē'li-os). Northern equivalent, 276.

HELMET OF DREAD, 242, 243; Sigurd uses the, 246, 251, 256.

HENGI-KIAPTR (heng'gē-kyäp'tr). Frodi's mill called, 122.

HENGIST (heng'gist). Descendant of Odin, 44.

HENRY. Murder of, 32; Ilse seen by, 215.

HERACLIDÆ (her-a-klī'dē). Northern equivalents, 279.

HERCULES (hēr'cu-lēz). Northern equivalents, 276, 281, 282, 286, 287, 289.

HERLA. Mythical king of England, 32.

HERLATHING. Wild Hunt called, 32.

HERMÆ (hēr'mē). Comparison between Northern boundaries and, 281.

HERMOD (hēr'mod). Heroes welcomed by, 26; Frigga mother of, 43; messenger of gods, 144, 146; journeys to Nifl-heim, 167, 189, 190–194; Greek equivalent, 286.

HEROD. Leader of Wild Hunt, 32.

HERU. Same as Tyr, 86; same as Heimdall, 141.

HERVOR (hēr'vor). Daughter of Angantyr, 219.

HIALLI (hyäl'lē). The trembling heart of, 259.

HIGH SONG. Same as Hávamál, 45.

HIMINBIORG (him'in-byērg). Heimdall's palace, 138, 143.

HIMINBRIOTER (him'in-bryō-ter). Thor slays, 175.

HINDARFIALL (hin'dar-fyäl). Sigurd comes to, 246; Brunhild asleep on, 248; Brunhild's story not ended on, 250.

HINDFELL (hind'fel). Same as Hindarfiall. 248

HIORDIS (hyôr'dis). Sigmund marries, 237; and leaves sword to, 238; Elf marries, 239; Sigurd obtains sword from, 244; death of, 256.

HIPPOMENES (hip-pom'e-nēz). Northern equivalent, 285.

HIUKI (hū'kē). Companion of Mani, 16.

HLADER (hlä'der). Thor's temple at, 82.

HLEIDRA (hlī'drå). Capital of Denmark, 53.

HLER. Same as Ægir, 171, 173; brother of Loki, 199; son of Fornjotnr, 212.

HLESEY. Ægir's palace in, 171, 174.

HLIDSKIALF (hlidz'kyålf). Odin's seat, 23, 25, 79; Odin sees sons of Hrauding from, 40; Frigga sits on, 46; Odin sees Vandals from, 49; Frey mounts, 114.

HLIN. Frigga's attendant, 51.

HLODYN (hlo'dēn). Same as Nerthus, 60.

HLORA. Thor fostered by, 61.

HLORRIDI (hlôr-rē'dē). Same as Thor, 61.

HNIKAR (hnē'kar). Same as Odin, 244.

HNOSS. Freya's daughter, 125.

HODMIMIR (hod-mē'mir). The forest of, 270.

HODUR (hō'der). Personification of darkness, 133, 197; Vali to slay, 152, 186; twin brother of Balder, 182; Balder to be slain by, 185; Balder slain by, 188, 189; Vali slays, 195, 287; explanation of myth of, 196; Loki guides hand of, 204; return of, 271.

HOENIR (hē'nir). Gives motion to man, 19; earth visited by, 101, 240; Loki joins, 102; hostage in Vana-heim, 107; peasant asks aid of, 201; survival of, 271.

HOFVARPNIR (hof-värp'nir). Gna's fleet steed, 51.

HÖGNI (hēg'nē). Son of Giuki, 250; Sigurd's death planned by, 254; warning given by, 257; captive, 258; the heart of, 259.

HOLDA. Same as Frigga, 54; Uller, husband of, 132.

HOLLAND. Frigga worshiped in, 59.

HOLLE, FRAU. Same as Frigga, 54.

HOLLER. Same as Uller, 132.

HOLMGANG. Thor's and Hrungnir's, 74, 75.

HOLY INNOCENTS. In Wild Hunt, 32.

HONEY. Drips from Yggdrasil, 20.

HORN. Same as Freya, 125.

HORSA. Descendant of Odin, 44.

HÖRSELBERG (hēr'sel-berg). Holda's abode in the, 56, 281.

HOSTAGES. Exchanged by Æsir and Vanas, 22.

HRAE-SVELGR (hrā-svelgr'). Giant eagle, 17; winds personified by, 277.

HRAUDING (hroud'ing). Agnar and Geirrod, sons of, 39.

HREIDMAR (hrīd'mar). Story of, 240–243.

HRIM-FAXI. Steed of Night, 15.

HRIM-THURS (hrēm-toōrs). Ice giants at creation, 11; Skadi, a, 109; architect of Valhalla, a, 203.

HROTHI (hrō'tē). Sword of Fafnir, 243.

HRUNGNIR (hrōōng'nir). Odin races with, 73; Thor's duel with, 74, 75; Greek equivalents, 282.

HRYM (hrēm). Vessel steered by, 266.

HUBERT, SAINT. Uller merged into, 132.

HUGI (hū'gi). Thialfi races with, 72.

HUGIN (hū'gin). Odin's raven, 24, 278; Od-hroerir discovered by, 94.

HULDA (hul'dà). Same as Holda, 54.

HULDRA (hul'drà). Same as Holda, 60.

HULDRA FOLK. Same as dwarfs and elves, 60, 217, 223.

HUNALAND. Gna flies over, 51, 234; Brunhild's home in, 248.

HUNDING. Helgi's feud with, 235; descendants of, 237, 257, 260, 262.

HUNGARY. Attila settles in, 87.

HUNS. Invasion by the, 87; Sigi, king of the, 226; Land of the, 257, 258, 260, 262, 292.

HUNTSMAN OF FONTAINEBLEAU. Leader of Wild Hunt, 32.

HVERGELMIR (hwer-gel'mir). The seething caldron, 10; Yggdrasil root near, 19; Nidhug in, 20; ice streams from, 168; wicked in, 169.

HYMIR (hē'mir). Story of Thor's visit and fishing with, 174–177.

HYNDLA (hēnd'là). Freya and Ottar visit, 129.

HYPERBOREANS. Northern equivalent, 276.

HYPERION. Northern equivalent, 276.

HYRROKIN (hēr'ro-kin). Ringhorn launched by, 190, 191.

IAFN-HAR (yåfn'här). Gylfi sees, 44.

IARN-GREIPER (yärn'grī-per). Thor's glove, 63.

IARNSAXA (yärn'sax-à). 1. Thor's wife called, 64; feeds wolves, 265. 2. A wave maiden, 137.

ICELAND. Thvera in, 118; Freya in, 124; maze in, 164; earthquakes and geysers in, 208; Norsemen settle in, 272; scenery of, 275.

ICELANDERS. Records of, 9, 139; call mountains Jokul, 211.

ICELANDIC. Shores, 224.

IDA. Same as Idavold, 187; gods return to, 271; same as Asgard, 277.

IDAVOLD. Plain where gods dwell, 18; gods play on, 187; Balder slain on, 188; last meeting on, 271.

IDISES (ē-dis'ez). Norns, 159.

IDUN (ē'doon). Daughter of Ivald, 98; story of, 100–106; returns to Asgard, 108; apples of, 155; Loki betrays, 199; Greek equivalents, 283, 284.

IFING (ē'fing). River surrounding Idavold, 18; Vafthrudnir asks about, 38; Loki flies across, 77.

ILDICO (il'di-co). Wife of Attila, 87, 88; same as Gudrun, 262.

ILSE (il'se). Story of Princess, 215; compared to Arethusa, 288.

ILSENSTEIN (il'sen-stīn). Home of Princess Ilse, 215.

INDIA. Languages of, 274.

INGLINGS. Frey's descendants called, 122, 279.

INGVI-FREY. Story of, 117–122.

INSPIRATION. The story of the draft of, 93–97.

IO. Northern equivalents for story of, 280, 281.

IÖRMUNGANDR (yēr'mun-gandr). Birth and banishment of, 89; Hel related to, 166; Thor angles for, 176; origin of, 200; rises from sea, 266; Loki leads, 268; tempests caused by, 288.

IRAN (ē-rän'). The plateau of, 9.

IRIS (ī'ris). Compared to Gna, 280.

IRMIN (ēr'min). Same as Odin, Heimdall, or Hermod, 36, 141, 146.

IRMIN'S WAY. The Milky Way, 36.

IRMINSUL (ēr'min-sŏol). Destroyed by Charlemagne, 36.

IRONWOOD. Iron leaves of, 167; wolves fed in, 265.

ISLANDS. Eglimi, king of the, 237.

ITALY. Golden Age in, 284.

IVALD (ē'väld). Dwarf blacksmith, 66, 86; Idun, daughter of, 98.

JACK AND JILL. Origin of story, 17.

JACK IN THE GREEN, 42.

JACK-O'-LANTERNS. Elf lights, 222.

JANUARY. Yule in, 121, Vali's month, 153.

JARL (yärl). The birth of, 143.

JASON. Northern equivalents, 282, 291.

JILL. The origin of Jack and, 143.

JOHN THE BAPTIST, 32.

JOKUL (yō'kŏol). Same as Jötun, 211.

JONAKUR. Gudrun, wife of, 260.

JÖRD (yērd). Daughter of Nott, 15; wife of Odin, 43, 46, 61.

JÖTUN-HEIM (yē'tŏon-hīm). Home of giants, 12; Vafthrudnir inquires about, 38; frost comes from, 69; Loki's journey to, 78; Odin gazes at, 79; Thor visits Geirrod in, 80; Loki's progeny in, 88, 89; Odin goes to, 94; Skirnir visits, 115; Thor personates Freya in, 127; Hel born in, 166; Hyrrokin dwells in, 190; Loki goes to, 198, 199; Loki's home in, 200; giants dwell in, 210; Tartarus compared to, 275; Idun in, 283.

JÖTUNS. Earth in the power of the, 48; the origin of, 210, 211; Thor feared by the, 211.

JOVE. Day of, in the North, 282.

JOYEUSE (zhwä'yēz). Charlemagne's sword, 165.

JUDEA (ju-dē'à). Bethlehem in, 122.

JUNO. Compared to Frigga, 280, 282; to Freya, 287.

JUPITER. Odin compared to, 275, 277, 278, 279, 280; Amalthea, nurse of, 278; quarrels with Neptune, 278; outwitted by Juno, 280; Thor compared to, 281; secures Ganymede, 283; compared to Frey, 284; wishes to marry Thetis, 286; wooing of Europa, 290.

JUSTICE. Compared to Forseti, 286.

JUTERNAJESTA (yōō-ter-na-jest′à). Senjemand loves, 212.

KARI (kär′ē). Brother of Ægir, 171; brother of Loki, 199; son of Fornjotnr, 212.
KARL. The birth of, 142.
KERLAUG (kēr′loug). Thor wades across, 62.
KNEFRUD (knef′rōōd). Invites Niblungs to Hungary, 257; death of, 258.
KOBOLD. Same as dwarfs, 18, 217; same as elves, 223.
KONUR. The birth of, 143.
KOPPELBERG. Children in the, 34.
KORMT. Thor crosses, 62.
KVASIR (kvä′sir). 1. Murder of, 93; Odin covets mead of, 94. 2. Loki surprised by, 206.

LAEDING (lā′ding). Chain for Fenris, 90; proverb concerning, 283.
LAGA (lä′gà). Same as Saga, 43.
LAMPETIA (lam-pe-tī′à). Northern equivalent for flocks of, 276.
LANDVIDI (länd-vē′di). Home of Vidar, 147, 149.
LANGOBARDEN. Story of, 50; Greek equivalent for, 280.
LAUFEIA (lou-fī′à). Mother of Loki, 199.
LAUGARDAG (lou′gar-dag). Saturday called, 209.
LAURIN (lou′rin). King of the dwarfs, 218.
LEIPTER (līp′ter). Sacred stream in Nifl-heim, 168.
LEMNOS. Northern equivalent for forge of, 291.
LERAD (lā′räd). Topmost bough of Yggdrasil, 20, 26; the animals upon, 20.
LESSOE. Island home of Ægir, 171.
LETHRA (leth′rà). Sacrifices offered at, 53.
LIF. One of the survivors of Ragnarok, 270; Greek counterpart of, 290
LIFTHRASIR (lif′thrä-sir). One of the survivors of Ragnarok, 270; Greek counterpart, 290.

LIGHT ELVES. Alf-heim, dwelling of, 118.
LIOD (lyōd). Same as Gna, 226.
LIOS-ALFAR ((lyōs′-alf-ar). Same as light elves, 221.
LIOS-BERI (lyōs′-bā-rē). Month of Vali, 153.
LIT, dwarf slain by Thor, 191.
LODUR (lō′dōōr). Gives blood to man, 19; same as Loki, 199.
LOFN (lōfn). Attendant of Frigga, 52.
LOGI (lō′gē). Cook of Utgard-loki, 71; wild fire, 72.
LOGRUM (lō′grum). Lake of, 53.
LOKI (lō′kē). God of fire, 19; Sif's hair stolen by, 65; Thor attacks, 66; different forms of, 66; wager with Brock, 67; flight of, 68; Brock sews lips of, 69; eating-wager of, 71; hammer recovered by, 76; marries giantess, 88; adventure with eagle, 101; called to account, 103; south wind is, 104; Skadi laughs at antics of, 109; the lightning is, 111; Brisinga-men coveted by, 127; falcon plumes borrowed by, 127; Freya urged by, 129; Freya accused by, 130; Hel, daughter of, 166; Ægir, brother of, 171; Frigga questioned by, 187; Hodur's hand guided by, 188; Thok, same as, 194; the jealousy of, 196; tempter personified by, 197; god of fire, 198–209; son of Fornjotnr, 212; visits the earth, 240; slays Otter, 241; secures hoard, 242; Æsir tolerate, 263; released from bonds, 265; boards Nagilfar, 266; foes led by, 267, 268; death of, 269; Greek equivalent for Loki's theft, 281; comparisons, 283, 286, 289, 290.
LOMBARDS. Story of the, 50.
LOMBARDY. The possession of, 50.
LONGBEARDS. The saga of the, 50.
LORELEI (lō′re-lī). Story of, 179, 180; Greek equivalent, 288.
LORRIDE (lor′ri-de). Thor's daughter, 64.
LUCIFER. Loki the mediæval, 198.
LYDIAN QUEEN. Northern equivalent, 281.

LYGNI (lĕg'ni). Wars against Sigmund, 237, 238; Sigurd slays, 244.

LYMDALE (lĕm'dāl). Brunhild's home at, 248.

LYNGVI (lēng'vi). Island where Fenris is bound, 91.

"MACBETH." The Norns in, 158.

MAELSTROM (māl'strom). Millstones form the, 123.

MAGDEBURG. Freya's temple at, 128.

MAGNI. Thor's son, 64, 75; survival of, 271; Greek equivalent, 282.

MAID MARIAN. On May day, 42.

MÄLAR LAKE (mä'lar). Legend of its formation, 53.

MANA-HEIM (man'à-hīm). Same as Midgard, 19; Greek equivalent, 276.

MANAGARM. The feeding of, 265; Greek equivalent, 290.

MANI (man'e). The moon, 14; his companions, 16; death of, 264, 265; equivalent, 276.

MANNIGFUAL (man'ig-fū-al). Ship, 214, 215; Greek equivalent, 290.

MARAS (mär'az). Female trolls, 220.

MARDEL (mär'del). Freya, 125.

MARS. Northern equivalents, 282, 285.

MARSYAS (mär'shў-as). Compared to Vafthrudnir, 279.

MAY FESTIVALS, etc., 42.

MEAD. Heidrun supplies mead, 20.

MECKLENBURG. Worship of Frigga in, 59.

MEGIN-GIÖRD (mä'gin-gyērd). Thor's belt, 63; Thor tightens, 72.

MELEAGER (mel-e-ā'jer). Nornagesta compared to, 287.

MEMOR. Same as Mimir, 36.

MENELAUS (men-e-lā'us). Northern equivalent, 291.

MENIA (men'i-a). Frodi's giantess slave, 122.

MENTOR. Eckhardt compared to, 281.

MERCURY. Northern equivalents, 279, 281, 282, 283.

MERMAIDS. In Ægir's palace, 288.

MEROVEUS (mer-ō've-us). Birth of, 212; Greek equivalent, 290.

MEROVINGIAN (mer-ō-vin'ji-an). Mythical descent of kings, 212.

MESNÉE D'HELLEQUIN (mä-nā del-ē-cang). Wild Hunt in France, 32.

MIDGARD (mid'gärd). Earth called, 13; man dwells in, 19; root of Yggdrasil in, 19; Bifröst spans, 20; fields of, 113; Uller rules, 131; rooster of, 265.

MIDGARD SNAKE. Thor attempts to lift, 73; Hymir fears, 175; Thor hooks, 176, 177; birth of, 199; rises from sea, 266; Thor slays, 268, 269; equivalent, 276; tempests caused by, 288.

MIDNIGHT. Part of day, 17.

MIDSUMMER. Balder disappears at, 133; night, fairy revels, 223; eve, festival, 197.

MILKY WAY in Germany and Holland, 36, 59.

MIMING (mē'ming). A sword, 165.

MIMIR (mē'mir). Well of, 19, 92, 94, 137, 138; god of ocean, 171; son of Hler, 212; Odin's last talk with, 268.

MINERVA. Northern equivalents, 278, 279, 285.

MINOS (mī'nos). Northern equivalent, 287.

MIÖLNIR (myēl'nir). Thor's hammer, 63; Thor receives, 68; Thor gives life with, 70; Thor slays with, 177; giant slain by, 204, 211; dwarfs make, 68, 218; Midgard snake slain with, 269; Greek equivalent for, 281.

MISTLETOE. Oath not sworn by, 184.

MÖDGUD (mud'gŏŏd). Warder of Giöll, 167, 192, 193; Greek equivalent, 288.

MODI (mō'dē). Thor's son, 64; survival of, 271.

MODIR. Heimdall visits, 143.

MŒRÆ (mē'rē). Compared to Norns, 278.

MOERI (mē'rē). Thor's temple at, 82.

MOKERKIALFI (mō'ker-kyålf-ē). A clay image which Thialfi fights, 74.

MORNING. Part of day, 17.

MORS. Northern equivalent, 288.
MOSELLE (mō-zel'). Celebrations along the, 119.
MOSS MAIDENS. Wild Hunt for, 31; Greek equivalents, 223.
MOTHER NIGHT. Longest night in year, 119.
MÜHLBERG (mül'berg). Battle of, 88.
MUNDILFARI (moon'dil-fär-ē). Father of sun and moon drivers, 14.
MUNIN (mū'nin). Odin's raven, 24; Od-hroerir found by, 94; Greek equivalent, 278.
MUSPELL (moos'pel). Sons of, 266.
MUSPELLS-HEIM (moos'pels-hīm). Home of fire, 10; sparks from, 14; host from, 266.
MYSINGER (mē'sing-er). Viking, slays Frodi, 123.

NAGILFAR (nag'il-fär). Launching of, 266.
NAGILFARI (nag'il-fär-i). Nott's first husband, 15.
NAIN. Dwarf of death, 98.
NAL. Mother of Loki, 199.
NANNA (nän'nà). Forseti's mother, 134; Balder's wife, 182; death of, 190; accompanies Balder, 193; sends carpet to Frigga, 194; emblem of vegetation, 196; compared to Greek divinities, 289.
NARVE (när'va). Son of Loki, 200; death of, 207.
NASTROND (nä'strond). The wicked in, 169, 272; compared to Tartarus, 288.
NECKAR (nek'kar). God and river, 178, 179, 288.
NECKS. Water sprites, 178, 179.
NECTAR. Compared to Northern drink, 277.
NEMEAN LION (nē'mē-an lī'on). Northern equivalent, 286.
NEPTUNE. Northern equivalents, 275, 278, 284, 288, 289.
NEREIDES (ne-rē'i-dēz). Northern equivalents, 288.
NEREUS (nē're-us). Niörd like, 284.
NERTHUS (nēr'thus). Same as Frigga, 59, 60; Niörd's wife, 108, 112, 124.

NIBELUNGENLIED (nē'be-loong-en-lēd). German epic, 225.
NIBLUNGS (nē'bloongz). Sigurd visits the, 250; Brunhild, queen, 251, 252; lament of, 256; visit Atli, 257, 258.
NICK, OLD. Origin of the name of, 178.
NICORS (nik'orz). Sea monsters, 178.
NIDA (nē'dà). Home of dwarfs, 273.
NIDHUG (nē'dhoog). Gnaws Yggdrasil, 20, 149, 169, 265; flies over Vigrid, 267.
NIDUD (nē'dood). King of Sweden, 163, 164, 165; comparison, 287.
NIFL-HEIM (nifl'hīm). Land of mist, 10; root of Yggdrasil, in, 19; Bifröst connects, 20; Odin gazes into, 39; Hel in, 89, 166; Hel's bird in, 265; Idun in, 105; Uller in, 133; horn heard in, 138; Odin visits, 184; Hermod visits, 189, 190; Balder in, 193; equivalents, 276, 283, 288, 289.
NIGHT. Birth of, 15; horses of, 37.
NIÖRD (nyērd). A hostage, 22; god of sea, 107–111, 171; Skadi marries, 109, 134; glove of, 111; Frey, son of, 112–114; semi-historical, 117; oath sworn by, 118; Freya, daughter of, 124; Greek equivalents, 171, 285.
NIP. Father of Nanna, 182.
NIXIES. Dwell with Ægir, water spirits, 178, 179, 288.
NÔATÛN (noo'à-toon). Niörd's home, 107, 108, 109, 110.
NOON. Part of day, 17.
NORDRI (nôr'drē). Dwarf, supports heaven, 14.
NORNAGESTA (nôrn-a-ges'tà). Story of, 157, 158; compared to Meleager, 287.
NORNS. Yggdrasil sprinkled by, 20; office of, 38, 154–159; decree of, 86; Odin questions, 145, 148; Valkyrs same as, 162; mortals visited by, 234; torn web of, 267; Greek equivalents, 278, 286.
NORSEMEN. Elves guide, 224; various beliefs of the, 272.
NORTH SEA. Mannigfual in, 214, 290.

NORVI (nôr'vē). Father of Night, 15, 154; ancestor of Norns, 154.

NORWAY. Landscape in, 9; Odin conquers, 43, 44; Thor, god in, 62–64; kings of, 111, 117; Maelstrom near, 123; Freya in, 124, 130.

NOTT. Goddess of night, 15.

NOVEMBER. Sacred to Uller, 132, 133.

NYMPHS. Compared to elves, 277.

OATHS. Sworn on Gungnir, 24, 279; on swords, 85; by Frey, 118; on boar, 120; by Uller, 133; by Leipter, 168; in favor of Balder, 184.

OBERON (ō'be-ron). Fairy king, 218, 223.

OBERWESEL (ō-ber-vä'zel). Fisherman of, 180.

OCEAN. Ymir's blood, 13.

OCEANIDES (ō-sē-an'i-dēz). Compared to wave maidens, 288.

OCEANUS (ō-se'à-nus). Northern equivalent, 276.

OD-HROERIR (od-hrē'rir). Kettle of inspiration, 93; Odin in quest of, 103; compared to Helicon, 283.

ODIN (ō'din). Birth of, 12; creates man, 19; hall of, 20; goat of, 20; brother of, 22; general account of, 23–45; attributes of, 24; mantle and spear of, 24; footstool of, 25; god of victory, 26; battle loved by, 28; the Wild Huntsman, 32; leader of souls, 34; constellation of, 36; one eye of, 36, 88, 92, 227, 267; Geirrod fostered by, 40; historical Odin, 40, 117, 280; serpents of, 45; statues of, 45; Frigga, wife of, 46; toast to, 46; return of, 48; Thor, son of, 61; present for, 66–68; Hrungnir races with, 73; downfall of, 268; Thrymheim viewed by, 79; Grid, wife of, 80, 147; compared to Tyr, 84; spear of, 68, 86, 218, 235; disposes of Loki's progeny, 89, 166; discovers Od-hroerir, 94; Gunlod won by, 96; runes of, 99; visits earth, 101; Loki joins, 102; Loki called to account by, 103; gives Idum wolfskin, 105; sky is, 106; Hoenir related to, 107;

throne of, 114; Freya marries, 129; Uller replaces, 131; drives Uller away, 132, 133; wave maidens, wives of, 137; Heimdall as, 141; Hermod, messenger of, 144; runic staff of, 145; to lose son, 146; prediction concerning, 149; Rinda courted by, 150–152. 195; visits Norns, 156, 267; Valkyrs attend, 160; decree concerning Völund's sword, 165; Balder, son of, 182, 183; Vala consulted by, 184-186; cheered by Frigga, 187; lends Sleipnir, 189; whispers to Balder, 190; Draupnir returned to, 194; emblem of sky, 196; Loki, brother of, 198; trilogy, 199; helps peasants, 201; Sleipnir, horse of, 204; Loki surprised by, 206; visits giants, 211; Sigi, son of, 225; gives sword to Sigmund, 227, 233; Helgi approved by, 236; receives Sinfiotli, 237; Sigurd advised by, 240, 244, 245; visits Hreidmar, 241; Brunhild punished by, 248; comparisons between Greek divinities and, 277, 278, 279, 280, 283, 284, 286, 291.

ODENSÖ (ō'den-sē). Founded by Odin, 43.

ODUR (ō'dōor). Freya's husband, 125; Freya finds, 126; Freya's search for, 127; sunshine is, 129; equivalents, 279, 285.

ŒNONE (ē-nō'ne). Compared to Brunhild, 292.

ŒTA (ē'tà). Northern equivalent for pyre on, 289.

OKOLNUR (o-kol'nōor). Giants dwell in, 273.

OLAF (ō'läf). Destroys statues, 45, 82, 83, 118; Yule changed by, 121; Nornagesta visits, 158, 287; giants in days of, 212.

OLAF, SIR. Captured by fairies, 222.

OLD NICK. Origin of name, 178.

OLDENBURG. Drinking horn, 214.

OLLER. Same as Uller, 131.

OLRUN (ol'rōon). Marries mortal, 163.

OLYMPUS (o-lim'pus). Northern equivalents, 276, 277, 278, 287.

OMENS. Wolves are good, 24.
OMPHALE (om'fa-lē). Northern equivalent for, 281.
OREADES (o-rē'a-dez). Compared to Northern divinities, 277.
ORGELMIR (ôr-gel'mir). Ice and fire giant, 11.
ORION (o-rī'on). Northern equivalents for, 47, 284, 286.
ORLOG (ôr'log). Irrevocable decrees of, 155, 186; equivalent, 278.
ORMT. Thor wades across, 62.
ORPHEUS (ôr'fūs). Northern equivalents, 280, 283, 289, 292.
ORVANDIL (ôr-van'dil). Thor brings home, 76; equivalent, 282.
OSTARA (os'tä-rà). Eástre, 57.
OTTAR. Freya helps, 128, 129.
OTTER. Slain by Loki, 241.
OXFORD. Yule at, 119.

PADERBORN (pä'der-born). Irminsul near, 36.
PARIS. Northern equivalent, 290, 292.
PEACE FRODI. Story of, 122.
PEACE STEADS. Of the gods, 18, 189.
PEGASUS (peg'à-sus). Blodug-hofi compared to, 284.
PELIAS (pē'li-as). Northern equivalent, 282.
PENEUS (pe-nē'us). Northern equivalent, 288.
PENTECOST. Princess Ilse appeared at, 215.
PENTLAND FIRTH. Whirlpool in, 123.
PERSEUS (per'sūs). Northern equivalent, 287, 291.
PHAETHUSA (fä-e-thū'sa). Northern equivalent, 276.
PHAETON (fä'e-ton). Northern equivalent, 285.
PHILEMON (fi-lē'mon). Northern equivalent, 279.
PHILOCTETES (fil-ok-tē'tez). Northern equivalent for arrows of, 291.
PHŒBE (fē'be). Equivalent, 276.
PHŒBUS (fē'bus). Equivalent, 276.
PHŒNICIAN (fē-nish'an). Dwarfs compared to miners, 220.

PIED PIPER. Story of, 33, 34; Greek equivalent, 280.
PLUTO. Northern equivalents, 275, 277, 281.
POLLUX (pol'uks). Northern equivalent, 292.
PRIAM (prī'am). Compared to Odin, 290.
PROCRIS (prō'kris). Northern equivalent, 277.
PROMETHEUS (prō-mē'thūs). Northern equivalent, 278, 289.
PROSERPINE (pros'er-pin). Northern equivalents for, 279, 281, 282, 283, 289.
PROTEUS (prō'tūs). Northern equivalent, 286.
PSYCHOPOMPUS (sī-ko-pŏm'pus). Compared to Odin, 280.
PUCKS. Same as dwarfs, 217.
PYRRHA (pir'à). Northern equivalent, 290.
PYRRHUS (pir'us). Northern equivalent, 290.
PYTHON (pī'thon). Compared to Fafnir, 291.

QUICKBORN. Magic fountain of, 57.

RAGING HOST. Same as Wild Hunt, 30, 32.
RAGNAR LODBROG (râg'nar lŏd'brog). Aslaug marries, 249.
RAGNAROK (râg'nà-rŭk). Heimdall to announce, 21; murder, precursor of, 204; recruits for battle at, 236; the tragedy of, 270; comparisons, 273, 290; Fenris dies at, 286.
RAN. Wife of Ægir, 172, 178; sister of Loki, 199; Loki makes a net like, 206; Loki borrows net of, 242; compared to Amphitrite, 288.
RANDWER. The death of, 260.
RAT TOWER. In the Rhine, 35.
RATATOSK (rä'tà-tusk). Squirrel, telltale, 20; equivalent, 278.
RATI (rä'tē). Odin's auger, 95.
REGIN (rā'gin). Sigurd educated by, 239; the story of, 240–243; Sigurd to slay Fafnir for, 243; sword forged by, 244; demands satisfaction, 245; death of, 246.

REINE PÉDAUQUE (rän pe-dōk'). Frigga same as, 59.

RENOWN. Compared to Heimdall, 286.

RERIR (rā'rir). Son of Odin, receives apple, 51, 52, 226; Greek equivalent for story of, 261.

RESURRECTION. Word whispered by Odin, 38, 190.

RHINE. Tower in the, 35; gold of the, 164, 225; divinity of the, 179, 288; Lorelei in the, 179–81; Brunhild and Gudrun bathe in the, 253; hoard sunk in the, 257.

RIESENGEBIRGE (rē'zen-ge-bēr-ge). Giant mountains, 211, 290.

RIGER (rē'ger). Heimdall visits earth as, 141.

RINDA (rin'dà). Wife of Odin, 43, 195; prophecy concerning, 146, 185; Odin courts, 150, 195; Greek equivalents, 277, 286.

RINGHORN. Balder's pyre on, 190, 191; Greek equivalent, 289.

RODENSTEIN (rō'den-stīn). Wild Hunt led by, 31, 32.

ROMANS. Æsir driven from Asia Minor by, 43; Vitellius, prefect, 86; Christianity, 224.

ROME. Tannhäuser visits, 56; Vitellius, emperor of, 86.

ROSKVA (ros'kvà). Thor's servant, 70.

ROSSTHIOF (ros'thēf). The prophecy of, 145, 150, 152, 185; compared, 286.

ROSTERUS (ros'ter-us). Odin as smith, 151.

RÜGEN (rē'gen). Nerthus's worship on island of, 59.

RUNES (rōōnz). Odin masters and uses, 39, 94, 182, 185.

RUSSIA. Æsir migrate to, 43; name for, 146.

RUTHENES. Odin visits the land of the, 146, 150.

SÆHRIMNIR (sā'hrim-nir). Boar in Valhalla, 27.

SÆMING (sā'ming). King of Norway, 44, 111.

SÆMUND (sā'mōōnd). Compiler of Elder Edda, 224.

SAGA (sä'gä). 1. Wife of Odin, 43, 279. 2. Records called, 10, 87, 262, 272.

SAGITTARIUS. Northern equivalent, 132.

ST. GERTRUDE. Belief in, 130.

ST. GOAR. Lorelei at, 179.

ST. HUBERT. Uller is, 132.

ST. JOHN'S DAY. Celebrations, 197.

ST. MICHAEL. Bears Cheru's sword, 88.

ST. VALENTINE. Replaces Vali, 153.

SARPEDON (sär-pē'don). Northern equivalent, 290.

SATAERE (săt'ā-re). God of agriculture, 209.

SATAN. Same as Loki, 209.

SATURDAY. Sacred to Loki, 209.

SATURN. Equivalent, 209, 284.

SAXNOT. God of Saxons, 86; Frey like, 112.

SAXON. Irmin, a god, 36; Hengist and Horsa, 44; Eástre, goddess, 57.

SAXONY. Conquered by Odin, 44.

SCALDS. Edda the work of, 10.

SCANDINAVIA. Worship in, 60, 108, 121, 223, 224; fairies in, 222.

SCANDINAVIANS. Belief of the, 132, 147, 211, 212; epic of the, 225; topographical belief of the, 211.

SCHWARTZE SEE (shvärt'se sā). Nerthus's car bathed in the, 60.

SCOURGE OF GOD. Attila the, 87, 262.

SCYLLA (sil'ä). Northern equivalent, 283.

SEASONS. The division of the, 17.

SEELAND. Gefjon plows, 53, 280.

SENJEMAND (sen'je-mänd). Story of giant, 212, 213.

SENJEN. Island of, 212, 213.

SESSRYMNIR (ses'rim-nir). Freya's home is, 124.

SHAKESPEARE. Norns used by, 158.

SIBICH (sē'bikh). The traitor, 260.

"SIEGFRIED" (sēg'frēd). Wagner's opera of, 225.

SIF. Wife of Thor, 64; hair stolen, 65–68, 199; Uller, son of, 131; Loki slanders, 205, 206; dwarfs make hair, 218; comparisons, 281, 282.

SIGGEIR (sig'ir). Marriage feast of, 226–228; treachery and death of, 228, 230, 233.

SIGI (sig'ē). Son of Odin, 44, 225; comparison, 261.

SIGMUND (sig'moönd). Völund's sword for, 165; brother of Signy, 227; sword won by, 228; a prisoner, 229; the vow of, 230; tests Signy's sons, 231; a werewolf, 232; prisoner of Siggeir, 233; escape and vengeance of, 234; the son of, 236; Hiordis, wife of, 237; death of, 238; Sigurd, son of, 239; the sword of, 244; comparisons, 261, 291.

SIGNY (sig'ni). Volsung's daughter, 226–229; vengeance of, 230–234.

SIGTUNA (sig-tū'nà). Odin founds, 43.

SIGURD (sē'goörd). Brunhild to marry, 165; story of, 225; birth of, 239; Grani selected by, 240; Regin speaks to, 243; sword of, 244; slays Fafnir, 245; rides through flames, 247; betrothal of, 248; marriage of, 249; Gudrun gives potion to, 250; Gudrun, wife of, 251; wooes Brunhild for Gunnar, 252; awakening of, 253; death of, 254–256; funeral pyre of, 255; Gudrun mourns, 257; Atli slain with sword of, 260; a sun myth, 261; Greek equivalents, 287, 291, 292.

SIGYN (sē'gēn). Loki's faithful wife, 200, 207.

SINDRI (sin'drē). Dwarf, smith, 67, 68; king of dwarfs, 273.

SINDUR (sin'doör). A wave maiden, 137.

SINFIOTLI (sin-fe-ot'li). Birth and education of, 231; Signy aids, 233; vengeance of, 234; career and death of, 235, 236.

SIR OLAF. Fairies beguile, 222.

SIRENS. Compared to Lorelei, 288.

SIRIUS (sir'i-us). Northern equivalent, 284.

SKADI (skä'dē). Wife of Odin, 43; in Asgard, 108, 109; wife of Niörd,

112, 124; wife of Uller, 132; punishes Loki, 207; comparison, 284.

SKIALF (skyälf). Same as Freya, 125.

SKIDBLADNIR (skid-bläd'nir). Dvalin makes, 66, 218; properties of, 66; Frey owns, 68, 113; comparison, 282.

SKIN-FAXI. Steed of Day, 15.

SKIOLD (shöld). King of Denmark, 44, 53.

SKIOLDINGS (shöld'ings). Descendants of, 53, 279.

SKIRNIR (skēr'nir). Servant of Frey, 90, 114, 117; journey of, 114, 115, 285.

SKÖLL (skul). Wolf pursuing sun and moon, 16, 265, 290.

SKRYMIR (skrim'ir). Thor's encounter with, 71, 72.

SKRYMSLI (skrims'lē). The story of giant, 201.

SKULD (skoöld). One of the Norns called, 154, 155, 157, 159, 162.

SLAGFINN. Marries a Valkyr, 163.

SLEEPING BEAUTY. Origin of myth, 158.

SLEIPNIR (slīp'nir). Odin's steed, 29, 39, 73, 75, 184, 268; Hermod rides, 145, 189, 193; Loki, parent of, 204, 290; Grani, son of, 240.

SLID (slēd). Stream in Nifl-heim, 168.

SNOR. Wife of Karl, 142.

SNORRO-STURLESON (snor'rō-stoör'-lä-sun). Author of "Heimskring-la," 117.

SNOTRA (snō'trà). Goddess of virtue, 53.

SOKVABEK (so-kvä'bek). Home of Saga, 43; comparison, 279.

SOL. The sun maid, 14, 264; death of, 265, 270; compared, 276.

SOMNUS. Northern equivalent for servants of, 291.

SON (sŏn). Bowl of expiation, 93.

SÖRLI (sēr'li). Son of Gudrun, 260, 261; compared, 292.

SPARTAN KING. Equivalent, 291.

STEROPES. Northern equivalent, 284.

STRAW DEATH. Northern contempt for, 168.

STROMKARLS. Water divinities, 178, 179.

SUABIANS (swä'bi-ânz). Tyr, a god of the, 84.

SUDRI (sū'drē). Supports heavenly vault, 14.

SURTR (sōōrtr). Flame giant, 10; progeny, 15; world destroyed by, 21; arrival of, 267, 268; Frey slain by, 269; world consumed by, 270.

SUTTUNG (sòòt'tōōng). The story of giant, 94, 95, 97.

SVADILFARE (svä'dil-fär-e). Horse of architect, 202, 203.

SVALIN (svä'lin). Shield tempered sun rays, 14.

SVANHVIT (svon'whit). Marries mortal, 163.

SVART-ALFA-HEIM (svärt-alf'a-hīm). Home of dwarfs, 18, 66, 90, 113, 127, 220.

SVART-ALFAR (svärt-alf'ar), 217.

SVASUD (svä'zood). Father of Summer, 17.

SWANHILD (swon'hild). Daughter of Gudrun, 256, 257, 260; compared, 292.

SWEDEN. Landscapes of, 9; Mayday in, 42; Odin conquers, 43, 44; Gylfi, king of, 41, 52; Thor in, 64; Frey, king of, 122; Frodi visits, 122; Freya in, 124, 130; Nidud, king of, 163; miners in, 220.

SWITZERLAND. Giants in, 211.

SWORD DANCES, 84, 85.

SYN (sēn). Goddess of truth, 52.

SYR (sir). Same as Freya, 125.

TANNGNIOSTR (täng'nyos-ter). Thor's goat, 64.

TANNGRISNR (tän'gris-ner). Thor's goat, 64.

TANNHÄUSER (tän'hoi-zer). Story of, 56, 57; equivalent for, 281.

TARNKAPPE (tärn'kap-pe). Invisible cap, 218.

TARTARUS (tär'tar-us). Northern equivalents, 275, 283, 288.

TELEMACHUS (te-lem'a-kus). Northern equivalent, 281.

TEUTON (tū'ton). Ostara, a goddess, 58.

TEUTONIC GODS. 209, 211.

THANATOS (than'a-tos). Same as Hel, 288.

THESEUS (thē'sūs). Northern equivalent, 291, 292.

THETIS (the'tis). Northern equivalent for, 286.

THIALFI (te-älf'e). Servant of, 69, 70, 72, 80; duel of, 74, 75; Egil's son, 174.

THIASSI (te-äs'se). Loki's adventure with, 101; Idun kidnapped, 102, 103, 104, 107-109, 199, 283; Loki pursued by, 104, 108; Gerda, relative of, 114; the eyes of, 283, 284.

THING (ting). Northern popular assembly, 30, 128, 129.

THOK (tok). Loki as, 194, 196, 204; comparison, 289.

THOR (thôr or tôr). Never crosses Bifröst, 21; Jörd, mother of, 43; toast to, 46; god of thunder, 61-83; infancy of, 61; anger of, 61, 65; description of, 62; hat of, 64; Alvis petrified by, 65; Miölnir given to, 68; drinking wager of, 72; duel with Hrungnir, 74; adventure with Geirrod, 80; temples and statues of, 82; Tyr like, 84; giants hated by, 113, 211; Yule sacred to, 118; Brisinga-men worn by, 127; Uller, stepson of, 131; Grid's gauntlet helps, 148; kettle secured by, 174; goes fishing, 175, 176, 177; consecrates Balder's pyre, 191; visits Utgardloki, 198; slays architect, 204; threatens Loki, 206; slays Midgard snake, 269; sons of, 271; Greek equivalents, 281, 282, 290.

THORA (tō'rà). Wife of Elf, daughter of Hakon, 256.

THORBURN. Origin of name, 81.

THORN OF SLEEP. Brunhild stung by, 248.

THORWALDSEN (tôr'wald-sn). Origin of name, 81.

THRALL. Birth of, 141, 142.

THRIDI (trē'dē). One of the trilogy, 44.

THRONDHJEIM (trōnd'yem). Temple of Frey at, 118.

THRUD (trōōd). Thor's daughter, 64, 65.

THRUDGELMIR (trōōd-gel'mir). Birth of giant, 12.

THRUD-HEIM (trōōd'hīm). Thor's realm, 61.

THRUNG (trōōng). Freya, 125.

THRYM (trim). Thor visits, 77, 78, 281, 282; Freya refuses, 129; son of Kari, 212.

THRYM-HEIM (trim'hīm). Home of Thiassi, 102; Loki visits, 103, 104.

THUNDERER. Same as Odin, 277.

THUNDERHILL. Named after Thor, 81.

THURINGIA (thū-rin'ji-å). Hörsel-berg in, 56; giants in, 215.

THURSDAY. Sacred to Thor, 82, 282.

THURSES (tōōrs'ez). Giants called, 210.

THVERA (tvā'rå). Temple of Frey at, 118.

THVITI (tvē'ti). Bowlder where Fenris is bound, 92.

THYR (tir or tēr). Wife of Thrall, 141.

TITANIA. Queen of fairies, 223.

TITANS. Northern equivalents for, 275, 283, 290.

TITYUS (tit'i-us). Northern equivalent, 289.

TIU (tū). Same as Tyr, 84, 282.

TOASTS. To Odin, 45; to Frigga, 46; to Bragi, 99; to Niörd and Frey, 111; to Freya, 130.

TORGE (tôr'ge). Story of giant, 213.

TORGHATTEN (torg-hat'ten). Mountain, 213.

TREE MAIDENS. Elves same as, 223.

TRENT. Superstition along the, 173.

TROLLS. Dwarfs known as, 18, 213, 217, 220, 291.

TROY. Northern equivalent for siege of, 280.

TÜBINGEN (tē'bing-en). Worship of Tyr in, 92.

TUESDAY. Tyr's day, 84.

TWELFTH-NIGHT. Wild Hunt at, 31; festival, 59.

TWILIGHT OF THE GODS, 263, 273.

TYR (tēr). Son of Frigga, 43; god of war, 84-92; one arm, 88, 267;

feeds Fenris, 89; like Frey, 112; like Irmin, 144; chains Fenris, 166; accompanies Thor, 174-177; fights Garm, 268; death of, 269.

TYRFING (tēr'fing). Magic sword, 219.

TYROL (tĭr'ul). Story of flax in, 54.

TYR'S HELM. Aconite called, 92.

ULFRUN (ŏŏl'froon). A wave maiden, 137.

ULLER (ŏŏl'er). Skadi marries, 111; winter-god, 131-133; equivalents, 286.

ULYSSES (ū-lis'sez). Compared to Tannhäuser, 281.

UNDINES (un'dēnz). Female water divinities, 178, 179, 288.

UPSALA (up-sä'lå). Temple at, 44, 82, 280; Ingvi-Frey at, 117; mound at, 284.

URD (ŏŏrd). One of the Norns, 154, 155.

URDAR (ŏŏrd'ar). Fountain, 19, 20, 21, 62, 148, 154, 155, 186, 268.

UTGARD (ŏŏt'gard). Realm of, 71, 72.

UTGARD-LOKI. Castle of, 71, 72, 73; evil, 198; Thor visits, 198.

VAFTHRUDNIR (väf-trōōd'nir). Odin's visit to, 37, 211, 279; fulfillment of prediction, 266.

VAK (väk). Odin as, 151.

VALA (vä'lå). Druidess, 86; grave of, 185.

VALAS. Norns called, 158; Odin consults, 184.

VALASKIALF (vä'la-skyålf). Hall in Asgard, 25; Vali in, 153.

VALENTINE. Vali as St., 153.

VALFATHER. Same as Odin, 26, 160.

VALFREYA. Same as Freya, 124.

VALHALLA (väl-häl'lå). Description of, 25-28, 38; masters of, 62; Hrungnir enters, 73; Tyr welcomed to, 84; Tyr's warriors in, 88; Bragi, bard of, 99; heroes in, 141, 145, 235; Vidar visits, 148; Valkyrs choose guests for, 160, 162; Ran's hall rivals, 172; mistletoe near, 184, 188; Helgi promised, 234,

235; Gudrun returns to, 236; Fialar above, 265; host of, 268.

VALI (vä'lē). Emblem of spring, 43. I. The avenger, 150-153, 186; slays Hodur, 195; survival of, 271. 2. Son of Loki, 200, 207.

VALKYRS (val'kirz). Attendants of Odin, 26; of the heroes, 26, 28; of Tyr, 88; led by Freya, 124; accompany Hermod, 145; Skuld a, 159; general account of, 160-165; Helgi marries a, 235; Gudrun a, 236; Brunhild a, 248; Freya a, 285; Hebe compared to the, 287.

VALPURGISNACHT (väl-pōōr'gēs-nähkt). Witches' dance on, 130, 159.

VALTAM (väl'tam). Vegtam, son of, 185.

VAN. Niörd a, 22, 284.

VANA-HEIM. Home of the Vanas, 21, 22, 107, 112, 124.

VANABRIDE. Freya, 124.

VANADIS (văn'à-dis). Freya, 124.

VANAS. Sea and wind gods, 21, 112, 124, 139, 171; quarrel between the Æsir and the, 93, 107; comparisons, 271, 278.

VANDALS. Story of Winilers and, 49, 280.

VARA (vä'rà). Oath keeper, 53.

VASUD (vä'sōōd). Father of Vindsual, 17.

VE (vä). Creation of, 12, 19, 278; replaces Odin, 42, 132; equivalent, 275.

VECHA (vech'à). Odin as, 151.

VEDFOLNIR (ved-fol'nir). Falcon, reporter, 20.

VEGTAM (veg'tam). Odin, 185.

VEIMER (vī'mer). Thor fords, 80, 282.

VELEDA. Warns Drusus, 159.

VENEUR DE FONTAINEBLEAU (vēn-ur duh fōn-tän-blō'). Wild Huntsman, 32.

VENUS. Northern equivalents for, 279, 282, 285, 291.

VERDANDI (vēr-dän'dē). Norn of present, 154; beneficent ways of, 155.

VESPASIAN (ves-pä'shan). Election of, 87.

VIDAR (vē'där). Parents of, 43; story of, 147-149; slays Fenris, 269; the survival of, 153, 271; comparisons, 286, 290.

VIENNA. Customs in, 120, 121.

VIGRID (vig'rid). Last battle on plain of, 38, 208, 266, 268, 271.

VIKINGS (vī'kingz). Valkyrs take, 161.

VILI (vē'lē). Creation, 12, 19, 278; replaces Odin, 42, 132; comparison, 275.

VINDSUAL (vind'su-al). Father of Winter, 17.

VINGNIR (ving'nir). Foster father of Thor, 61.

VINGOLF (ving'golf). Tyr welcome in, 84.

VINGTHOR (ving'tôr). Same as Thor, 61.

VINLAND. Norse settlement in, 224.

VIRGIN. Sponge called hand of, 111; health of, 130.

VITELLIUS. Has Cheru's sword, 86, 87.

VJOFN (vyofn). Goddess of concord, 52.

VOLLA. Same as Fulla, 50, 51.

VOLSUNG (vol'sōong). Saga of, 225, 292; birth of, 52, 226; career and death of, 225-230; descendants of, 231, 235, 238, 261.

VÖLUND (vēl-oond). Story of the smith, 163-165, 287.

VÖLUNDARHAUS (vēl'oond-ar-hous'). Maze, 164; compared to Cretan labyrinth, 287.

VON. River from Fenris's mouth, 92.

VÖR (vēr). Same as Faith, 53.

VROU-ELDE (vrou-eld'e). Same as Frigga, 59.

VROU-ELDEN-STRAAT. Milky Way in Holland, 59.

VULCAN. Northern equivalents for, 277, 285, 287, 291.

VULDER (vōol'der). Same as Uller, 132.

WAGNER. Four operas from Volsunga Saga, 225.

WAIN. Same as Great Bear, 36.

WANDERER. Same as Odin, 37.

WAVES. Ægir's daughters, 173, 288.

WEDNESDAY. Sacred to Odin, 45.

WELDEGG. King of East Saxony, 44.

WEREWOLF. Sigmund a, 232.

WESER (vā'zer). Rats drowned in, 33.

WEST SAXONY. Conquered by Odin, 44.

WESTERBURG. Ilse loves knight of the, 215.

WESTRI (wes'trē). Dwarf supporting heavenly vault, 14.

WHITE LADY. Last appearance of, 58, 59.

WILD HUNT. Leaders of, 30, 32, 59, 132.

WILD HUNTSMAN, 30, 32.

WILL-O'-THE-WISP. Mediæval superstition concerning, 222.

WIND. Waves play with, 173.

WINGI (wing'ē). Same as Knefrud, 257.

WINILERS (win'i-lerz). Story of Vandals and, 49, 280.

WINTER. Odin supplanted by, 42.

WODE (wō'da). Same as Frigga, 59.

WODEN. Same as Odin, 23, 30, 45.

WODEN'S DAY. Same as Wednesday, 45.

WOOD MAIDENS. Elves known as, 223.

WUOTAN (wō'tan). Same as Odin, 23, 59.

WURD (wŏŏrd). Same as Urd, 155.

WYRD (wērd). Mother of Norns, 148, 149.

YDALIR (ē-däl'ir). Abode of Uller, 131.

YGGDRASIL (ig'drá-sil). Creation of, 19; stags pasture on, 20; assembly under, 21; spear from, 37; Odin hangs from, 39; Thor goes to, 62; Idun falls from, 105; Bifröst reaches to, 137; Giallar-horn hung on, 138; Norns dwell under, 154; Nidhug eats, 169, 265; consumed, 269; comparison, 283.

YMIR (ē'mir). Giant of fire and ice, 11; sleep of, 12; death of, 12, 210; earth created from, 13; dwarfs from, 17, 217, 277; Fornjotnr same as, 199, 212; comparisons, 275, 277.

YOUNGER EDDA. Gylfi's delusion described in the, 44.

YULE. Month and festival of, 118, 119.

YULE LOG, 121.

YULE-TIDE, 82, 99.

ZEPHYRUS (zef'i-rus). Frey like, 284.

ZEUS (zūs). Northern equivalents for, 280.

ZIU (zū). Same as Tyr, 84.

ZIUSBURG (zūz'berg). Same as Augsburg, 84.